LITERACY IN THEORY AND PRACTICE

D1380098

Cambridge Studies in Oral and Literate Culture

Edited by PETER BURKE and RUTH FINNEGAN

This series is designed to address the question of the significance of literacy in human societies: it will assess its importance for political, economic, social and cultural development, and examine how what we take to be the common functions of writing are carried out in oral cultures.

The series will be interdisciplinary, but with particular emphasis on social anthropology and social history, and will encourage cross-fertilisation between these disciplines: it will also be of interest to readers in allied fields, such as sociology, folklore and literature. Although it will include some monographs, the focus of the series will be on theoretical and comparative aspects rather than detailed description, and the books will be presented in a form accessible to non-specialist readers interested in the general subject of literacy and orality.

Books in the series

1 NIGEL PHILIPPS: *'Sijobang': Sung Narrative Poetry of West Sumatra*
2 R. W. SCRIBNER: *For the Sake of Simple Folk: Popular Propaganda for the German Reformation*
3 HARVEY J. GRAFF: *Literacy and Social Development in the West: A Reader*
4 DONALD J. COSENTINO: *Defiant Maids and Stubborn Farmers: Tradition and Invention in Mende Story Performance*
5 FRANÇOIS FURET and JACQUES OZOUF: *Reading and Writing: Literacy in France from Calvin to Jules Ferry*
6 JEAN-CLAUDE SCHMITT: *The Holy Greyhound: Guinefort, Healer of Children since the Thirteenth Century*
7 JEFF OPLAND: *Xhosa Oral Poetry: Aspects of a Black South African Tradition*
8 RICHARD BAUMAN: *Let Your Words be Few: Symbolism of Speaking and Silence among Seventeenth-Century Quakers*

LITERACY IN THEORY AND PRACTICE

BRIAN V. STREET

CAMBRIDGE
UNIVERSITY PRESS

Published by the Press Syndicate of the University of Cambridge
The Pitt Building, Trumpington Street, Cambridge CB2 1RP
40 West 20th Street, New York, NY 10011-4211 USA
10 Stamford Road, Oakleigh, Melbourne 3166, Australia

First published 1984
Reprinted 1993, 1995

Library of Congress catalogue card number: 83–23938

British Library Cataloguing in Publication Data

Street, Brian V.
Literacy in theory and practice.–
(Cambridge studies in oral and literate culture; 9)
1. Literacy
I. Title
306′.4 LC149

ISBN 0 521 28961 0

Transferred to digital printing 1999

To Joanna, Chloe, Alice and Nicholas

CONTENTS

Acknowledgements   *page*   viii
Prolegomenon   x
Introduction   1

Section 1 Literacy in Theory

1 The 'Autonomous' Model: I Literacy and Rationality   19
2 The 'Autonomous' Model: II Goody   44
3 Literacy and Linguistics   66
4 The 'Ideological' Model   95

Section 2 Literacy in Theory and Practice

Introduction   129
5 'Maktab' Literacy   132
6 'Commercial' Literacy   158

Section 3 Literacy in Practice

7 Unesco and Radical Literacy Campaigns   183
8 Adult Literacy Campaigns in the UK and the USA   213

Bibliography   233
Index   240

ACKNOWLEDGEMENTS

The ideas expressed in this book developed, on the one hand, out of anthropological field work in Iran during the 1970s and, on the other, out of a course on the anthropology of literacy that I offer as part of the Social Anthropology major at Sussex. Friends, colleagues, students and others in both contexts have contributed to the book in a variety of ways. In current circumstances, it is not appropriate to name the very many Iranians to whom I am indebted, but any who see this work should understand my appreciation of their friendship and assistance. (The village in which I conducted field work has been given a fictitious name, as have the individuals referred to, but this does not disguise my gratitude to the villagers for their hospitality and friendship.)

The British Institute of Persian Studies provided a Research Fellowship that helped me to continue doing field work in Iran and I would like to express my gratitude both for this support and for the hospitality shown me at the Institute's Tehran lodging house, especially by Dr David Stronach the then Director of the Institute and the Assistant Director, Sandy Morton. Officials of the British Council in Iran also provided both hospitality and intellectual community and some earlier drafts of this book were used as briefing papers for the Council's staff in Iran. In particular I would like to thank R. X. Hindmarsh, English Language Officer for the British Council, Iran, in 1972, Rosalind Wilson who taught at the British Council in Mashad in 1972 and Rafe Isaacs, Director for the Council in Mashad when I returned in 1976–7 and his wife Ruth. I would also like to thank Directors and teachers at the Iran–America Society in Mashad for similar help and support, in particular Carter and Judy Bryant, Jim and Ginny Goode and Greg and Jean Gary. André Singer, a colleague and friend, has provided considerable help and support, particularly during my period in Iran.

It would be invidious to single out from my University of Sussex classes individuals whose comments and own work have contributed to this book. But I would like to express my gratitude to all of the students in these classes for the stimulation they provided: there are references in the bibliography to those final-year student extended essays to which I owe a specific debt. Some of the more recent developments in my ideas about literacy owe much to the lively University of Sussex workshop in anthropology and linguistics which has provided a stimulating environment for interdisciplinary work in recent years and I would particularly like to thank the convenors, Dr R. Grillo and Dr M. Deuchar, who have also taken time and trouble to discuss drafts of this book and to make extensive comments upon them.

I would also like to thank others who have discussed the ideas with me or read and commented upon parts of the work: Professor John Lyons, Jane Freeland, Lourdes de Léon, Johnny Parry, Suzanne Romaine, Joanna Lowry, Bernard Gabony and Mike Smith. The University of Sussex Arts Support Fund also contributed towards the costs of further field research in 1976 and 1977.

The responsibility for the ideas expressed in this book is, of course, mine alone.

PROLEGOMENON

A surprising number of general arguments about society, language and thought appear to rest upon claims made, whether implicitly or explicitly, regarding the nature of literacy. It is assumed that we 'know' what literacy is and can therefore appeal to it in the resolution of more uncertain areas of knowledge. Many western academics, for instance, in claiming objectivity, neutrality and greater logic for what they have to say, appeal to the 'technical' qualities of literacy, in which they are proficient, to legitimise assertions that might otherwise appear self-interested and ethnocentric. Some linguists, for instance, have recently argued that certain languages 'enable their users to approximate to neutral objective description' and they support the argument by reference to the 'intrinsically greater objectivity of written language'. Some anthropologists, attempting to explain messianic religious movements, have appealed to theories of literacy, in order to describe the supposed 'mistaken' nature of native thought: the natives, it is suggested, use literacy in a 'ritualised' way as opposed to the 'rational' uses evident in the western writer's own particular practices.

Similarly, tests by developmental psychologists for an ability to make neutral, objective and logical statements are frequently related to groups of literates and illiterates: the researcher's assertions regarding 'deprivation' in cognitive skills, which might appear to be culture-based and even ethnocentric when applied to native language and speech, can more easily be represented as 'neutral' when made with regard to literacy. The apparent 'technical' qualities of literacy thus disguise the cultural bias in some of these kinds of research. This has practical implications too, since claims made by educationalists for funding often rest on assumptions concerning the intellectual and developmental consequences of students learning to acquire the 'technology' of reading and writing.

I intend to question these assumptions, to open up what is taken for granted about literacy, and to assert the need for the practitioners cited above to apply as much rigour to the description and analysis of literacy as they do to their own primary objects of study. I begin with a critique of the kinds of general arguments cited above, following through the consequences of the writer's assumptions about literacy for his or her general position and demonstrating the contradictions and problems they lead to. I then pose what I term an 'alternative model' of literacy and attempt to pursue the consequences of this approach for the kinds of problems various disciplines are currently concerned with. I shall use anthropological field work which I conducted in Iran during the 1970s in order to test out the model I am proposing in more detail and I shall attempt to suggest some directions for further research and some of the bases for a more general theory of literacies. Finally, I shall attempt to show how the model applies to certain Unesco programmes for literacy and also to adult literacy campaigns in the UK and the USA.

INTRODUCTION

Section 1: Literacy in Theory

I shall use the term 'literacy' as a shorthand for the social practices and conceptions of reading and writing. I shall be attempting to establish some of the theoretical foundations for a description of such practices and conceptions and will challenge assumptions, whether implicit or explicit, that currently dominate the field of literacy studies. I shall contend that what the particular practices and concepts of reading and writing are for a given society depends upon the context; that they are already embedded in an ideology and cannot be isolated or treated as 'neutral' or merely 'technical'. I shall demonstrate that what practices are taught and how they are imparted depends upon the nature of the social formation. The skills and concepts that accompany literacy acquisition, in whatever form, do not stem in some automatic way from the inherent qualities of literacy, as some authors would have us believe, but are aspects of a specific ideology. Faith in the power and qualities of literacy is itself socially learnt and is not an adequate tool with which to embark on a description of its practice.

I shall demonstrate that, nevertheless, many representations of literacy do rest on the assumption that it is a neutral technology that can be detached from specific social contexts. I shall argue that such claims, as well as the literacy practices they purport to describe, in fact derive from specific ideologies which, in much of the literature, are not made explicit. I claim, then, that analysis of the uses and consequences of literacy frequently fails to theorise, in a way that is adequate for cross-cultural comparison, just what is the nature of the practice which has these 'uses and consequences'.

In order to clarify the differences between these different approaches to the analysis of literacy, I shall characterise them as the 'ideological' model and the 'autonomous' model of literacy respectively. I shall deal firstly with the 'autonomous' model. This model is often at least partially explicit in the academic literature, though it is more often implicit in that produced as part of practical literacy programmes. The model tends, I claim, to be based on the 'essay-text' form of literacy and to generalise broadly from what is in fact a narrow, culture-specific literacy practice. The main outlines of the model occur in similar form across a

1

range of different writers and I shall summarise these before investigating variations. The model assumes a single direction in which literacy development can be traced, and associates it with 'progress', 'civilisation', individual liberty and social mobility. It attempts to distinguish literacy from schooling. It isolates literacy as an independent variable and then claims to be able to study its consequences. These consequences are classically represented in terms of economic 'take off' or in terms of cognitive skills.

An influential example of the former representation is the claim by Anderson (1966) that a society requires a 40% literacy rate for economic 'take off', a hypothesis that recurs with apparent authority in many literacy programme outlines. What is not specified is what specific literacy practices and concepts 40% of the population are supposed to acquire. Yet comparative material, some of which Anderson himself provides, demonstrates that such practices and conceptions are very different from one culture to another. The homogenisation of such variety, which is implied by the statistical measures and the economic reductionism of these approaches, fails to do justice to the complexity of the many different kinds of literacy practice prevalent in different cultures. It also tends implicitly to privilege and to generalise the writer's own conceptions and practices, as though these were what 'literacy' is.

The theory behind these particular conceptions and practices becomes apparent when we examine the claims made for the cognitive consequences of literacy by many writers in the field. These claims, I argue, often lie beneath the explicit statistical and economic descriptions of literacy that are currently dominant in much of the development literature. The claims are that literacy affects cognitive processes in some of the following ways: it facilitates 'empathy', 'abstract context-free thought', 'rationality', 'critical thought', 'post-operative' thought (in Piaget's usage), 'detachment' and the kinds of logical processes exemplified by syllogisms, formal language, elaborated code etc.

Against these assumptions I shall pose an 'ideological' model of literacy. Those who subscribe to this model concentrate on the specific social practices of reading and writing. They recognise the ideological and therefore culturally embedded nature of such practices. The model stresses the significance of the socialisation process in the construction of the meaning of literacy for participants and is therefore concerned with the general social institutions through which this process takes place and not just the explicit 'educational' ones. It distinguishes claims for the consequences of literacy from its real significance for specific social groups. It treats sceptically claims by western liberal educators for the 'openness', 'rationality' and critical awareness of what they teach, and investigates the role of such teaching in social control and the hegemony of a ruling class. It concentrates on the overlap and interaction of oral and literate modes rather than stressing a 'great divide'.

The writers I am discussing do not necessarily couch their argument in the terms I am adopting. But, nevertheless, I maintain that the use of the term 'model' to describe their perspectives is helpful since it draws attention to the underlying coherence and relationship of ideas which, on the surface, might appear unconnected and haphazard. No one practitioner necessarily adopts all of the characteristics of any one model, but the use of the concept helps us to see what is entailed by adopting particular positions, to fill in gaps left by untheorised statements about literacy, and to adopt a broader perspective than is apparent in any one writer on literacy. The models serve in a sense as 'ideal types' to help clarify the significant lines of cleavage in the field of literacy studies and to provide a stimulus from which a more explicit theoretical foundation for descriptions of literacy practice and for cross-cultural comparison can be constructed.

In the light of these different perspectives on literacy, and following the critique of the 'autonomous' model, we will, I hope, be in a position to pose some general questions of both a sociological and practical kind. Are there, for instance, any significant general or universal patterns in the practices associated with literacy in different cultures? What concrete practices and ideological formations have been characteristically associated with shifts from memory to written record, and how can the associations be explained? How can the findings of theorists and in particular of those associated with the 'ideological' model be fruitfully put into practice?

Chapter 1 offers an exposition and critique of what I take to be a 'strong' version of the 'autonomous' model of literacy – that put forward by Olson, Hildyard and Greenfield. Hildyard and Olson argued that written forms enable the user to differentiate the logical from the interpersonal functions of language in a way that is less possible in oral discourse (1978). Patricia Greenfield, whose work they refer to for ethnographic support, applied aspects of Bernstein's concepts of elaborate and restricted codes to schooled and unschooled children amongst the Wolof of Senegal (1972). Her conclusions were that unschooled children lacked the concept of a personal point of view and the cognitive flexibility to shift perspective in relation to concept-formation problems. All three authors then related such differences to the intrinsic qualities of writing. I argue that such conceptions are mistaken on a number of grounds:

1 The work of social psychologists, social anthropologists, philosophers and linguists challenges the representation of certain forms of language use, in different cultures or social groups, as 'embedded' and 'illogical'. This work, notably by Evans-Pritchard (1937), Lévi-Strauss (1966),

Labov (1973), Rosen (1972), Stubbs (1980), Crystal (1976) etc., demonstrated the logic beneath unfamiliar conventions. It challenged the general significance attributed to tests that are claimed to demonstrate the working of logic and suggested that they often test instead such factors as explicitness, the nature of which is more clearly dependent on the cultural context.

2 From this and other literature it can be argued that the 'rationality' debate is itself embedded in particular ideological and political contexts. The introduction of literacy to the classic debate can be seen as an attempt to give the legitimacy of the 'technical' to statements about rationality that would otherwise appear to be culturally loaded.

3 The justification made by Hildyard and Olson of elaborate and expensive education systems on the grounds that they foster improved 'logic' and 'scientific' thought are circular in that the tests for 'success' are those of the education systems themselves.

4 It is, in any case, virtually impossible to set up a measure by which different performances of logic across different social groups can be reliably assessed.

5 Claims for the objectivity and neutrality of 'sentence meaning *per se*' (Olson, 1977) are themselves socially constructed conventions, developed within specific social traditions. They should not be taken at face value since they serve more often to privilege the users' own beliefs than as rigorous standards of 'truth'.

6 The claims that texts embody 'autonomous' meaning which does not change over time and space is not proven. The 'meaning' of texts lost for years and then rediscovered (Popper's World Three) in fact depends upon the learnt conventions of the discoverer's society.

7 The actual examples of literacy in different societies that are available to us suggest that it is more often 'restrictive' and hegemonic, and concerned with instilling discipline and exercising social control.

8 The reality of social uses of varying modes of communication is that oral and literate modes are 'mixed' in each society. There is nothing absolute about a shift to greater use of literate modes, which is better described as a change in the 'mix'. Oral conventions often continue to apply to literate forms and literate conventions may be applied to oral forms.

9 What is taken in the 'autonomous' model to be qualities inherent to literacy are in fact conventions of literate practice in particular societies.

While the descriptions of literacy provided by the writers described in Chapter 1 probably represent the most extreme version of the 'autonomous' model, the most influential presentation of it has probably been that of the social anthropologist Jack Goody. In a number of publications since the 1960s he has attempted to outline what he sees as the importance, 'potentialities' and 'consequences' of literacy. His views have been adopted by, amongst others, fellow anthropologists as the authoritative position on the subject, particularly where they themselves have devoted little explicit attention to the question of literacy. This implicit acceptance leads, I argue, to problems not only in the representations of literacy itself made by these anthropologists but also in their more general accounts of social change, religious thought and ideology in the societies they describe. It is, therefore, important for anthropological work in general that the concepts underlying Goody's representation of literacy should be made explicit and their implications followed through.

Goody's perspective, which I examine in Chapter 2, includes many of the characteristics of what was outlined in Chapter 1 as the 'autonomous' model of literacy, but he extends its scope across grand sweeps of culture and history (Goody, 1968, 1977). He would explicitly replace the theory of a 'great divide' between 'primitive' and 'modern' culture, which had been employed in earlier anthropological theory and which is now discredited, with the distinction between 'literate' and 'non-literate'. He believes that this distinction is similar to, but more useful than, that traditionally made between 'logical' and 'pre-logical'. This, he claims, is because of the inherent qualities of the written word: writing makes the relationship between a word and its referent more general and abstract; it is less closely connected with the peculiarities of time and place than is the language of oral communication. Writing is 'closely connected to', 'fosters', or even 'enforces' the development of 'logic', the distinction of myth from history, the elaboration of bureaucracy, the shift from 'little communities' to complex cultures, the emergence of scientific thought and institutions, and even the growth of democratic political processes. Goody does, in fact, enter caveats against taking these views too literally and, in particular, claims that he is not arguing a determinist case.

But the language, the texture of the argument, and the treatment of the ethnography tend to override such warnings and justify the claim that Goody does lay himself open to being interpreted in this way.

I argue that Goody overstates the significance that can be attributed to literacy in itself; understates the qualities of oral communication; sets up unhelpful and often untestable polarities between, for instance, the 'potentialities' of literacy and 'restricted' literacy; lends authority to a language for describing literacy practices that often contradicts his own stated disclaimers of the 'strong' or determinist case; and polarises the difference between oral and literate modes of communication in a way that gives insufficient credit to the reality of 'mixed' and interacting modes. Despite the density and complexity of social detail in Goody's descriptions of literacy practice, there is a peculiar lack of sociological

imagination in his determination to attribute to literacy *per se* characteristics which are clearly those of the social order in which it is found.

I also argue that the use by social anthropologists in particular of the
'autonomous' model of literacy, notably in the Goody version of it, affects
not only their representation of literacy practices in specific societies but
also their descriptions of the processes of social change and the nature of
religious and political ideology in those societies.

Clammer's work on Fiji, for instance, assumes uncritically many of the
tenets of the 'autonomous' model of literacy and illustrates what this can
lead to for the unwary anthropologist (1976). His unconscious adoption
of the 'autonomous' model is revealed in his use of the concept of 'ritualised' literacy. This leads to representations of the uses of literacy in Fiji in
terms which emphasise native simple-mindedness and lack of 'logic' at the
expense of accounts of the real political and ideological significance of the
response to colonisation. The model misleads us as to what literacy meant
to the participants themselves in the social upheavals that were taking
place at that time and in which it played a significant part. In anthropological terms, the 'autonomous' model of literacy entails 'intellectualist'
assumptions about the nature of 'primitive' thought which have generally
been rejected in the discipline. Although anthropologists have in other
contexts helped to clarify to some extent the theoretical foundations for
descriptions of non-European religion and belief, they have left largely
untheorised their representation of the uses and consequences of literacy.
This leads to adverse consequences for their general descriptions and
analyses of social change and of unfamiliar belief systems. The 'autonomous' model of literacy, then, leads anthropologists like Clammer to
descriptions which are in conflict with the explicit anthropological assumptions on which their studies otherwise claim to be based. Clammer's
own later work in fact rejects these assumptions and represents an important example of the shift towards the 'ideological' model (1980). A re-
analysis of some of the material on cargo cults in terms of the 'ideological'
model of literacy rather than the 'autonomous' model is an important
task awaiting anthropologists.

Many of the claims that I examine regarding literacy rest upon theories
that were developed within the discipline of linguistics. I devote Chapter 3
to an examination of these theories, noting that recent developments in
linguistics suggest little justification for such claims. Those linguists who
have paid explicit attention to literacy (and they are as yet few) have been
forced to question the early assumptions of the discipline with regard to
literacy and to cast doubt on the 'autonomous' model. Writers in other
areas, however, have continued to use these assumptions as though they
were secure and certain.

Many influential linguists of an earlier generation, such as Bloomfield, and grammarians and educators deriving their practice from such theorists, assumed that there was little significant difference between speech and writing. The assumption that speech and writing were fulfilling the same functions and the inability to recognise their separate character made it possible to use one as the model for another. In England the 'traditional grammatical rules of school text books' were derived from written language which was taken as the standard for spoken language (Crystal, 1976). Linguists themselves built up models of language based on what in fact were the conventions of writing in their own culture. Recent writers (Crystal, 1976; Linell, 1983; Deuchar, 1983; Stubbs, 1980) have challenged this view and have argued for more precise descriptions of the variety of spoken and written forms. 'Ethnolinguists' have discovered that the 'grammars' developed for their own language, or developed by missionaries for native languages, were inadequate for understanding and describing the variety of languages they were encountering. There was, then, a resistance to 'universalism', partly on the empirical grounds that it was often no more than ethnocentrism in disguise, and partly on general theoretical grounds.

Recognition of variety can, however, be used to maintain hierarchies of languages, whether implicitly or explicitly. I examine in this light claims by John Lyons that English is different from a great many other languages in 'allowing its users to approximate to neutral, objective description' and I argue that the basis of this argument is the by now familiar assumptions regarding literacy and its relationship to 'objectivity' (1982). I cite recent work in sociolinguistics (Stubbs, 1980; Rommetveit, 1982) which challenges theories of 'autonomous' meaning, on which Lyons' arguments appear to rest, and which thus challenges also the 'autonomous' model of literacy. This brings me back to the work of David Olson, and I examine in the context of these linguistic theories the general claims which he made in a famous Harvard Review article (1977) regarding the nature of '"autonomous" text'. I conclude with a classic anthropological comparison of the underlying similarity between the concepts used to represent 'self' amongst the Dinka tribe of the Sudan and those employed by an Oxford professor of philosophy (Lienhardt, 1980), a comparison which undermines the notions of 'autonomous' and 'objective' meaning and of a 'great divide' on which the 'autonomous' model of literacy has been shown to rest.

A number of writers from many different disciplines and over a period of time have, therefore, expressed doubts about the grander claims made for literacy. These criticisms have not previously cohered in an explicit alternative model of the kind I describe as the 'ideological' model of literacy.

However, work produced in the last few years in this field has made it possible to begin such a process. In Chapter 4, I examine some of this work, link it with the arguments examined above, and attempt thereby to lay the foundations for the construction of such a model.

Ideas being developed in a number of different disciplines can be seen to have significant underlying premises in common which, I argue, provide a coherent challenge to the 'autonomous' model of literacy. This coherence can be usefully presented through the representation of these ideas as forming an 'ideological' model of literacy. Those working through these ideas do sometimes make explicit the challenge to the theories which I have collectively labelled as the 'autonomous' model, although they do not necessarily address it in those terms. I argue that the application of those terms enables us to see more clearly the underlying theoretical assumptions in writing on literacy, to recognise cleavages in the field, to expose hidden contradictions, and to begin the work of cross-cultural comparison and generalisation on the basis of a worked out model of literacy.

This model has the following characteristics:

1 It assumes that the meaning of literacy depends upon the social institutions in which it is embedded;
2 literacy can only be known to us in forms which already have political and ideological significance and it cannot, therefore, be helpfully separated from that significance and treated as though it were an 'autonomous' thing;
3 the particular practices of reading and writing that are taught in any context depend upon such aspects of social structure as stratification (such as where certain social groups may be taught only to read), and the role of educational institutions (such as in Graff's (1979) example from nineteenth century Canada where they function as a form of social control);
4 the processes whereby reading and writing are learnt are what construct the meaning of it for particular practitioners;
5 we would probably more appropriately refer to 'literacies' than to any single 'literacy';
6 writers who tend towards this model and away from the 'autonomous' model recognise as problematic the relationship between the analysis of any 'autonomous', isolable qualities of literacy and the analysis of the ideological and political nature of literacy practice.

I examine these conceptions, then, as they are represented in the work of a number of writers. The writers I cite are identified with a range of disciplines and, significantly, many of them have themselves consciously attempted to cross disciplinary boundaries.

Within the collection of essays on literacy edited by Goody in 1968 there was already a challenge to his position. Gough, for instance, argued that he had overstated the case for the 'consequences' of literacy (Goody, 1968 p. 69). She emphasised that literacy is perhaps a necessary but not a sufficient cause for specific social developments (ibid. p. 153). She showed, for instance, that within the centralised bureaucratic states which Goody claimed are facilitated by literacy, varieties of political formation are in fact possible and not just the single outcome that his 'literacy determinism' suggests. Classes and the development of individualism, which Goody related to the spread of literacy, were taken by Gough to derive from the 'division of labour and the relationship to the mode of production'. Differences 'in levels of literacy and reading habits tend to spring from these arrangements rather than giving rise to them' (ibid.). History may be re-constructed in literate as well as in oral societies. The scientific exploration of space and the sceptical questioning of authority are widely variable 'as between comparably literate societies'. Literacy 'forms part of both the technological and ideological heritage of complex societies as well as being intrinsically involved with their social structures' (ibid. p. 84). These arguments and others put forward by contributors to the 1968 volume and elsewhere, worked out in close relation to ethnographic data, provided an important early check to the easy acceptance of Goody's ideas and therefore to the 'autonomous' model with which I would link them.

Goody's later work, while repeating many of these formulations, does also present material and ideas that could be construed as lending support to the 'ideological' model of literacy and as a challenge to the 'autonomous' model. In *The Domestication of the Savage Mind* (1977) he emphasises the importance of tables, lists and bureaucratic devices as being part of the corpus of 'literacy', and in doing so moves attention away from the cognitive consequences of literacy and towards the social practice. He does not, however, make this explicit. I maintain that an analysis of his work in terms of the models of literacy that I have outlined exposes and helps to resolve contradictions which Goody himself has not so far confronted.

Within social psychology too there has been some challenge to the 'autonomous' model without entirely confronting its implications. Cole and Scribner (1981) argue that studies of the kind that I describe in Chapter 1 make inferences about 'cognitive' consequences of literacy that are too general and vague to be of any use. Instead they propose testing for specific language skills rather than for 'cognition' and they relate these skills to particular social practices. What is acquired in a particular literacy, they argue, is closely related to the practice of that literacy. They conducted social psychological surveys, linked with anthropological field research by M. Smith, amongst the Vai peoples of Liberia. These people have three forms of script available, Latin, Arabic and Vai, and different individuals make use of different ones in different contexts. Cole and Scribner and their team of researchers tested different Vai literates for the transfer of specific skills that were practised in different literacies. They then formulated their findings in specific terms. If those literate in Vai script, for instance, develop certain skills of contextualisation and word recognition which are transferable to other contexts, it is in very specific ways. If, for instance, particular uses of Vai script promote memorisation, it has to be established which aspects of memory are involved: it cannot be assumed that memory in general is facilitated by literacy in general. Since Vai script is not learnt in schools but through personal tuition, Cole and Scribner hoped that their study would contribute towards an analysis of the significance of literacy separately from the influence of schooling, with which it is generally conflated.

Although this approach provides a useful corrective to the grander claims of Goody and others, it poses an unresolved contradiction between the possibility of isolating ever more precisely the 'technical', 'autonomous' qualities of literacy and the understanding that any literate practice is a social practice and thus cannot be described as 'neutral' or in isolation. Vai literate practices may be usefully isolated from formal schooling, but they are embedded in other socialising practices and in the beliefs and customs which accompany them and give them meaning. The Vai material poses and highlights the basic sociological questions about literacy to which the 'ideological' model of literacy addresses itself.

Michael Clanchy, an historian, describes the shift from memory to written record in medieval England in such a way as to highlight the social and ideological nature of literacy practice (1979). He argues that the shift was facilitated by the continuing 'mix' of oral and literate modes and that written forms were adapted to oral practice rather than radically changing it. He thus provides evidence to challenge the grander claims for the radical shift supposedly entailed by the acquisition of literacy. His carefully documented account of the growth of a 'literate mentality' emphasises the necessity of examining the real social practice involved rather than attempting to infer the nature of literacy itself from introspection or experimentation.

Harvey J. Graff, a social historian, likewise provides a basis for an alternative more socially based view of literacy (1979). He challenges what he calls the 'literacy myth' whereby it is contended that literacy of itself will lead to social improvement, civilisation and social mobility. With reference to nineteenth century Canada he analyses the statistics for occupational and ethnic groupings in relation to evidence of their respective literacy achievements. He discovers that literacy itself made very little difference to occupation and wealth as compared with the significance of ethnic and class origin. He argues that the presentation of literacy as 'autonomous' and 'neutral' is itself part of the attempt by ruling groups to assert social control over the potentially disruptive lower orders. Schooling and the techniques for teaching literacy are often forms of hegemony and it would be misleading in such contexts to represent the process of literacy acquisition as leading to greater 'criticalness' and logical functioning.

Developments in sociolinguistics, of the kind examined in Chapter 4, can also be linked with recent work in literacy criticism which lends support to the 'ideological' model of literacy and helps to move us away from the 'autonomous' model.

Some of the writers I identify as contributing towards the development of an 'ideological' model of literacy may be more aware of the points outlined above than others. Certainly no one of them necessarily represents all of the features outlined, and the model itself is a development from them. But I will attempt to justify the claim that taken together their work represents a significant challenge to the ideas about literacy that have been generally accepted until recently and provides the essential starting point from which to construct an alternative approach.

Section 2: Literacy in Theory and Practice

I provide an analysis of the political and ideological context in which education provision in general and literacy programmes in particular are to be found in a particular area of Iran. I suggest that the detailed study of one such area provides a concrete test of the ideas formulated in Chapters 1–4 and that the material from this area has some general significance.

The area under analysis is that around Mashad, the holy city and capital of Khorosan province in North East Iran on the border with Afghanistan. I did anthropological field work there, as well as teaching in the University of Mashad, at various times between 1970 and 1977. I describe the relations of rich fruit-growing villages in the mountains (concentrating particularly on the village of Cheshmeh where I lived for some time), to the central city and to the poorer grain-producing villages of the plains. I relate some of the significant differences in their response to the oil boom of the mid-1970s to the different ways in which literacy practice was developed there.

I attempt to provide a model of the literacy practice that developed out of the religious schools or 'maktabs' that preceded State schools in the village and compare this with what I term 'commercial' literacy, which developed as a means of handling the economic expansion generated by the oil money. In the village, the leading 'tajers' or middlemen who organised the fruit trade learnt as children in the 'maktab' a particular form of literacy which they then adapted to the requirements of their new commercial position. I argue that this adaptation provides a good example of what I mean by the 'ideological' nature of literacy practice. It was rooted in village institutions, and in the social relations of 'tajers' with other villagers and with city dealers on which their commercial success depended. The construction of this particular literate form was neither an individual matter nor was it a product of specific formal training. Although it emerged from 'maktab' literacy, for instance, it was not a product of 'maktab' pedagogy, which was directed towards a different cluster of meanings and usage. It was a development at the level of ideology, a social construction of reality embedded in collective practice in specific social situations.

I describe in detail the elements of the different literate practices in the village (e.g. use of lists, bureaucratic devices, personal notes, labelling, cheques, religious commentary, signs, poetry etc.) identifying the different perceptions and uses of literacies by different groups within the village. I compare this with the introduction by State schools of a different literacy, less directly integrated into village production and social relations (involving, for example, text books, magazines, newspapers, legal documents, political pamphlets etc.). This literacy has now acquired some significance, but for a different social segment. Newly literate youths, even those trained in city schools, do not apply this 'school' literacy to the commercial activities of the village; they do not become 'tajers'. It represents a different ideology and is employed in different social contexts for different purposes. The nature of the relations between these forms of literacy and the ideologies in which they are embedded is the central theme of Chapters 5 and 6. 'Maktab' literacy was successfully transformed into 'commercial' literacy for a particular social group in the village; what adaptation is likely by either of them to 'school' literacy? And what is the relation of 'school' literacy to the real social practices that Iranians were engaged in at that time?

What are the consequences of applying different models of literacy to the Iranian material? This material was used as a test case for the alternative model of literacy I have been trying to develop. How successfully does its application here suggest that the model can be used? Is a more general application indicated? Can we begin the work of cross-cultural comparison of literacy practices on the theoretical foundation built so far? What practical consequences and political programmes follow from the adoption of the 'ideological' model of literacy? The final section of the book will be concerned particularly with this latter question.

Section 3: Literacy in Practice

In the first chapter of this section, I shall examine examples of Unesco literacy programmes, such as those in Tanzania and Iran, and attempt to elicit the underlying theories on which they are based in the light of the analyses developed in Sections 1 and 2. This will involve attention to the general statements of aims and perspectives provided by Unesco conferences, programme statements etc., and in the literature about these programmes. Anderson's hypothesis that about 40% adult literacy is a threshold for economic development has been taken more literally than he intended and underlies many programmes. What such assumptions fail to specify is what particular literacy practices and concepts that proportion of the population is supposed to acquire; literacy is treated as a single homogenous thing, its variety and relation to different social conditions is reduced to statistical measures and economic functions.

An Iranian work-oriented literacy programme, for instance, was accepted as increasing 'the social exclusiveness of general secondary higher education in order to secure greater economic efficiency in resource utilisation' (Unesco, 1973, Vol. 1, p. 69). The underlying premises of this can be identified as those of the 'autonomous' model of literacy. A Tanzanian programme, recognising that teaching literacy to people who would afterwards have no personal use for reading and writing was futile, proposed the creation of a 'literacy environment' in which the skills learnt would not atrophy (Unesco, 1971). This begged the question as to what, in that case, literacy was being taught for. Carol and Lars Berggren (1975) offer one answer: literate people are perceived by companies contemplating investment as a market for goods that could not otherwise be sold to them. They relate the Unesco concept of 'functional literacy' to crude commercial exploitation and see Unesco idealism as a thin veneer for multinational interests. Arguments about cognitive consequences of acquiring literacy are, for them, to be seen in terms of this larger economic and political context. I shall attempt to place this classic debate into the general context of the models of literacy described in Sections 1 and 2.

Academic writing on social change and development has been significant in contributing concepts of literacy that underlie many Unesco development programmes. I argue that much of this literature tends towards the 'autonomous' model of literacy, as I have described it, and in particular towards individualistic explanations of the 'meaning' of literacy. Lerner, for instance, in his influential *Change in Traditional Societies* conceived of there being a relationship between levels of literacy and such characteristics as 'empathy' and 'cosmopolitanness' – loose and somewhat ethnocentric terms that are employed all too frequently in this field. Oxenham, while relating literacy more closely to social variety than most developmentalists, nevertheless gives credence to the vague and culture-loaded belief that literacy increases people's sense of 'personal efficacy' and that attainments in literacy are associated with 'dispositions favourable towards planned change in a society' (Oxenham, 1980, p. 15). These individualistic, psychologistic approaches to literacy in development programmes, as well as the economistic utilitarian ones cited above, can be seen to rest on assumptions about the nature of literacy itself that, I claim, are often those of the 'autonomous' model. With reference to the critique of this model developed in Section 1, I shall attempt to make explicit what often lies embedded in both the theoretical work and the campaign practice.

What is taken as the 'Unesco view' of literacy has been strongly challenged in the work of P. Freire and his followers (Freire, 1978; cf. also Mackie, 1980). He sees the acquisition of literacy as an active process of consciousness, not just as the passive acquisition of content. He rejects the 'problem solving' ideology within which many literacy programmes operate, and substitutes for it the notion of 'problematising' social reality. The person acquiring literacy should have his or her consciousness raised in the process, enabling them for instance to analyse the historical and social conditions in which particular 'problems' arose in the first place.

Freire's work has been taken as a direct political challenge to the hegemony of ruling capitalist states and of the Unesco programmes that are taken to subserve their interests. But his analyses often appear to be rooted in the kinds of theory of cognitive development and of the relationship of literacy to rationality that are explored in Section 1. Moreover examples of societies where Freire's work has been applied, such as Cuba and Nicaragua, would seem to reinforce the intuition that his work is less radical than has been generally believed. While representing in some ways a shift towards an 'ideological' model of literacy, Freire seems to have not entirely shrugged off the assumptions of the 'autonomous' model.

In Chapter 8 I consider literacy campaigns in the UK and the USA from the point of view of the theories expounded above and their possible practical implications.

In the mid-1970s literacy (or rather perceptions of illiteracy) became a public issue in the UK and the USA. In the UK a Bill in Parliament and a British Broadcasting Corporation (BBC) campaign led to the 'discovery' that as many as one million adults in the country lacked basic literacy skills, as defined in Unesco and developmentalist terms. In the USA the figure cited was as large as 64 million and similar campaigns were conducted both to set up research projects and to 'do something' about 'illiteracy'. Money was set aside to support voluntary teaching schemes and Quangos were set up to co-ordinate the work. Teaching methods were, at first, based on one-to-one relations between the volunteer and the 'illiterate' with various support systems available. One direction in which this experience led the participants was to a rejection of conventional models of literacy and towards an understanding similar to that which I have labelled as the 'ideological' model. It was realised that teaching literacy was not just about phonetics or technical 'skills' but about a whole approach to the use of one's own language and control over one's own life. Methods were evolved for teaching literacy that took account of this perception, such as the creation of learning material by the students themselves in contrast with the previous tendency towards passive reading of whatever had been made available, a tendency that had been generated to some extent by the prevalence of the 'autonomous' model of literacy amongst teachers and educators. Many students who had blamed themselves for their 'failure' to learn to read and write came to recognise that the system had failed them. In some sectors of the literacy programme, students were encouraged not only to produce their own written material for classroom use etc. but to work through the whole production process themselves including binding and distributing their own books. The meaning of 'literacy' to these participants was significantly altered by this practice. In some cases this approach has been challenged by the literary and political establishment, with the refusal of Arts Council grants on the grounds that the work produced in this way was not 'literature', and complaints by at least one Member of Parliament that the content of students' own materials was too politically radical. Such challenges have served to highlight the ideological nature of literate practice and to polarise different approaches to literacy teaching in the adult sector. The 'radicals' argue that the one-to-one approach, while providing a useful transition for those alienated by their experience at school, serves to marginalise and individualise the notion of 'illiteracy' and they point to press reports which concentrated on individual 'illiterates' and how they 'managed' their 'disability'. Mace in *Working with Words* (1979) has drawn attention to these radical directions, while Jones and Charnley (1980 etc.) have produced official reports concentrating on individual attainment and ways of testing it which challenge the establishment view without altogether rejecting it. Levine (1980), in a Social Science Research Council (SSRC) study of 'adult illiterates' has criticised the assumption that 'illiterates' lack 'self-esteem' and has argued that they often manage perfectly well and have positive self-images until some crisis occurs, so that the Mace approach fails to meet their own self image and stated needs.

In the USA similarly the 'discovery' of illiteracy (between 50 and 60 million are quoted as illiterate by Hunter and Harman (1979)) has led to practical programmes that raise the same fundamental issues. I examine these issues, and the approaches and practice developed in relation to them, in the light of the general theoretical models of literacy outlined in Sections 1 and 2 with a view to putting into broader perspective what the practice of literacy now means and is taken to mean in these societies. I conclude with some proposals regarding the practical application of the theories I have been analysing.

SECTION 1

Literacy in Theory

1

THE 'AUTONOMOUS' MODEL:
I LITERACY AND RATIONALITY

I shall attempt to establish the general outlines of what I term the 'autonomous' model of literacy by examining in detail the work of some writers who have explicitly addressed themselves to questions of literacy and its cognitive consequences. Highlighting its features in this way will, I hope, enable us to recognise them more easily when they occur in embedded form in other writers.

Angela Hildyard and David Olson have put forward a 'strong' version of the 'autonomous' model in a recent article. They begin by challenging the current opinion that all peoples share basic functions of the mind such as logical and abstract abilities. They find this view 'alarming' since 'if it is indeed the case that intellectual resources of Savage and Modern minds are essentially equivalent [then] what legitimises the extraordinary efforts and resources that go into compulsory schooling?' (1978, p. 4). There are a number of sociological and political answers to this question, such as the contention that compulsory schooling serves a variety of social functions, including those of social control, transfer of dominant values etc. In the language of some recent approaches, 'compulsory schooling' asserts the 'hegemony' of a ruling class (cf. Dale et al. 1976; Graff, 1979). I will examine such contentions below. They entail quite different assumptions about the nature of literacy than those put forward by Hildyard and Olson. *Their* answer to the question they pose is to say that education systems are to be justified on the grounds that they develop 'intellectual competence that would otherwise go largely undeveloped' (1978, p. 4). They conjecture that literacy plays a central part in this process. The qualities which they attribute to literacy thus take on the more general significance of justifying the vast expense on western education systems. Seen in this perspective, the claims already have political and ideological significance – they are not as neutral or detached as internal presentation of the argument would appear to suggest. The 'autonomous' model is, then, constructed for a specific political purpose.

This is apparent in their claim that differences in intellectual performances of modern and traditional societies are 'sufficiently deep and of sufficient significance to warrant, at least in a literate society, the continued emphasis on schooling and the acquisition of literacy' (ibid. p. 5). They attempt to justify the claim and the assumptions that underlie it, by 'advancing some conjectures and some evidence regarding the ways in which language and thought change under the impact of the specialised forms of written text' (ibid.). Their central conjecture is that there are functions of language that are significantly affected by the mastery of a writing system, particularly its logical functions. Written forms, they argue, enable the user to differentiate such functions in a way less possible in oral language. They distinguish between the function of language as imparting meaning, 'making statements which can be assigned a set of truth conditions' (ibid.), and its function of regulating and maintaining social or interpersonal relations between people. Most utterances, they claim, serve both functions but written forms facilitate the differentiation and separation of the functions. It thus becomes possible, through writing, to specialise language, to use it to serve a specific function rather than conflating different functions. Writing has the effect of distancing the speaker from the hearer; what is said need not be suited to the requirements of the listener because the listener is absent. Consequently the interpersonal or social functions of the language can be more or less held constant. The logical functions of language are given free rein. The invention of writing and particularly the attempt to create autonomous text has resulted in a realignment of the two primary functions of language. Oral language is always directed to a particular individual usually with some intended effect such as influencing his views, maintaining a certain relationship or controlling his actions. It can be constantly modified according to its effect and thus the social function dominates the logical. Written language, on the other hand, makes such interpersonal functions less critical; it can be conducted over time and space and is less subject to immediate feed-back. It thus comes to serve the logical function rather than the interpersonal one. It develops the 'ability to operate within the boundaries of sentence meaning, on the meaning expressly represented in the sentence *per se*, and thereby to operate within the boundaries of an explicitly presented problem' (ibid. pp. 8–9).

It follows from these conjectures that members of literate societies have the possibility of developing logical functions, of specialising in the 'truth functions' of language, and of extracting themselves from the embeddedness of everyday social life. As Hildyard and Olson put it: 'the authority of rhetorical conditions are collapsed onto the truth conditions so that if a statement is true to the facts or to the text itself, that is sufficient condition for its being interpersonally appropriate' (ibid. p. 9). To support these conjectures they cite cross-cultural research into cognitive difference, in particular Patricia Greenfield's study of the differences between schooled and unschooled children amongst the Wolof of Senegal (1972).

Greenfield argues that the significant differences that are revealed by her tests on schooled and unschooled groups derive from fundamental differences between oral and written language. She maintains that 'speakers of an oral language rely more on context for the communication of their verbal messages' (1972, p. 169), and this has implications for cognitive processes. Her hypothesis is 'that context-dependent speech is tied up with context-dependent thought, which in turn is the opposite of abstract thought' (ibid.). She glosses 'abstraction' in a sense close to the literal one: a separation from. Abstraction is, therefore, 'the mental separation of an element from the situation or context in which it is embedded' (ibid.). Oral speech depends on context to communicate meaning; it is therefore egocentric and takes for granted a common point of view as though no others were possible. This quality derives from the fact that oral speech involves face-to-face contact and also that oral languages are less widespread than written languages and so are shared by smaller groups. Written language is also more widespread across cultural groups, and its users do not share a common frame of reference.

She pursues the consequences of these differences for educational modes and for cognitive operations. Education in oral language is context-based and imitative. Kpelle education, for instance, is largely nonverbal, the child learning by imitation. She infers from this: 'thus, in the appropriate real-life situation he learns concrete activities, not abstract generalisations' (ibid. p. 170). Even where words are used, this form of education 'avoids the classificatory and analytic isolating functions which words have in Western culture' (ibid.). I shall return to these quite unwarranted inferences later. Schools in 'technical societies', she continues, develop reading and writing which, unlike oral education systems, emphasise 'telling out of context rather than showing in context' (ibid.). School is isolated from life and 'the pupil must therefore acquire abstract habits of thought if he is to follow the teacher's oral lessons' (ibid. p. 171). Indeed, written language in itself entails higher levels of abstraction because 'while the spoken word stands for something, the written word stands for something that stands for something' (ibid.).

Tests on working class black people are then cited as evidence that in oral contexts education is by demonstration and is 'totally dependent on the concrete physical situation' (ibid.). This has grave consequences for their children who 'do not learn as much from their mothers as do their middle-class counterparts' (ibid.). Moreover these children are deprived intellectually by such an upbringing: 'Thus, a context-dependent teaching style on the part of the mothers is associated with a lesser development of an ability to form conceptual and linguistic abstractions on the part of the children' (ibid. p. 172). One vital consequence was highlighted by Bernstein in his tests of working-class children in England. Much of Greenfield's paper derives from the theoretical foundations laid by Bernstein and she is surprised how closely the 'verbal deprivation' he identifies in working-class English youths corresponds to that which she found amongst the

Wolof. He argued (1971) that the working-class spoke in 'restricted code' which entailed a failure 'to perceive the informational needs of the listener as being different from their own' (Greenfield, 1972, p. 172). Greenfield picks up as most pertinent to her own argument his attempt to trace 'this failure to a lack of conscious differentiation of self from others' and his prediction that this will be 'reflected in the structure of communication, as, for example, in failing to make one's point of view known' (ibid.).

Greenfield's comparable studies and conclusions are related to her research into different groups of Wolof children in Senegal, namely: 'rural unschooled', 'bush schooled' and those who attended westernised schools in the cosmopolitan capital, Dakar. She provided tests for three different age groups in each set, corresponding to six- and seven-year-olds, eight- and nine-year-olds and eleven- to thirteen-year-olds. In tests designed to examine 'concept formation' she asked children to put together those pictures or objects in an array that were most alike, and then to explain the reasons for their choice. Unschooled children gave answers that lead Greenfield to frighteningly large conclusions:

> It seemed that the unschooled Wolof children lacked Western self-consciousness; they did not distinguish between their own thought or statement about something and the thing itself. The concept of a personal point of view was also absent to a greater degree than in Western culture, for the unschooled children could group a given set of objects or pictures according to only one attribute, although there were several other possible bases for classifications. The Wolof school children, in contrast, did not differ essentially from Western children in this respect. It appeared that school was giving both urban and rural children something akin to Western self-consciousness for they could answer questions implying a personal point of view; and as they advanced in school they became increasingly capable of categorising the same stimuli according to different criteria or 'points of view'. (Greenfield, 1972, p. 173.)

She cites Bernstein and others as testing for uses of the form 'I think'. She infers that using such forms means 'absence of cognitive flexibility' and quotes the studies by Bereiter and others (Osborn, 1967) of lower-class children who, it is argued, 'cannot conceive of a single object having two attributes' (ibid.). These findings, she claims, parallel her own amongst the Wolof: 'Thus the absence of self consciousness and the resulting presence of an ego-centrically unified perspective seem to be associated with an inability to shift perspective in concept formation problems' (ibid.).

Her tests for the relation between grammatical structure and context formation similarly show the unschooled Wolof children in a poor light.

Asked to select all the objects in an array that shared a particular attribute and to name the attribute, these children could provide an answer but the grammatical form revealed, according to Greenfield, inferior cognitive facility. Thus, if they said of a group of red objects simply 'red', their answer is taken to be unsatisfactory because 'we are not told *what* is red'. Its communication value is 'more dependent on the situational context'. Saying 'this' or 'they' 'red' is better practice because it entails use of pronouns which 'symbolise what concrete objects belong to the category'. The 'superordinate grouping' has been 'explained by linguistic predication'. 'Schooled children did this more often than unschooled and so were less context-bound' (ibid. p. 174).

Further refinements proposed by Greenfield include an analysis of the significance of grammatical forms for cognitive facility. In Wolof language it is possible to say either 'this is round' or 'this— round'. Greenfield found that the particular form used corresponded to the degree of what she calls 'abstractness'. 'A superordinate grouping in which it is explicitly stated that all members share a single attribute was, however, much more likely when linguistic predicates were formed as complete sentences with copula ["they are round"] than as incomplete sentences without. For a schooled child the probability was increased threefold; for an unschooled child, it was increased sixfold' (ibid.). Similarly, schooled children were more likely to say 'they— round' than to itemise each member of the array 'this— round; this— round' etc. Greenfield takes this to be further evidence of the greater degree of abstraction being learnt in schools.

She links such abstraction explicitly with the fact that schools teach literacy:

> The results led to the hypothesis that school is operating on grouping operations at least partly through the training embodied in the written language. Writing is practice in the use of linguistic contexts as independent of immediate reference. Thus the embedding of a label in a total sentence structure (complete linguistic predication) indicates that it is less tied to its situational context and more related to its linguistic context. The implications of this fact for manipulability are great; linguistic context can be turned upside down more easily than real ones. Once thought is freed from the concrete situation the way is clear for symbolic manipulation and for Piaget's stage of formal operation in which the real becomes a sub-set of the possible. (ibid. p. 175.)

Greenfield's appeal, here, to literacy as the source of significant cognitive differences is crucial. It demonstrates, I would argue, the ideological use to which conceptions of literacy are being put in current academic practice. The appeal to literacy as the basis for mental differences is apparent in her claim that the superior cognitive operations of schooled children amongst the Wolof were 'learnt through the training embodied in written language' (ibid.). The reference to literacy in this context is what induced Hildyard and Olson to quote Greenfield in their own work in order to support their conjectures about the consequence of literacy for such aspects of thought as 'abstractness', 'logic' and 'embeddedness'. Furthermore, its application to class differences has been recognised by many commentators, most notably in the work of Basil Bernstein (1971) on whom Greenfield leans heavily. Stubbs, for instance, notes that 'Bernstein's distinction between restricted and elaborated codes' has often 'been related to distinctions between spoken and written languages respectively (Milroy 1973; Cook-Gumperz 1977; Lunzer and Harison 1979)' (Stubbs, 1980, p. 111).

This trend represents, I would argue, a shift in traditional representations of the differences in thinking between members of different cultures. Writers concerned to establish a 'great divide' between the thinking processes of different social groups have classically described them in such terms as logical/pre-logical, primitive/modern and concrete/scientific. I would argue that the introduction of literate/pre-literate as the criterion for making such a division has given the tradition a new lease of life just as it was wilting under the powerful challenge of recent work in social anthropology, linguistics and philosophy. I would maintain that claims for the cognitive consequences of literacy must take account of this challenge. They cannot simply side-step it by claiming that the appeal to literacy has altered the nature of the 'great divide' theory.

In order to sustain the argument that I am putting forward here, it is important to establish what were the major arguments levelled by anthropologists and others against the 'great divide' theory. We can then proceed to apply them to the work on literacy that we have been examining.

The major challenge has been to question the evidence on the basis of which the distinction 'logical/pre-logical' was made. Analysis has been brought forward to show that what was taken as proof of a lack of logical processes amongst 'primitive' peoples was often simply misunderstanding by ill-informed European commentators of the meaning of what was being said and done. They were ill-informed in the sense that the conceptual basis for understanding such meaning was not carefully theorised, as well as in the more obvious sense that the travellers often simply did not know the language and did not spend enough time living in a particular society. A powerful challenge to such approaches was made as long ago as the 1930s by Professor E. E. Evans-Pritchard who lived with and studied the Azande of Central Africa, a technologically simple society whom Europeans therefore tended to assume were intellectually simple as well. He argued, however, that their views on witchcraft were not, in fact, irrational, illogical or 'mystical' as European conceptions commonly supposed them to be. Once one had accepted the initial premise of statements about witchcraft, the processes of thought could be shown to be the same as those entailed in scientific thought. Other writers have enlarged on these insights, comparing the mechanisms for establishing proof in scientific practice with those of the Azande for establishing the nature of witchcraft. Michael Polanyi, for instance, argued that the way in which a proposition is protected, through such mechanisms as 'nucleated suppression' etc., is exactly the same in both cases (1965). Differences in the content of thought, such as concern with witchcraft or with physics, should not blind us to similarities in the fundamental processes of thought. Robin Horton, in a widely cited article on African systems of thought (1967), likewise attempted to break down the elements of scientific thinking in order to demonstrate that so-called 'primitive' peoples such as the Azande did in fact make use of the same elements of thought, although applied to different content. He argued that it is too simplistic, and indeed ethnocentric, to dismiss such peoples as irrational and unscientific. Too often all that is at fault is the observer's understanding of what other people's statements and actions mean.

Evans-Pritchard and others have also pointed out that the divisions between scientific and non-scientific thinking as such, if they can indeed be reliably established, do not necessarily correlate with different social groups. Members of supposedly 'primitive' societies clearly engage in scientific practices, such as empirical testing of hypotheses, when they plant seeds, the successful growth of which is vital for their survival. Lévi-Strauss has shown, further, that the classification of the natural world amongst South American Indian tribes is as complex and as interesting as those of the academic biologist, at an intellectual as well as a utilitarian level (1966). Conversely, in many contexts in western 'scientific' society, it is clear that what some writers have labelled 'non-scientific' thought is as evident as in non-western societies. This has been investigated in close detail by such social anthropologists as Edmund Leach, who attempted to describe the 'expressive' and symbolic aspects of thinking in industrial and non-industrial society alike (1954, 1976). Wedding rituals in either case are a classic example of how the statements made by participants in a particular context should not be taken literally or at face value but must be interpreted as standing for something else, rich in ambiguity and figures of speech. The extent to which it would be mistaken to take our own rituals literally provides a standard from which to assess our understanding of the rituals and statements of other cultures. Too often what has been taken as 'illogical' or 'mystical' is, in reality, pregnant with symbolic meaning which the observer has failed to appreciate through attempting to interpret it literally.

The anthropological evidence, then, suggests that there is scientific and non-scientific thought in all societies and within all individuals. Observers have simply failed to remark the scientific nature of much of the thinking of so-called 'primitive' peoples and have perhaps overstated the 'scientific' nature of thinking in their own societies.

The recognition of these misunderstandings, and of the amount of dead wood that has to be cleared away before a reliable account of cognitive operations and differences can be provided, is also apparent in recent work by sociolinguists. This work complements that of the anthropologists in the sense that it uses a cross-cultural perspective to study the thinking processes of different social groups within the researcher's own society.

Labov (1973), studying negro youths in the New York ghetto, discovered, as did anthropologists studying other cultures, that representations of cognitive 'deprivation' were founded upon misunderstanding of the real meanings of such people's statements and actions, and upon ethnocentric assumptions about the ways in which logic can be recognised. On investigation, the speech of supposedly retarded New York ghetto youths turned out to have all of the qualities generally associated with logical thought – facility with complex propositions, meaningful sequence, rule recognition, syllogistic reasoning etc. Forms of speech which had been labelled 'ungrammatical', and taken as evidence of cognitive deprivation, are shown by Labov to be simply forms of dialect with no fundamental consequences for cognitive performance. Leaving out the copula (to be), using double negative, interchanging subjective and objective pronouns (he and him) can all be shown to be rule governed and consistent dialect practices, not evidence for an inability to express logical relations as Greenfield and some of the writers she cites had claimed (1972, p. 173).

Noting the similarity between such claims, and those by early travellers regarding the 'illogicality' of the thought of 'primitive peoples', Labov writes: 'When linguists hear Negro children saying "He crazy" or "Her my friend", they do not hear a primitive language' (1973, p. 61). Rather, they recognise that such 'nonstandard dialects are highly structured systems' and that 'the adult or child who uses these rules must have formed at some level of psychological organisation clear concepts of "tense marker", "verb phrase", "rule ordering", "sentence embedding", "pronoun" and many other grammatical categories which are essential parts of any logical system' (ibid. p. 45). I shall examine below (Chapter 3) what recent writers have said about the relationship between such language uses and literacy. For the moment it is sufficient to establish the fact that to speak a language at all is to employ abstraction and logic.

One reason for the previous misrepresentation of the logical abilities of such social groups is that the tests carried out to assess such abilities were unreliable both in method and in conception. The test situation itself was often authoritarian and unfamiliar, discouraging response, and leading to bright children being labelled unresponsive and subnormal. Labov, by simply altering the test situation, such as by creating informality or having two youths to one researcher etc., came up with far 'better' results for clever youths who had been labelled ESN (educationally subnormal) by the conventional system.

He further demonstrates that what is being tested is often the social conventions of a dominant class, rather than universal logic. The convention most often mistaken for logic is explicitness, which, he shows, is not the same thing at all. In relation to a repetition test, he argues that the negro children who failed because they did not repeat the teacher's utterance in the same form were really being failed for a different attitude to surface detail. 'They do not need a new logic; they need practice in paying attention to the explicit form of any utterance rather than its meaning. Careful attention to surface features is a temporary skill needed for language learning – and neglected thereafter by competent speakers' (ibid. p. 51). Such attention to surface forms is also, of course, necessary for the researcher; one aspect of the form of English I am using now, and of that used by Labov, Greenfield and Olson, is its attempt at explicitness. Labov recognises that certain forms of standard English may well have developed such explicitness further than some dialect forms. He argues, however, that this is quite different from logic. 'The logic of standard English cannot be distinguished from the logic of any other dialect of English by any test that we can find' (Labov, 1973, p. 52). Most anthropologists and linguists would add that this is true also of comparisons between different languages: 'there is nothing in the vernacular which will interfere with the development of logical thought' (ibid.).

In the light of Labov's researches it is apparent that Bernstein's famous experiments, which have deeply influenced such writers as Greenfield and Olson, in fact test mainly for explicitness, although they assume this to be 'cognitive flexibility' and logic. For example, when Bernstein showed working-class children a sequence of pictures and asked them to tell the story contained there, they began so to speak from inside it: 'he kicks the ball through the window then the woman chases them' etc. (1971). Middle-class children, on the other hand, drew explicit attention to the test conditions: 'this is a picture; in the picture a boy is depicted as kicking a ball through a window ...' (ibid.). To Bernstein this demonstrates not simply the convention of explicitness which the middle-class child has learnt and has recognised as appropriate for this context, but the development of 'elaborated code' with all its associations of abstraction, logic etc. One might remark that the working-class child considered it redundant to constantly refer to the presence of a picture since he knew that the researcher was present and could see it for himself. There was no need to say 'a' ball, 'a' window, since the researcher was looking at them too and so they were, in common to both viewers, 'the' ball, 'the' window. Were researcher and student both watching an actual event in which someone kicked a ball through a window, the use of 'the' would be obvious and the 'frame' as it were would not need to be drawn. Learning to frame written material, particularly in test conditions, is a convention of our education system. It can be shown to have uses and it may well be advantageous for working-class children to learn it for certain purposes. Its use for examination purposes is clearly a rather restricted justification, although it may account for much of the labelling of 'failure' which the working-class child experiences. Its uses for other social purposes, however, would need to be specified and justified in relation to the context. Moreover, it is only one convention amongst many. The conventions of working-class speech also have their uses, and one could provide an argument for some of these being taught to middle-class children. Perhaps some of the middle-class verbosity found by Labov could be eradicated in this way.

What is clear from this, though, is that what we are talking about are conventions, and it is obvious that conventions derive their meaning from social contexts. What some researchers have done is to shift the significance of their findings away from such socially precise conditions, and to claim a kind of extra-social status for their own conventions by associating them with supposedly general logical qualities. Greenfield in testing Wolof children is really testing for such conventions, although she describes her results in general cognitive terms as though they represented general mental qualities.

In doing so she is reviving the 'great divide' theory that has been so discredited by social anthropologists and sociolinguists. Any researcher who still poses the problem of cognitive difference across cultural groups must confront this literature and take account of these arguments. Although Hildyard and Olson do cite this literature in their article, they do not confront the arguments it raises but simply respond to them with 'alarm'. If these arguments are true, they ask, then 'what legitimizes the extraordinary efforts and resources that go into compulsory schooling?' (1979, p. 5). Finding no answers, partly because they do not spend much time looking for them, they assume that it cannot be true; the differences must be 'sufficiently deep and of sufficient significance to warrant, at least in a literate society, the continued emphasis on schooling and the acquisition of literacy' (ibid.). This is the political and ideological basis of their analysis of literacy which, by a sleight of hand, is presented as the 'neutral', 'objective' findings of the scientist, appropriately couched in the technical language of their academic discipline.

They and others who employ what I term the 'autonomous' model of literacy appear, then, to believe that this model insulates them from the arguments I have been discussing. The supposedly technical and neutral nature of the 'autonomous' model of literacy which they employ appears to absolve them from the charge that they are making ideological claims about cultural difference. They can argue, whether implicitly or explicitly, that this new version of the 'great divide' – the division between literate and non-literate – does not discriminate between cultures but simply between technologies. Since technologies are 'neutral', then no aspersions are being cast on individual members of cultures which happen to lack a particular technology and are thus taken to lack certain intellectual advantages. Where Lévy-Bruhl's (1926; cf. also Evans-Pritchard, 1970) version of the 'great divide' theory claimed differences in cognitive *capacity* between members of different cultures, those appealing to literacy simply claim differences in cognitive *development*. The suggestion is no longer that a culture has acquired such technological skills as literacy because it is intellectually superior, as earlier racist theories had argued. Rather, it is claimed that a culture is intellectually superior because it has acquired that technology.

Although this may sound appealing, it is not, I contend, tenable. The argument must still confront the anthropological and linguistic evidence for intellectual development as well as capacity in different cultures. It cannot side-step this challenge by claiming to be neutral and value-free because of its appeal to the technology of literacy. This technology is, in fact, ideologically charged; any version of literacy practice has been constructed out of specific social conditions and in relation to specific political and economic structures, as I hope to demonstrate below. A statement about cognitive difference based on assessment of the nature of literacy is as socially-embedded and open to challenge as are statements about cognitive differences based on race, ethnicity and class.

If we can establish that literacy practice involves a socially variable set of conventions (as I hope this book will make a contribution to doing), then claims for its consequences will not so easily be disguised as universal truths. Such claims will be shown to rest, instead, on faith in the value, indeed superiority, of particular conventions. The faith of Greenfield, Hildyard and Olson in the consequences of the particular literacy practices which they describe will appear as faith in the particular social conventions within which such practice became established.

The claim that unschooled Wolof children have not developed the 'logical functions' of language will appear then as no more than a statement that the conventions in which their thinking is expressed are different from those of the researcher herself. Greenfield tries to claim more than this, as do Hildyard and Olson. They attempt to maintain that their own conventions are superior. However, they do not do so directly, as earlier writers in the 'great divide' tradition did. Instead they do so indirectly, by appealing to the supposed intrinsic and culture-free nature of literacy. If they can establish that literacy in itself constructs superior logical functions, then it will follow that those without it have inferior logical functions. The assertion is supposedly absolved of its racist and ethnocentric connotations by the neutrality of literacy. 'Scientific' tests for cognition can be conducted not on social groups and individuals as such, with all the political implications that involves, but on a newly constructed, asocial category of 'literates' and 'non-literates', as though the culture they belonged to were incidental. The implications of the findings can then be claimed to follow directly from scientific experiments conducted in an open-minded way with no prior assumptions. The fact that the Wolof turn out to be less 'logical' when in their own environment than when in contact with European influences just happens to follow from the tests, whatever we might want to believe. The 'great divide' has been reestablished, by the appeal to literacy, apparently on a 'scientific' basis and apparently without the offensive appeals to inherent cultural and intellectual superiority that discredited its early phases.

If, however, we do apply anthropological and linguistic perspectives to this recent work on the consequences of literacy, as I claim we must despite its claim to protection from them, then that work in fact turns out to be as biased as that of the earlier phases. If we strip it of the insulation apparently provided by its appeal to the technology of literacy, we will expose the same ethnocentric claims and uncritical faith in the observer's own ways of thinking.

When Greenfield claims that oral speech is context-dependent, the anthropological evidence would challenge her to demonstrate what speech, whether oral or written, was not. If she is simply referring to degrees of context-dependency, then she must establish a scale on which such things can be measured. She must also show the relationships of such a scale to the claims for detachment made within particular cultural conventions. Merina orators in Madagascar, for instance, make claims for detachment similar to those of westernised educators in Senegal (Bloch, 1976). Greenfield's scale must be capable of distinguishing such local claims from 'true' evidence of detachment. The example, however, demonstrates the conceptual problems in devising such a scale since 'detachment' and 'context-dependency' are themselves culturally-loaded terms. Greenfield attempts to avoid this by claiming to test for 'abstractness'. When, however, we examine her definitions and her evidence we find that the differences she discovers in performance skills are no more than differences in explicitness, of the kind noted by Labov. She defines abstraction, for instance, as 'a separation from' or 'the mental separation of an element from the situation or context in which it is embedded' (1972, p. 169).

When she applies this to her test situations, however, she tends to interpret it in the narrow sense of explicitness rather than with reference to the higher orders of logic to which abstractness usually refers and which the general weight of her argument implies. If, in fact, we apply the higher order definition to the evidence she adduces from Wolof schoolchildren we will find that it applies to schooled and unschooled alike. When unschooled children group the members of an array according to some such criterion as 'red' or 'round', they reveal exactly the higher processes of 'abstraction' even if their language use stops short of explicitness. Indeed, Labov's work and that of other linguists argues that any user of language is of necessity involved in abstraction in its higher order sense. The simple fact of referring to something not present is already a separation from the immediate context, while the concepts and terms employed in any language involve degrees of such separation. The word 'red' separates the colour of an object from its form. The word 'round' separates form from function etc. Furthermore, the grammatical structure and the rules it entails are, as Labov points out, 'essential parts of any logical system' (1973, p. 45). In observing such rules, as they clearly do since otherwise they would not communicate, unschooled Wolof children are demonstrating a use of logic, and of abstraction. The differences between schooled and unschooled children that Greenfield's material suggests are at a less universal and profound level than her descriptions imply.

On the least culture-bound scale for determining cognitive operations, that of 'degree of abstractness', the anthropologist and the linguist would tend, then, to argue that all societies and social groups share common capacities. Further, most would argue that all peoples have evidenced certain basic developments of these capacities, notably with regard to language facility and abstract thought. Where differences can be found in language use and mental skills, they are more appropriately described as cultural conventions than seen as evidence for profound disjunctures in mental development between members of different groups. The differences between schooled and unschooled Wolof children are more appropriately described as differences in conventional uses of explicitness than as differences in 'abstraction'. The reasons for such different conventions must then be sought in the social context.

Unschooled children, if the evidence does demonstrate that they are being less explicit, may in fact be taking it for granted that the questioner can see what is being referred to so that there is no apparent need to be explicit. Schooled children, on the other hand, may have been taught that in formal school situations such assumptions must be suspended, however strange that may appear to be. They have learnt the convention of adopting a 'detached' role, of not indicating their own presence in a situation and of not acknowledging what they know about others. Such conventions are common in English education where students are taught to use impersonal and passive forms rather than the first person. But these conventions do not tell us anything about the student's facility with abstraction nor about his or her logical performance. They might, in some cases, indicate a facility of explicitness, but even here we have to be careful since what is or is not explicit is always relative. The schooled children may be aptly described as speaking explicitly when they say 'they are red' but they are not being as explicit about what they are doing as Greenfield, for instance, is attempting to be. She is trying to make explicit what lies hidden at another level, one which the participants, whether schooled or unschooled, are not drawing attention to themselves: the cognitive level. Similarly, I, as an anthropologist, am attempting to draw attention to another level at which Greenfield is not being explicit: namely, the fact that what schooled children are doing has been learnt as a convention within a school system. I am attempting to make explicit what is for the participants a shared and implicit agreement on the structure within which the practice is taking place. I can argue that Greenfield does not make this explicit because she is taking for granted conventions that she herself has learnt in the western education system and which she expects her readers to share. She addresses herself in this article not to the schoolchildren whom she describes but to an audience of fellow academics. So she does not feel the need to make these 'academic' conventions explicit. Knowledge of when to make a convention explicit is culturally learnt, and use varies according to context. Unschooled Wolof children know when to make certain things explicit in their own culture; it would appear that they are not triggered off to do so by Greenfield's questions. Not having been trained in school formalities, there is no reason why they should associate her test questions with the need to make explicit answers, or why they should pretend that the questioner is not there as the 'detached' answer requires. Schooled children, on the other hand, had learnt these conventions and this is why their answers accord with them.

Greenfield herself provides some evidence that the test situation was not entirely culture-free although she does not allow this to restrict her from making large inferences from the results. When the Wolof children were asked to put together the pictures or objects in an array that were most alike and to give their reasons, the question was at first put in the form 'Why do you say (or think) that these are alike?'. American and European children had been known to respond well enough to this form of words and schooled Wolof children did so too. But the unschooled children met 'this type of question with uncomprehending silence'. The testers might have got a clue from this that such a question was entirely artificial, constructed out of test situations and irrelevant to children who did not go to school and so were not used to being exposed to such tests.

Instead the researchers changed the form of the question and asked not 'Why do you say (or think) that these are alike?' but 'Why *are* these alike?' The children then answered the questions. But their initial difficulty is recorded as a 'lack of western self-consciousness; they did not distinguish between their own thought or statement about something and the thing in itself' (p. 173). This is a somewhat exaggerated inference to draw from such narrowly based data. To infer that because Wolof children were not familiar with western school practices they were therefore unable to distinguish between their thought and its object unjustifiably inflates the significance of the western school and its practices. If we really wanted to find out whether the unwesternised Wolof were capable of expressing different points of view, we could do worse than to look for instance at their political activities and see whether, in factional disputes, the lobbying that takes place indicates such an awareness. To rest the whole so-called 'cognitive skill' of 'variable points of view' on a single convention is greatly misleading. Moreover, an explicit claim to multiple points of view tells us nothing about the actual practice of using them. School children who have learnt to express insights explicitly in terms of various points of view do not necessarily, in practice, make much political, intellectual or other use of such variety. Conversely, indigenous politicians, who do not make explicit reference to the individual actor as having multiple points of view, may nevertheless in practice make considerable use of those multiple points of view that are implicit in the existence of different political factions. The concept of the individual actor is itself a political construction, highly charged and central to much western political practice; it can be used, for instance, to give the impression that 'choice' is being exercised when analysis of the deeper political and economic structures would indicate that there is no real choice. The expression of individual choice and of multiple points of view is, in that sense, 'ideological', since it disguises the true situation behind an appearance of reality. It leads participants to put up with exploitation, for instance, with lack of real choice and an inability, despite exercising different points of view, to alter the real political and economic situation. If we recognise the possibility of such an argument in relation to the concept 'multiple points of view', then we must recognise that the ability to exercise multiple points of view is not very fully tested by Greenfield's school tests. Conversely, the school tests for explicitness do not tell us very much about the exercise of multiple points of view.

Moreover, particular examples of the use or non-use of multiple points of view are not necessarily indicators of cognitive deprivation. I might argue that a particular capitalist economist is so embedded in the political and economic structure of the society that employs him that he fails to represent adequately the challenge levelled by 'political economy' to the perspective he purveys, and thus fails to take into account multiple points of view. Whether I would be justified in couching this political criticism in terms of cognitive deprivation – that he lacks 'cognitive flexibility' or 'cannot distinguish between his own thought about something (e.g. capitalism) and the thing itself' (Greenfield, p. 173) – seems to me doubtful. It might strengthen my case to appeal to apparently neutral, non-political standards but I do not suppose that I would be saying anything useful about the nature of cognition. If I were to write of Milton Friedman: 'the absence of self-consciousness and the resulting presence of an egocentrically unified perspective seem to be associated with an inability to shift perspective in concept formation problems', I do not suppose that many psychologists would accept such an application of the language of psychology. It might be argued that, even if such a statement were true of certain of Friedman's works, it would not necessarily reveal anything about the man himself and also that the appeal to cognition was irrelevant. It would have been more appropriate to limit oneself to making political comment and to exploring the limitations of the ideas and concepts that underly a capitalist system rather than directing the criticism towards the cognitive capacity or development of particular groups or individuals. The flaw, to which I should address myself, if there is one, lies in the ideas not in the individual mind.

The same is true, I would argue, of the ideas and concepts of the unschooled Wolof. If they do not express the concept of multiple points of view in a way familiar to those schooled in western ways, we might be justified in exposing the limitations of their expressions and of the thought system within which they operate, but this would not tell us anything about the individuals or groups themselves as thinkers. Moreover, the Wolof may retort that they do have ways of expressing multiple points of view and that we should attempt to understand these before dismissing them *en bloc*. They may, indeed, wish to defend the particular concepts and ideas they hold, as Friedman might wish to defend his, and to point out the limitations of their critic's own conventions, such as the conventions for 'self consciousness' developed by western schooling. In such intellectual dispute and discourse, the claim by one side that the other lacks cognitive skills appears as part of the political process of debate. In a society that legitimises its forms of truth by appeal to 'science' and 'objectivity', a person's case will certainly appear stronger if she or he can demonstrate that the other side is 'context-bound' and limited in their deployment of such logical abilities as 'abstraction'. One does not get the impression, however, that Greenfield recognises this polemical and ideological aspect of her description of unschooled thinking. Instead it is presented as though it really were neutral, detached and scientific, and that the description reliably tells us of Wolof mental states rather than of Wolof cultural conventions.

That the ideological purpose of such work is to justify and defend western educational practice is, indeed, made explicit in the article by Hildyard and Olson (1978) as we have seen. In Greenfield, however, it remains implicit although it is not too difficult to uncover. In comparing oral and literate societies in terms of their education systems, for instance, she represents oral systems as decidedly inferior. They are not only context-based, they are also imitative and that has severe cognitive consequences. Kpelle children, she asserts, do their learning in the appropriate real-life situation and thus they learn 'concrete activities, not abstract generalisations' (p. 170). The leap in the argument here reveals an underlying interest akin to that expressed more explicitly by Hildyard and Olson: namely, in justifying the large and expensive western education systems that teach children away from the real-life situation. There is, in fact, no justification for Greenfield's inference here. Learning a practice in the situation where that practice is conducted must involve some abstraction if the practice itself does. It is impossible, for instance, to fully imitate the practice of making political speeches that analyse, summarise and comment upon a social situation without also developing the abstract skills that such practice entails. Anthropologists have produced considerable evidence of such analytical and abstract speech-making in oral cultures, as they have of other practices that involve such abilities (Bloch, 1975). Indeed, much 'practical' scientific learning in a western education system takes place in a laboratory where students imitate, learn concrete activities and at the same time are assumed to be developing logical and abstracting abilities.

Greenfield further claims that where Kpelle 'concrete' education is also verbal, it is still inferior to western verbal education: 'It avoids the classificatory and analytic isolating functions which words have in Western culture' (p. 170). The consequences of such a claim are enormous. Does Greenfield really believe that oral societies lack these functions of language? Linguists and anthropologists alike have carefully documented the complex classification systems apparent in non-literate societies and have recognised the presence of abstraction in both. Pulgrum, for instance, writes:

> If communication takes place acoustically or optically (through speech or writing) then this is due to the faculty of abstraction of the auditory and visual centres of the brain, that is, the ability of the brain to recognise the class in a specimen of the class, regardless of the individual features of the specimen. This intellectual process is of greatest linguistic and epistemological importance, because thanks to it human beings can devise and use common nouns, which are class names and not merely proper names for

each individual of a species of beings or class of things. Phoneme and grapheme are precisely such class abstractions. In the absence of classes of phones or phonemes valid for all members of a linguistic community, all oral communication would cease, for every individual could talk intelligibly only to himself, because he could meaningfully use, actively and passively, only one set of phones, namely his own. Even animals can do better than that. (Pulgrum, 1951, p. 16.)

The very use of language, then, whether oral or literate involves classification, abstraction and the selection by specific criteria of elements from a largely undifferentiated universe. Greenfield, on the other hand, would appear to be arguing that only graphemes and not phonemes involve class abstractions. This would imply, according to Pulgrum's argument, not only that the Wolof could not communicate with Greenfield but also that they could not communicate with each other. Lévi-Strauss, amongst others, has provided ethnographic validation for Pulgrum's position. In detailed descriptions of 'oral' cultures he has shown how such systems of classification work in practice. Classification, he shows, involves selection and isolation of elements whose meaning derives from their being part of a system rather than from any intrinsic significance. Thus, a member of another culture can never know without exploring that system, what criteria have been used to link elements in a set. The Ojibwa Indians of Parry Island, for instance, number the eagle and squirrel among their 'totems'. Lévi-Strauss explains the connection: 'Fortunately a native text explains that these animals are included as symbols of the trees they each inhabit; hemlock trees and cedar trees respectively. The interest which the Ojibwa have in squirrels is therefore really an interest in a kind of tree' (1966, p. 60). Like phonemes themselves, words only have significance in relation to other words and as part of a total system of classification. To suggest that some oral forms of education involve a use of words that lack 'classificatory and analytic isolating functions', as Greenfield does, is meaningless. To claim that such functions are peculiar only to western cultural uses of words is plain ethnocentrism easily refuted by the evidence available.

Lévi-Strauss' reference to the Ojibwa use of squirrels as symbols for trees also highlights another aspect of Greenfield's case. She argues that writing provides 'practice in using linguistic context as independent of immediate reference. Thus the embodying of a label in a total sentence structure ... indicates that it is less tied to its situational context and more related to its linguistic context' (1972, p. 175). She is thinking here, specifically, of the way in which schooled Wolof children in her tests described the sets they selected in terms of 'complete linguistic predication', using such terms as 'they are round' rather than 'they— round'. This complet-eness and therefore detachment, she claims, facilitates manipulability: 'linguistic contexts can be turned upside down more easily than real ones. Once thought is freed from the concrete situation the way is clear for symbolic manipulation and for Piaget's stage of formal operation in which the real becomes a sub-set of the possible' (ibid. p. 172). It would appear from her article that she believes that the unschooled Wolof have not passed through this stage. Lévi-Strauss' example is drawn from a society which, like the unwesternised Wolof, is oral. Yet he demonstrates that symbolic manipulation is a complex part of their linguistic and social practice. Squirrels are not treated literally as 'things' in the outer world but as, firstly, parts of sets defined by such criteria as 'those that live in trees' and, secondly, 'available for symbolic manipulation' since they can be taken to stand for the very trees they live in. Other peoples, however, use the same apparent elements for different purposes. Amongst the Fang of the Gabon, for instance, pregnant women are forbidden to eat squirrels due to quite other considerations:

> Squirrels shelter in the holes of trees and a future mother who ate their flesh would run the risk of the foetus copying a squirrel and refusing to leave the uterus. The same reasoning could equally well apply to weasels and badgers, who live in burrows, but the Hopi follow a quite different line of thought; they hold that the meat of these animals is favourable to child-rearing because of their habit of working their way through the ground and 'getting out' at some other place when they are chased into a hole. They therefore help the baby to 'come out quickly'. (Lévi-Strauss, 1966, p. 61.)

Nor should these statements necessarily be taken literally: the animals are interesting and people adopt attitudes to them not because of any beliefs in the direct material effect of squirrels on child-birth but because of their usefulness in helping people to make intellectual and symbolic discrimina-tions – they are 'good to think'. Given the vast symbolic and metaphorical potential of the natural world, it is obvious, says Lévi-Strauss, that the same characteristics could be given different meaning and that different characteristics could be selected to make up a set. But: 'Arbitrary as it seems when only its individual terms are considered, the system becomes coherent when it is seen as a whole set' (ibid.).

In this sense the elements of a people's 'real' universe can be 'turned upside down' as easily as those of its linguistic universe, since their appre-hension of both stem from the same fundamental principles of thought and meaning construction. These principles involve the attribution of meaning through placing elements in relation to each other. The characteristics of both the phonemes and of the things in the natural world that are selected for specific purposes are arbitrary in themselves but they become meaningful when contrasted with others to form a set. Linguistic contexts are not, as Greenfield supposes, more easily 'turned upside down' than 'real ones'. The 'real' is a sub-set of the possible for all language users. All peoples manipulate elements of linguistic and 'real' systems in ways that involve symbolic and logical operations.

The unschooled, oral Wolof do not, then, lack the abilities of abstraction, symbolisation and formal logic that schooled, literate children are claimed to have. The differences between the two groups cannot be couched in such grandiose terms. There is not a 'great divide' between them as Greenfield would have us believe. Her data provides us, in fact, with evidence of very little comparative value.

What we do learn, however, from the article and the use of it by Hildyard and Olson is something of the ideological nature of recent claims for the consequences of literacy. These claims are made in the context of attempts to justify expenditure on western education systems and to represent the ideals of the writers' own culture as 'universal'.

In this sense the claims for literacy can be described as 'ideological'. They are part of an armoury of concepts, conventions and practices that give meaning to and protect the writer's own social formation and specifically their own place within it. What Greenfield and others are privileging and providing ideological support for is, in fact, their own academic establishment, their own work practice within it, their own values and rules. Moreover, although what they are testing other people for are their own conventions, their own work does not necessarily provide evidence of them in practice. The conventions are, in fact, ideals. Much academic language is, in practice, obscure and verbose. Labov's work to redeem, as it were, underprivileged speech also entailed a revealing critique of more privileged forms. He compared the speech of a negro ghetto youth with that of a middle-class, educated man in terms of their underlying coherence and clarity rather than their surface form. He found that the ESN youth Larry was arguing cogently and pithily, once the dialect conventions of his speech were recognised, while the middle-class speaker circled around his subject, waffled and got side-tracked (1973, p. 53). Work by Rosen (1972) in England, which challenges some of Bernstein's claims regarding working-class thought, also provides an analysis of middle-class speech that shows it to be less than clear, precise or detached.

The same is true of much written academic language, despite the claims of Olson and Greenfield to the contrary. Indeed, much of their own writing is embedded, context-laden and ethnocentric, as the current argument attempts to demonstrate. They represent the classic disproof of their own claims for the detached and context-free qualities of writing. What they are writing about in reality are the ideal standards of their own social group, those that give meaning to their work practice even if they do not always live up to them. Greenfield's testing, for instance, of those who variously succeed and fail by these ideal standards has the quality of a social ritual to establish the true order. Her account has some of the qualities of myth in validating shared beliefs and providing a charter for social action. The 'truth' value of statements is classically tested in such ways in different societies. The particular forms adopted by Greenfield, Hildyard and Olson can be related to the social formations and institutions that generated them, in this case specific academic institutions, just as in oral societies statements about truth are expressed and validated in terms of such complex forms and institutions as witchcraft, religion, cosmology and ritual.

It is in this sense that the claims that we have been examining concerning the consequences of literacy are 'ideological'. They derive from the writers' own work practice and belief system and serve to reinforce it in relation to other groups and cultures.

That Hildyard and Olson have in mind their own academic establishment is apparent not only from the standards and ideals to which they appeal, but also from the explicit nature of the examples which they use. They support their conjecture that writing enables interpersonal meanings to be dominated by the logical functions of language, for instance, by citing the Royal Society of London. 'Just such a re-alignment [from interpersonal to logical functions of language] in historical fact characterised the philosophical bias of the British empiricists as represented, for example, in the charter of the Royal Society of London which demanded "a mathematical plainness of language" and a rejection of "all amplifications, digressions and swellings of style"' (1978, p. 9). Literacy, in this case, is taken to involve attention to the 'meaning expressly represented in the sentence *per se*' to the exclusion of the interpersonal and social implications that dominated oral language. The example appears to be offered in order to demonstrate the relationship of literacy to a scientific tradition. It presents the Royal Society as evidence of the logical and socially detached nature of language.

Yet this is the very example that one would have used to challenge their argument. For the origins and development of the Royal Society of London, far from demonstrating the objectivity and truth of scientific inquiry, is a classic example of the extent to which such inquiry is contingent on social pressures, political interests and the nature of the institutions in which it is conducted (cf. Smith, 1960, Ch. 1). The competition for status and patronage between the Royal Society and the British Academy, for instance, demonstrates how alternative theories of knowledge are embedded in real ideological and political circumstances and are not as rarified and detached as they are commonly claimed to be. The charter that was drawn up represents, in fact, just such a claim: it was a political weapon in the battle for status and funding and is not to be taken simply at face value. Similarly, the description of the conventions regarding the form of language to be used are to be interpreted more as a parody and critique of the rival Academy than as evidence of what members of the Royal Society really did. The aims set out in the charter do not, in any case, represent the only form in which scientific progress can be achieved; other conventions than 'mathematical plainness of language' could also be appealed to as significant for intellectual endeavour. As with all claims made by competing groups for the objective nature of their own discourse, those made by the Royal Society are tainted by the contingencies of the world in which they were made. Observers from other periods attempting to make sense of such discourse have to understand the conventions and to unpack the ideology. Far from doing this, Hildyard and Olson simply reproduce those very conventions in their own work making the same claims for objectivity as those made by the Royal Society. The claims which they make for the consequences of literacy belong to the same tradition. They are not made any more convincing to a modern reader by the assumption that this tradition really was 'objective'.

That they are really writing about the superiority of their own academic tradition, rather than about some universal characteristics of literacy in itself, becomes apparent when they pursue the implications of literacy for language forms. The result of acquiring literacy, they conjecture, 'is not an ordinary language ... it is the language of analytic thinking and explicit argument and it is the tool that has been adopted by science and philosophy and to a large extent by the formal school system' (ibid. p. 10). If they are saying that 'analytic thinking and explicit argument' are the sole province of literate cultures, and by implication their own, then they must confront the counter-evidence provided by social anthropologists of the intellectual achievements of so-called 'primitive' societies that do not have literacy. Without this cross-cultural breadth their argument appears parochial and ethnocentric.

What is also required is some analysis of the social practice of 'science and philosophy' in different contexts. We might find, for instance, that 'analytic thinking' of the kind they describe, free of interpersonal bias and 'meaning what they say with little or no room for interpretation' is no more apparent within university institutions and the formal school system than within other social institutions. Such practice needs investigation before we can accept it, *en bloc*, as evidence for objectivity and logical thought. The investigations by social anthropologists of the conventions of other societies for detaching utterances from their immediate context would provide a useful model for such an inquiry. Forms of oratory described by Bloch in Madagascar and Turton for the Mursi of East Africa (Bloch, 1975), for instance, involve conventions for distancing the speaker and separating out some aspects of meaning from contingent social pressures, without the use of written forms. They do, nevertheless, reveal implicit social bias and have political implications, just as does the work done in British universities. While societies do themselves construct devices for specialising and separating out levels of meaning, this does not mean that they ever achieve in reality the claims that they make about such discourse. As we saw earlier, the very writers whom we are discussing themselves make ritualistic claims for objectivity that function more to support their own ideology than to convince a sceptical reader of the 'truth'. But writers do not have a monopoly on such claims; they are part of oral practices too. There has not been any demonstration of a necessary correlation between the incidence of claims to objectivity and the development of literacy. Even less has there been evidence of any real correlation of objectivity itself with literacy practice.

Moreover, the representation of literate practice that is offered by writers like Olson, Hildyard and Greenfield is a limited one in relation to the whole range of literate practices that could be described. Olson's claims for the consequences of literacy refer only to the essay-text form of writing, as though this was what is generally meant by 'literacy'. Yet the evidence we have available suggests that this is too specific and narrow an example from which to generalise. Goody's examination of historical records, for instance, suggests that for many centuries very few 'texts' were produced, the vast bulk of writing being concerned with lists, tables, charters, headings, business records etc. (Goody, 1977). Recent ethnography of writing has demonstrated that the same is true for many contemporary societies now labelled 'literate'; much of the practice turns out to be, as in Iran (see below, Section 2), writing names on crates of produce, keeping records of business transactions, writing cheques etc., or, as in English factories, reading warning or instruction labels, one-word sign symbols and signing names or filling in forms (see Section 3). The generalisations made about the essay-text form already assume a social formation in which it is significant and embedded in specific social institutions. Thus, what is said about the text is contingent on the nature of those institutions: it will differ across literate societies, as it does for instance between those with a tradition of novel-writing or of academic institutions etc. and those without, and its consequence will depend on the social role, functions and meanings of its practice.

The essay-text is not the same, then, as 'literacy'. If Hildyard and Olson were saying that the form of literacy represented by its essay-text development in European academic institutions facilitates certain social, political or ideological functions that other forms of literacy and oral forms handle less efficiently, then one could test the hypothesis against the social facts. Even then, when formulated in this more precise and sociological way, the hypothesis is not yet proven. But their argument is not couched in these terms. Rather it is couched in absolutist terms that reify literacy as though its very essence were being described and that unjustifiably relate specific cultural manifestations of it to such universals as logic, abstraction etc. Expressed in this way the hypothesis does not do justice to the variety and complexity of literate practices, undervalues the character of oral practices, and sets up a 'great divide' that they themselves reject when it is made explicit.

Indeed, Hildyard and Olson do recognise the dangers of stating their case in such strong terms and they attempt to qualify it. 'We do not wish to imply that all written language is autonomous and that all oral language is context-based. Clearly some forms of written language, for example personal letters, do rely on a shared knowledge base and some oral language, for example lectures, can employ the autonomous language of text' (ibid. p. 10). But they go on to represent these examples as limited qualifications to their general thesis and to argue that nevertheless 'literacy fosters the specialisation of the logical functions of language resulting in a focus on sentence meaning *per se*' (ibid.).

If the examples cited by Hildyard and Olson of oral language being 'autonomous' and of written language being 'context-based' were the rare exceptions that the reference to letter writing and to lectures suggests them to be, then their conjectures about literacy would have some credence, though the argument could not be as absolute as they sometimes make it appear. But the many complex descriptions of the real social practice of literate and oral modes that are now becoming available suggest that literacy and orality are not so vastly differentiated as these writers claim. The examples which they cite as exceptions in fact correspond more closely to the norm: literate practices are everywhere 'context-based' while oral language has everywhere developed techniques for separating out different contexts. This can be illustrated from a wide variety of cases: the uses of literacy for social control in nineteenth century Canada, for instance, where any 'critical' element was carefully excluded (Graff, 1979); the restriction of the content of written forms to religious tracts by the Methodist missionaries who introduced literacy to Fiji in the nineteenth century (Clammer, 1976); the examples from British literacy campaigns that show how illiteracy developed in schools because of the class-based nature of schooling (Mace, 1979); the uses of literacy for religious and symbolic purposes in Ghana (Goody, 1968); the greater trust placed by thirteenth century knights in England on seals and symbols as means of legitimating charters and rights to land and their suspicion of the written document as more likely to be forged and inaccurate

(Clanchy, 1979); the development in Iranian villages of forms of literacy taught in Koranic schools into forms of literacy appropriate for commercial trading in a rapidly modernising and urbanising economy (Section 2). All of these descriptions of literacy practice, which I shall deal with in more detail below, suggest that attention to the 'interpersonal', socially-conditioned aspects of literacy is central to understanding the nature of that practice. These are not just minor counter examples that prove the rule, as Olson's reference to the personal nature of letters attempts to suggest: they are what literacy is. It is always embedded in some social form, in conventions such as letter writing, charters, catechisms, business styles, academic 'texts' etc., and it is always learnt in relation to these uses in specific social conditions. These conditions include theories of pedagogy and practices of hegemony that help to determine the meanings of literacy for particular practitioners. As Graff argues, literacy can only be understood in context: 'it can be established neither arbitrarily nor uniformly for all members of the population' (1979, p. 292).

I shall now examine these works in more detail in order to develop my critique of the 'autonomous' model and to move towards an alternative 'ideological' model. I have cited the work of Olson, Hildyard and Greenfield as representative of the 'strong' version of the 'autonomous' model, although other writers could have served the purpose equally well so my criticisms are not intended as specific to them. In the next chapter, I shall examine the work of Goody, which appears to justify the 'autonomous' model from a more detached, anthropological perspective and which is probably the major source of general conceptions about literacy outside that discipline. We will see from this how deeply the 'autonomous' model is rooted in contemporary thought and at what levels, therefore, the challenge to it must be conducted.

2

THE 'AUTONOMOUS' MODEL:
II GOODY

The most influential presentation of the 'strong' version of the 'autonomous' model has probably been that of the social anthropologist, Jack Goody. Frustrated by his colleagues' lack of attention to the problems of literacy, partly because of their tradition of studying 'pre-literate' societies, Goody has attempted in a number of articles and books (1963, 1968, 1977) to describe the importance and 'potentialities' of writing. This polemical concern to highlight the importance of what had been ignored is significant in helping to explain why Goody so overstates the case. For, despite his explicit recognition that 'writing is not a monolithic entity' and that 'in the study of behaviour, there are few, if any "sufficient causes"' (1968, p. 4), Goody can quite legitimately be charged with arguing for the 'autonomy' of literacy and with reducing its significance – as the 'technology of the intellect' – to a kind of technological determinism.

The various versions of Goody's case comprise major characteristics of what I term the 'autonomous' model. He believes that the distinction literate/non-literate is similar to, but more useful than, that traditionally made between logical and 'pre-logical'. This, he claims, is because of the inherent qualities of the written word – writing makes the relationship between a word and its referent more general and abstract, it is less closely connected with the peculiarities of time and place than is the language of oral communication. Writing is closely connected to, 'fosters' or even 'enforces' the development of 'logic', the distinction of myth from history, the elaboration of bureaucracy, the shift from 'little communities' to complex cultures, the emergence of 'scientific' thought and institutions and even the growth of democratic political processes. These views of the consequences of literacy, held with greater or lesser attention to the explicit caveats which Goody enters, deeply permeate the work of his fellow anthropologists as well as that of developmentalists and some social psychologists. It is important, then, in attempting to establish the study of literacy practices on a sounder basis, to examine Goody's argument as a test case for those of many other writers who have paid less explicit attention to the questions than he has. I shall argue that he overstates the significance that can be attributed to literacy in itself: that he lends authority to a language for describing literacy practices that often contradicts even his own stated disclaimers of the 'strong' case; that he understates the qualities of oral communication; that he sets up unhelpful and often untestable polarities between, for instance, the 'potentialities' of literacy and 'restricted literacy'; and that he polarises the differences between oral and literate modes of communication in a way that gives insufficient credit to the reality of 'mixed' and interacting modes. Despite the density and complexity of social detail in Goody's descriptions of literacy practice, there is a peculiar lack of sociological imagination in his determination to attribute to literacy *per se*, characteristics which are clearly those of the social order in which it is found.

In an essay written with Watt in 1963 (in Goody, ed. 1968), Goody sets out to counter-balance the relativism of his colleagues in anthropology which, he feels, 'has now gone to the point of denying that the distinction between non-literate and literate societies has any significant validity'. The 'personal observation' of Goody and Watt is contrary to this so they intend to pursue 'the traditional dichotomy between literate and non-literate societies' (1968, p. 28) in order to see if any genuine illumination can be found in it. They begin from a description of 'the ways in which the cultural heritage is transmitted in non-literate societies' and then inquire 'how these ways are changed by the widespread adoption of an easy and effective means of written communication' (ibid.).

What characterises oral societies, and justifies drawing the distinction between them and 'literate' societies, is that 'all beliefs, and values, all forms of knowledge, are communicated between individuals in face-to-face contact; and, as distinct from the material content of the cultural tradition, whether it be cave-paintings or hand-axes, they are stored only in human memory' (ibid. p. 29). From this sharply drawn difference Goody and Watt draw all their inferences concerning the thought process, cognitive skills and social achievements of the two kinds of societies.

Yet the distinction is clearly overdrawn. Goody himself in a later essay points out that 'at least during the last 2,000 years the vast majority of peoples of the world (most of Eurasia and much of Africa) have lived in neither kind of situation, but in cultures which were influenced in some degree by the circulation of the written word, by the presence of groups or individuals who could read or write' (1968, p. 4). Ruth Finnegan, in a recent article that challenges many of Goody's contentions regarding literacy, expands the area of the world to which this comment can be applied:

> Even in areas outside this great span – in Australia for example, the South Pacific or Amerindia – the main detailed knowledge that we have of these cultures is – almost by definition – in neither kind of situation, but in cultures which were influenced in some degree by the circulation of the written word, by the presence of groups or individuals who could read or write. By now, at least, it

would be hard to find an example of either of the supposed
mutually exclusive 'pure' types of culture; indeed, there are few, if
any, historical cases where we have detailed and solid (rather
than speculative) evidence about the processes of communication
in a purely 'oral' society. It is in practice the 'mixed' rather than
the 'pure' type that in one form or another provides the typical
case and – furthermore–the available evidence for analysis (Finnegan, 1981, p. 5).

So it is not possible to test Goody's hypothesis since one cannot find an
isolated society on which to test the cognitive and other consequences of
'purely' oral communication. Every society represents some 'mix' of oral
and literate modes of communication. Even in the so-called 'developed'
societies, which claim 'high' literacy rates according to various measures,
people experience a variety of different forms and meanings of literate and
oral communication, according to such aspects of the social context as,
for instance, class, gender, age and ethnicity. Moreover, recent surveys
have suggested that not so many members of these societies are 'literate'
by the standards expected than had previously been assumed: in the UK it
is now held that over one million people have an acquaintance with
literacy that is insufficient for the demands made on them by this kind of
society (DES, 1980). Such measures and judgements are themselves, however, imprecise and depend upon political and ideological positions, so
they, too, must be part of our object of study. Although within Goody's
own terms they do provide a challenge to his claims for the consequences
of a shift from oral to literate culture, they do not provide an unambiguous or 'scientific' starting point from which to test those claims.

In his study of the development of literate practices in medieval England, *From Memory to Written Record 1066-1307* (1979), Michael Clanchy has suggested that the problem is better formulated in a different way.
He considers the ways in which oral conventions persisted in twelfth and
thirteenth century English society at a time when larger numbers of
people were beginning to use literacy for more purposes. He recognises
that the 'shift' from memory to written record involves changes in conventions for which social explanations have to be offered, rather than a
change in 'cognitive' processes or at the radical, absolute level that Goody
implies. This kind of change is simply disguised by the use of quasi-
scientific measures and statistics of 'literacy'. The change is in the 'mix' of
oral and literate modes and this is related to changes in the conventions
associated with them. In medieval England what came under pressure
were the conventions by which claims to land rights were legitimated;
while some sectors of society were attempting to make written records the
prime guarantor of 'truth' and legitimacy, others were suspicious that

such records could easily be forged and preferred to put their faith in seals and in the oral testimony of 'twelve good men and true'. The researcher, interested in different modes of communication, has to investigate the framework of thought within which decisions regarding what is legitimate are made and to explain how a particular group succeeds in making its ideology dominant in specific contexts. Certain groups managed to extend the uses of writing to subserve their political and ideological interest in centralisation through the construction of what Clanchy calls a 'literate mentality'. What is crucial for our concerns here is that such a 'mentality' or ideology is *constructed*; it is not something imposed by the form of literacy itself as though the 'technology of the intellect', as Goody terms it, were determinate. I shall suggest below just what insights and new directions of inquiry can emerge from this more 'ideological' approach to literacy practices. As regards Goody's sharp distinction between oral and literate cultures, it demonstrates not only that the social reality does not correspond to this 'great divide' but also that developing a model which enables one to proceed as if it did so is not the only or most fruitful way of proceeding.

Despite his own caveats, Goody proceeds to base fundamental and far-reaching aspects of human reasoning and achievement on the distinction between oral and literate cultures. In the essay with Watt he writes: 'The intrinsic nature of oral communication has a considerable effect upon both the content and transmission of the cultural repertoire (1968, p. 29). In the first place, he says 'it makes for a directness of relationship between symbol and referent'. In oral cultures the meanings of words are ratified in specific concrete situations where they are used, whereas in literate cultures words accumulate 'successive layers of historically validated meanings' (ibid.). This 'immediacy' of meaning in oral society he relates to the society's functional needs, citing Malinowski's claim that 'in the Trobriands the outer world was only named in so far as it yielded useful things' (ibid.). Since such a cultural repertoire is held only in the memory it is subject to constant change according to the new interests of the moment 'and whatever parts of it have ceased to be of contemporary relevance are likely to be eliminated by the process of forgetting' (ibid. p. 30). What follows from this apparently technical account of the abstract nature of communication are quite radical consequences for the intellectual potential of members of these different societies. The development of logic, the distinction of myth from history, the emergence of scepticism, and the ability to challenge and reinterpret social dogma are all taken by Goody to follow from these initial pronouncements on communication. Since so much else rests on it, it is clearly crucial to assess the validity of the initial analysis of communication itself.

Once again it is Goody himself who points out the counter arguments, although, again, he proceeds to ignore them. He is not, he claims, denying the existence of social change in oral societies, nor of the 'survivals' which this change leaves in its wake. These 'survivals' would, of course, be evidence that oral societies can and do 'fix' some aspects of the cultural repertoire; they do not simply roll on in perpetual immediacy, responding to each new need in a new way and changing the meanings of words and communication accordingly. There are, for instance, mnemonic devices in oral cultures which offer some resistance to this process: 'formalised patterns of speech, recital under ritual conditions, the use of drums and other musical instruments, the employment of professional remembrancers – all such factors may shield at least part of the content of memory from the transmuting influence of the immediate pressures of the present' (1968, p. 31). He might also have added the examples he cited earlier of the 'material content of the cultural tradition', such as cave-paintings and hand-axes, since these also serve as repositories of meaning which may persist over time. More recently, Bloch's work (1975) on political language and oratory has provided evidence of ways in which speech is formalised and is used for functions which Goody attributes solely to writing. These formal devices enable cultural heritage to be maintained beyond the lives of single individuals and offset what Goody sees as the ephemeral nature of 'face-to-face' communication. The distinction between literate and non-literate societies based on the contrast between 'immediacy' and 'storage' of the cultural repertoire thus becomes less clear cut. Even if an idealised model of the two kinds of society could be constructed, it is apparent that the nature of communication in each of them would have to be less strongly differentiated than Goody is claiming.

The notion that 'primitive' societies classify and organise their intellectual world simply in terms of their crude 'needs', which Goody derives from Malinowski and uses to further characterise 'oral' societies, has also been subject to some radical revision in recent years. In his latest publication on literacy, *The Domestication of the Savage Mind* (1977), Goody acknowledges this work, but does not allow it to deflect from his design. Lévi-Strauss, he acknowledges, has criticised Malinowski's claim that the interest of 'primitive' peoples in totemic plants and animals was inspired by 'nothing but the rumblings of their stomachs'. Lévi-Strauss' counter argument was that 'the universe is an object of thought at least as much as it is a means of satisfying needs' (Goody, 1977, p. 5). 'Classifying as opposed to not classifying has a value of its own, whatever the form the classification may take' (ibid.). In other words 'primitive' peoples do not simply construct words and meanings in relation to the felt needs of everyday life but classify according to more general intellectual interests and concerns. The characteristics of 'storage', 'indirectness', and the construction of 'successive layers of historically validated meanings' which

Goody attributes to literacy alone are, then, part of the intellectual framework of any society. In oral as well as in literate culture, it would appear that there are techniques whereby the directness and immediacy of everyday experience are contrasted with the holding of traditions over time, and with the 'fixing' and ratifying of definitions and meanings. It is not true to say of oral cultures that there is a peculiar 'directness of relationship between meaning and referent', that 'the meaning of each word is ratified in a succession of concrete situations' only, that meanings in oral cultures are always particular and specific.

Goody however attempts to evade the implications of Lévi-Strauss' argument by pointing out that, ultimately, Lévi-Strauss himself provides a dualistic model of the world: one which distinguishes between 'primitive' and 'modern', mythological and scientific (Goody, 1977, pp. 7–8). Goody claims to reject these distinctions as ethnocentric and suggests that we 'should look for more specific criteria for the differences' between these kinds of societies. These criteria will include 'the material concomitants of the process of mental "domestication", for these are not only the manifestations of thought, invention, creativity, they also shape its future forms. They are not only the products of communication but also part of its determining features' (ibid. p. 9). In other words it is the development of literate modes of communication that provides the basis for making a distinction between two kinds of society, and those modes themselves have determining effects: if some societies are more 'scientific' and 'logical' than others, it is not on account of the nature of their thought processes but because their acquisition of literacy has released these capacities.

There is a dangerous circularity about this argument. If it begins from the assumption of difference and then adduces literacy as the explanation, the argument is open to the same criticism that Goody himself levels at Lévi-Strauss' dualism; if, on the other hand, it begins from the assumption that literacy is the crucial source of difference and that the mental differences follow from this, then it is beginning from the very assumption that it claims to be setting out to prove. This circularity is apparent in the seminal article written by Goody and Watt where they lay down the reasons why they attribute such importance to literacy. Summarising the previous versions of a 'great divide' between primitive and modern societies they write:

> Nevertheless, although we must reject any dichotomy based upon the assumption of radical differences between the mental attributes of literate and non-literate peoples and accept the view that previous formulations of the distinction were based on faulty premises and inadequate evidence, there may still exist general

differences between literate and non-literate societies somewhat along the lines suggested by Lévy-Bruhl. One reason for their existence, for instance, may be what has been described above: the fact [sic] that writing establishes a different kind of relation between the word and its referent, a relationship that is more general and more abstract, and less closely connected with the particularities of person, place and time than obtains in oral communication. There is certainly a great deal to substantiate this distinction in what we know of early Greek thought ... It was only in the days of the first widespread alphabetic culture that the idea of 'logic' appears to have arisen. (Goody, 1968, p. 44.)

Goody and Watt, and Goody himself in later developments of these ideas, lay great store on the example of classical Greece. It is presented as virtually the defining case for the argument that there is a crucial distinction between literate and non-literate societies and that this difference relates to differences in cognitive processes and the development of 'logic'. Classical Greece is for them the 'prime historical example of the transition to a really literate society' without the interference of 'other cultural features imported from the loan country along with the writing system. Greece thus offers not only the first instance of this change but also the essential one for any attempt to isolate the cultural consequences of alphabetic literacy' (ibid. p. 42).

Looked at more closely, however, the Greek example is not as powerful or effective as Goody and Watt would have us believe and we would need to be cautious in drawing any general implications from it. To begin with, literacy in general was not, of course, independently invented in Greece, as Goody and Watt recognise: the form of literacy particular to Greece developed from the Semitic writing system over a long period of time. This system was widely adopted in the ancient world, although the 'social diffusion of writing' was slow, mainly due to 'the established features of the societies which adopted it. There was, for one thing, a strong tendency for writing to be used as a help to memory rather than as an autonomous and independent mode of communication' (ibid. p. 40). To this extent, then, the adoption of a writing system in classical Greece does not in itself provide an example of development without the cultural 'interference' that goes with diffusion, nor of the characteristics of writing independent of oral modes of communication.

What Goody and Watt have in mind, however, in citing their Greek example, is not simply the adoption of a writing system in general but the development of a particular form of writing in a particular way: 'in the sixth and fifth centuries BC in the city states of Greece and Ionia ... there first arose a society which as a whole could justify being characterised as literate' (ibid.). What they take 'literate' to mean, then, delimits the term considerably in relation to the larger world experience of forms of writing. They mean an easy, phonetic (or rather phonemic) system such as alphabetic literacy and they think of a 'literate society' as one in which such a script is widely assumed in public life, as they claim it was in sixth century Greece. It is this form of 'literacy' which has the consequences they then describe. According to Goody and Watt, the development of alphabetic script and its wide diffusion throughout society – the two criteria for 'literacy' as they mean it – happened independently within Greece and were not the result of cultural borrowing. It is in this sense that Greece represents 'the prime historical example of the transition to a really literate society'.

It is important to bear this definition in mind, since elsewhere Goody employs the term 'literacy' in ways which appear more general than this. In his latest book (1977), for instance, he includes under 'literacy' such graphic devices as lists, tables and Ramus systems. Definitions, of course, are only relevant to the interests they are constructed to serve and it would be fruitless to enter into a definitional argument as to what 'literacy' really is. But, if Goody is going to draw significant consequences from what he defines as 'literacy', then it is important to be clear as to just what it is that is supposed to have these consequences. If this varies, as seems to be the case in Goody's work, then the general argument about consequences loses some of its force.

If, for the moment, we accept the narrow definition offered by Goody and Watt (in Goody, 1968) and remember not to draw general conclusions about 'literacy' as such from the arguments presented there, we nevertheless still find some problems about accepting the kinds of consequences they assume for even that limited form of 'literacy'. A major problem is that, despite the socially specific nature of their definition of Greek literacy, they still couch the argument in a way that tends towards technological determinism. The reasons for the widespread development of the particular form of alphabetic literacy evident in Greece must clearly be sought in the social structure; Goody and Watt, however, insist that 'considerable importance must surely be attributed to the intrinsic advantages of the Greek adaptation of the Semitic alphabet, an adaptation which made it the first comprehensively and exclusively phonetic system for transcribing human speech' (ibid. pp. 40–1). Social factors are then suggested as somehow additional to this essentially technical breakthrough: 'The extensive diffusion of the alphabet in Greece was *also* materially assisted by various social, economic and technological factors' (ibid. p. 41) (my emphasis). I shall discuss later the theoretical objections to technological determinism; Goody in any case recognises the dangers and in a later essay himself rejects such determinism, refuting the claims that this is what he was doing. To counter these claims he tempers the language slightly: 'The article should perhaps have been entitled the "implications" rather than the consequences of literacy.' (1968, p. 4.)

The tenor of Goody's general statements on literacy often seems at variance with such caveats, but even couched in these terms the argument is overstated. The 'implications' of literacy are not so obvious nor so easily elicited or described as Goody suggests. He argues, for instance, that the intrinsic advantages of the Greek adaptation of the Semitic writing system were that it became 'easy, explicit and unambiguous'. Yet Goody and Watt themselves provide evidence to refute such a judgement:

> It must be remembered, of course, that Greek writing throughout the classical period was still relatively difficult to decipher as words were not regularly separated; the copying of manuscripts was a long and laborious process; and that silent reading as we know it was very rare; until the advent of printing in the ancient world books were used mainly for reading aloud, often by a slave. (1968, p. 42.)

The 'ease' of any writing system is, clearly, relative. But if Greek literacy is not, in fact, as easy or as unambiguous as Goody sometimes claims, then its 'implications' may not be so important as those claims assert. It is, however, the grand claims rather than the caveats that other writers tend to follow. An example of this can be found in the volume of essays edited by Goody in 1968, *Literacy in Traditional Societies* where, in an article by Meggitt, we find uncritical use of the claims for the 'ease' and lack of ambiguity of writing. Meggitt contrasts the 'ritualised' literacy supposedly apparent in Melanesian politico-religious movements with a model of what literacy 'really' is in a way that obviously owes much to Goody: 'It seems that writing was rarely treated as a straightforward technique of secular action, one whose prime values is repeated and surrogate communication of unambiguous meanings in a variety of situations' (1968, p. 302). These assumptions about what literacy 'really' is generate misleading representations of the political and ideological nature of Melanesian responses to colonialism. But what the example also indicates is that Goody's claims for the consequences of Greek literacy, for all the qualifications that he and Watt make, do lay themselves open to more general and misleading applications. Despite their recognition that even the model example of Greek literacy was not always 'unambiguous', explicit and easy, they nevertheless tend to represent these qualities as 'intrinsic' to literacy and as the source of its great potential. They can hardly be surprised when others make use of this representation rather than the narrower and more qualified one.

But even in its narrow definition and with the actual limitations of its practice in classical Greece, literacy is still taken by Goody to have conse-quences, or implications, of a far-reaching kind. We have already seen that, whatever doubts Goody may have about the distinction 'logi-cal'/'pre-logical', he is still inclined to identify 'general differences between literate and non-literate societies somewhat along the lines suggested by Lévy-Bruhl' (Goody, 1968, p. 44): i.e. that the idea of 'logic' is connected with the growth of alphabetic culture. Linked with this is the notion that writing is responsible for the distinction between myth and history and this distinction, like the idea of logic, he associates with classical Greece. Again, however, the precise definition of literacy, and its location in that particular society, tends to get forgotten in grand general claims for the consequences of 'literacy' itself and in the general distinction between 'literate' and 'non-literate' societies.

In oral cultures, he claims: 'The individual has little perception of the past except in terms of the present; whereas an analysis of a literate society *cannot but enforce* a more objective recognition of the distinction between what was and what is' (1968, p. 34) (my emphasis).

He goes on to say 'The pastness of the past, then, depends upon a historical sensibility which can hardly begin to operate without perma-nent written records' (ibid.).

There are, again, problems for the researcher hoping to test out such hypotheses. About whom is he speaking? Which individuals or groups are being 'objective' as a result of having writing? Is he referring to the whole of a literate society in the reference to 'historical sensibility'? The unit of study is, in fact, unlikely to be a whole society since, as an anthropologist, Goody is fully aware that the ways in which a society represents its own past are always entangled in the present ideological and political concerns of particular groups and factions. One has only to think of the way in which the Shah of Persia reinforced his position by claiming direct descent from the Achaemenids of the third century BC, to give depth to a geneal-ogy that in fact started with his father – a Cossack officer – assuming the throne in 1920 when the previous dynasty collapsed (see Avery, 1965); or the use in Britain of the 'historical' roots of the Royal Family to support such current political structures as the House of Lords.

In line with these more specific uses of the 'past' by specific groups, Goody's claims for changes in perceptions of the past as a result of the development of literacy in classical Greece appear to refer specifically to scholars and intellectuals rather than to the society as a whole. It was the writing down of the poems of Homer and Hesiod that led scholars to ask, for the first time apparently: 'How far was the information about their gods and heroes literally true?'. Goody traces the development of written forms in early Greece until the point when alphabetic literacy enabled 'groups of writers and teachers ... to take as their point of departure the belief that much of what Homer had apparently said was inconsistent and unsatisfactory in many respects' (1968, p. 46). In this context 'critical' and 'rational' powers were developed and Goody sees this as connected with the beginnings of religious and natural philosophy and ultimately with science (ibid.). He reads the texts that remain to us from sixth century Greece as evidence of 'a more thoroughgoing individual challenge to the orthodox cultural tradition ... than occurred elsewhere' (ibid.).

Since it is difficult to find independent evidence with which to test the interpretations of their own past offered by Greek historians, we cannot know whether they were 'really' being exceptionally 'rational' and 'scientific'. What we can glean, though, and what Goody appears to take at face value, is some insight into how they represented themselves, such as in the statements they made about the reliability of their own accounts. Thucydides, for instance, made 'a decisive distinction between myth and history, a distinction to which little attention is paid in non-literate society. Thucydides wanted to give a wholly reliable account of the wars between Athens and Sparta; and this meant that unverified assumptions about the past had to be excluded.' (ibid. pp. 47–8.) The fact that Thucydides wanted to do this, or said he did, does not of course provide evidence of whether he actually did.

Some recent interpretations of Greek history, and of the Greek historians' versions of it, have suggested that there was, in fact, a gap between such ideals and the actual practice and that we should not take their own statements too literally. Professor John Boardman, for instance, Lincoln Professor of Classical Art and Archaeology at Oxford University, recently shocked an audience of classicists by claiming that: 'The exploits of Theseus, the ancient Greek hero who tamed the Minotaur and repulsed the Amazon invasion of Attica, were probably no more than state propaganda invented to rouse nationalistic pride' and were 'manufactured to glorify the role of Athens in the Ionian revolt of 499 BC' (*Times Higher Educational Supplement* 7.8.81). His version of the 'reality' of what happened is that: 'In 499 BC Athens sent half her fleet to help the Ionians fight the Persians. The story was recast to raise the popularity of Theseus, the rising star, to show how the Athenians taught the barbarians a sharp lesson' (ibid.).

It is difficult to believe that the historians were not party to such constructions, although Goody might justifiably envisage that such honourable men as Thucydides would have been shocked if his material had been manipulated in this way by the politicians. The social reality is that the uses of 'history', if not always as crude and blatant as this, always involve selection, speculation and hypothesised connections, and that the scholars operating this process are products of a specific society, speak its language and are imbued with its ideology, so their work must always bear a complex if not tangential relationship to 'reality' and 'objectivity'. A recent work on political theory in ancient Greece has pursued this question more explicitly than has traditionally been the case in classical scholarship and provides a further check to our ready acceptance of Goody's grander claims for the consequences of literacy in classical Greece.

Ellen and Neal Wood, in *Class, Ideology and Ancient Political Theory* maintain that the 'classics of political theory are fundamentally ideological' (1978, p. ix) and they set out to relate them 'more closely and systematically' to their social contexts. They consider the 'lives, class affiliations and social circumstances' in which Socrates, Plato and Aristotle were writing and 'try to establish that their political theories are essentially partisan in origin and ideological in content' (ibid.). These writers were, the Woods claim, defending the declining way of life of the landed aristocracy, challenged by urban developments which saw the rise of traders, manufacturers, artisans and wage-labourers many of whom had migrated from rural areas where they had worked as slaves and peasants for the old nobility. The writers, while condemning the failings of the old nobility, notably their decadence and degradation, thought that their way of life could be revitalised and could become the foundation of a civil life that stemmed the rising tide of democracy and, as they feared, mob rule. Their philosophical idealism was at once a retreat from the material world of unruly mobs and declining privilege and a programme for maintaining their position while accommodating some change: 'Socratic political thought was an intellectually sophisticated and ingenious justification for counter-revolution in democracy and the maintenance of the status quo in oligarchy' (ibid. p. 4). One can recognise easily why so many later European commentators extolled classical Greece as the model for their contemporaries since the material conditions of these changes from rural to urban, from aristocracy to bourgeoisie, and from oligarchy to proto-democracy similarly characterised their own social situation. As Wood and Wood argue, the sympathy of the classicists for the social class represented by the Socratics of classical Greece made them 'more than ready to accept rather uncritically their account of the situation in Athens and throughout the Greek world'. Plato's claims, for instance, that his work enabled him to 'rise above ideology and the immediacy of mundane affairs' (ibid. p. 9) have been accepted faithfully by classicists who wanted to believe what he said because of its significance for their position in and views of their own society. Goody's claims that Greek historians have distinguished myth from history is of a kind with the uncritical faith of these classicists. His grander claims for the significance of literacy are based, then, upon assumptions about the 'objectivity' of Greek historians that turn out, on closer scrutiny, to be unfounded.

The historians and the political theorists (as well as recent commentators on them) must themselves be seen in their historical and social contexts. Their work is relevant to us and speaks of the human condition not because it attains universality and 'objectivity', as Goody and others would imply, but on the contrary precisely because of its articulation with the real social experience in which they participated. As Wood and Wood comment, 'relating ideas to their social context' far from 'depriving them of their universal meaning' in fact 'rescues them from the emptiness of ethereal abstractions which have no human meaning at all' (ibid. p. x). Not only is it impossible to demonstrate whether the writers of classical Greece really attained 'objectivity'; but our regard for them and our ability to learn from them do not require it.

However, Goody's claims for the 'consequences' of literacy are couched in such a way that they do require it: he imposes upon himself the obligation to establish that the Greeks really did achieve the distinction of 'myth' from 'history' if his claims for literacy are to be credible. If his foundation is insecure, as the arguments of the Woods and others would suggest, then the structure he builds upon it must also be unsafe. If we have no evidence or proof of a 'real' distinction of myth from history, as opposed to an ideological claim or commitment to it, either in society as a whole, or amongst the community of scholars or even, it now appears, in the exalted ranks of classical Greek historians and political theorists, then to ask whether literacy, however defined, is a cause of such a distinction becomes fruitless.

That some individuals or groups challenge received opinion in their society, as Goody claims some Greek historians did, is obviously true. But the conditions in which this challenge becomes significant are social ones rather than 'technological' as Goody would have us believe. An analysis and cross-cultural comparison of such circumstances would involve study of political and ideological structures rather than technologies. Despite the claims by many that advanced levels of technological development somehow lead to democracy and scientific thought, the 'advanced' states of the modern world would not necessarily emerge very favourably from a comparison of degrees of historical 'objectivity', however defined. Conversely, Goody himself recognises that 'In non-literate society ... there are usually some individuals whose interests lead them to collect, analyse and interpret the cultural tradition in a personal way' and the work of his fellow anthropologists is ample testimony to the variation and potential for challenge in non-literate societies.

Goody, nevertheless, believes that such individuals are more likely to appear and to have scope for challenge in societies with the 'technology' of literacy. Apart from the 'evidence' of classical Greece, another main plank of the argument in favour of this belief is the hypothesis that one is more likely to put together two statements in writing and then compare them than two oral utterances. As a result of acquiring writing 'one can compare side by side utterances that have been made at different times and places' (1977, pp. 11–12). This, he claims, helps foster criticalness and awareness of contradiction. This property is, he argues, intrinsic to literacy and the reason for many of the grand consequences which, given the right circumstances, arise from the spread of literacy.

However, even at the hypothetical level, the proposition is not as obviously true as Goody seems to assume. One can, for instance, easily imagine circumstances in which oral utterances including recollections from different times and places are, as it were, placed side by side as in a debating chamber and where the listeners could then recognise contradictions and employ their 'critical' faculties. There are many examples of this. Bloch's work (1975) on political language and oratory, as we saw above (p. 41), provides evidence of ways in which speech is formalised in non-literate and in literate societies alike and is used for the functions which Goody attributes to writing alone. A sense of the past may be retained by the use of remembrancers whose representations of it are differentiated from the everyday casual memories of people. The formal devices of political oratory amongst the Mursi, a technologically primitive people of Ethiopia described by D. Turton (Bloch, 1975), similarly perform functions which Goody appears to restrict to literacy. The context of speech-making and the techniques and conventions that have been developed ensure that many sides of a case are put at the same time as maintaining the proprieties due to different statuses. There is, in a sense, an ideology of scepticism within clearly defined boundaries and as old men die out of the system and younger ones join it the tradition becomes cumulative and socially-constructed rather than just an individual matter. Goody, however, claims that if the processes of political scepticism do occur at all in non-literate societies, they must always be limited and individual.

> In non-literate society ... the cultural tradition functions as a series of interlocking face-to-face conversations in which the very conditions of transmission operate to favour consistency between past and present, and to make criticism – the articulation of inconsistency – less likely to occur; and if it does, the inconsistency makes a less permanent impact, and it is more easily adjusted or forgotten. While scepticism may be present in such societies, it takes a personal, non-cumulative form; it does not lead to a deliberate rejection and reinterpretation of social dogma so much as to a semi-automatic readjustment of belief. In literate society, these interlocking conversations go on; but they are no longer man's only dialogue; and in so far as writing provides an alternative source for the transmission of cultural orientations it favours awareness of inconsistency. (1977, p. 48.)

Despite the general level of the analysis, which offers 'scepticism' as a further quality to add to 'logic' and 'objectivity' as characteristics associated with literacy, this passage does offer a more precise formulation of what Goody has in mind as the consequences of literacy. Just as the term 'literacy' itself turned out to be more precise than in general use, and we were able to pin down the distinction 'literate/non-literate' to 'literacy in classical Greece' as opposed to literacy or non-literacy elsewhere, so the grand consequences of the literacy being described can be seen from this passage to hinge on very particular distinctions. The crucial difference is between two categories of social thought and action: those defined, on the one hand, by 'deliberate rejection and reinterpretation of social dogma' and, on the other, by 'semi-automatic readjustment of belief'. It is by reference to this distinction that we are to test for 'scepticism' and, presumably, can expect to find the Mursi lacking. What Thucydides and his contemporaries were doing was 'challenging' social dogma, not simply 'readjusting' it, and it is in this characteristic of classical Greek scholarship that we can identify the crucial consequence of acquiring literacy.

The researcher, unfortunately, has the same problems with testing this hypothesis, despite its greater precision, as he or she has with the grander ones. In order to test it he or she would presumably have to examine a number of literate and non-literate societies from the point of view of their degree of 'scepticism'. The difficulty of finding such clearly defined 'literate' and 'non-literate' societies has already been alluded to and Goody himself recognises that there are few societies today not touched in some way by literate practices. The difficulties in Goody's use of classical Greece as the defining example are also apparent. But what we are now faced with more clearly than in his other claims for the consequences of literacy is an argument based on socially relative judgement and ideology. The distinction he adduces as the crucial consequence of literacy depends upon interpretation of what is 'readjustment' as opposed to 'reinterpretation' and 'rejection' of ideas and beliefs. That is, of course, a personal and ideological matter. To the capitalist, socialist countries would represent the situation where deliberate 'rejection' and 'reinterpretation' of social dogma is not widely evident, since the capitalist rejects the underlying philosophy of those countries himself but finds that its inhabitants do not. Conversely, a Marxist is scornful of the supine, uncritical level of political consciousness in western 'liberal' societies, where readjustments of ideas and practices are allowed but no general challenge to capitalist theory is evident. In Goody's terms either one of these would provide an example of the characteristics of non-literate societies – lack of scepticism and of radical challenge to social dogma. Couched in these terms, where the political nature of the interpretation is not hidden behind the language of 'cognitive' structures and 'intellectual' abilities, the argument for the consequences of literacy appears less absolute, less 'technical' and more obviously dependent on ideologically-based assumptions.

Looked at from this perspective, however, the distinction itself is not a very fruitful one. The notion that some societies 'reinterpret' and some 'readjust' does not provide a very helpful model for the analysis of social change and for understanding why certain historical events appear to involve more radical and revolutionary changes than others. A causal explanation for these events is not to be found by looking at the mental processes of particular social groups or categories involved in them since any traits so identified are as likely to be effects as causes. The explanation is better sought in the specific social and material circumstances and their articulation with political and ideological structures.

Gellner (1973), for instance, provides a more complex intellectual framework for analysing such change. He argues that no social units can be treated in isolation as though they had no contact with others: all groups, whether tribes, villages, nations or families interact with other groups. Our representation of them as groups is an intellectual device for handling them, just as the people themselves use names and labels, but this does not correspond to the empirical reality which is of constant contact and flow between 'peoples': a continuum rather than a series of separate but interlocking units. It is, therefore, impossible to isolate such a unit for the purpose of testing it for 'closed' or 'open' minds or for 'reinterpretation' as opposed to 'readjustment of belief'.

'Readjustment of belief' is, in fact, the norm and all social groups are continually undergoing the process. They may construct artificial representations of a fixed reality at any one point of time as a means of handling the continuous flow of social change, but these are simply data for the social scientist and not to be taken at face value. Constant contact with other social groups, whether within or between identifiable political units, means that new ideas are being constantly encountered. At different points of time, one set of ideas may be abandoned and another adopted, and the history of any society consists of a series of such adjustments, some more radical than others. Why a particular adjustment or radical change is made, and by what sectors of a society, depends on the conjuncture of a number of factors. When this process becomes revolutionary upheaval is not always easy to identify and the decision as to whether it was a radical reinterpretation rather than simply an adjustment depends on the observer's standpoint. This, then, makes for serious definitional and methodological problems in identifying and pursuing Goody's distinction between the two kinds or levels of thought. It is doubtful, therefore, whether pursuing the 'consequences' of literacy in this direction is very fruitful.

Moreover, there are serious theoretical problems in attempting to isolate those intellectual factors that might be held to account for social change, apart from then attempting to associate these factors with particular social groups on the one hand or with literacy on the other. As Kuhn argues in *The Structure of Scientific Revolutions*, intellectual rigour and purity are seldom major factors in changes even in the scientific world. The adoption, for instance, of Darwinian views of evolution depended not simply on the intellectual breakthrough of a brilliant mind but on the conjuncture of social movements that made these propositions more acceptable then than they might have been at other periods. Contemporary breakthroughs in nuclear science depend on large funding and on the construction of elaborate institutions geared to that end, which in turn depend on political decisions, not those of the neutral scientist in the laboratory.

Parry, for instance, cites the scientific achievements of ancient India, such as logic and medicine, astronomy, grammar and mathematics, as arising out of 'non-scientific' institutions and ideologies: 'essentially religious preoccupations seem to have provided the stimulus for developments in all these fields; – the discipline of yoga, for physiological knowledge, the construction of sacrificial altars for geometry and so on, (1982, p. 23).

Goody himself provides a telling example of how 'scientific' progress may be the product of social forces which, in themselves, do not represent the kind of scholarly community and logical thought which he extols. The development of Pythagoras' theorem, he notes, is not related to the separation of mathematical, scientific thinking from mythological and non-literate practices but rather was associated with 'the use of number magic' and:

> was discovered in the course of such numerological experimentation. The theorem is now recognised to be older than Pythagoras, much of whose mathematics has an eastern origin. But the interpenetration of mathematics and magic in the school is well attested; Dodds, for example, sees Pythagoreanism partly as 'a development of shamanism and partly as a development of number mysticism and the speculations about cosmic harmony'. The world of nature was for them constructed on a mathematical plan, things were generated from numbers – an idea to whose mystical overtones Aristotle objected. (1977, p. 17.)

Elsewhere Goody cites Guthrie's comment that the Pythagoreans were 'highly arbitrary and inconsistent' (ibid. p. 11). Goody, then, sees the activities of Pythagoras and his followers as quite different from the flowering of logic, scientific clarity, lack of ambiguity, scepticism etc. for which he praises classical Greece. Indeed he explicitly opposes the secretive and mystical practices of the Pythagoreans to the 'spirit of enquiry' which, he believes, literacy 'fosters'. 'Pythagoras scarcely typifies the Greek reaction to the growth of learning' (1968, p. 11). Despite the attempt to treat the Pythagorean example as an exception, it cannot but weaken Goody's case. For it illustrates well how literacy co-exists with arcane mystical practices and how such practices co-exist with and even help to account for scientific progress. The flowering of the very Greek culture that Goody takes as the example par excellence of rationality, philosophy and science is inextricably linked with mysticism, secrecy and ambiguity. The distinction between these apparent opposites is, in fact, an ideological one common in Goody's own culture. The social reality is always a mix of such modes and practices.

Goody, however, retreats from the implications that this more flexible model of scientific progress hold for his claims regarding literacy. He continues, instead, to insist on the existence of a 'real' distinction between scientific and mythological deriving from that between literate and non-literate.

The counter-evidence that we have been considering is, in a sense, defined away. Where, for instance, the characteristics which he attributes to oral communication persist in a society with literacy, and would thus appear to undermine the case for the 'intrinsic' qualities of literacy, Goody draws a further distinction which enables him to maintain the purity of his ideal model. This distinction is one between 'restricted' literacy and the 'full' realisation of the 'potentialities' of literacy. Where the ideal type of literacy is not found in a particular practice that practice is taken as an example of 'restricted' literacy. This provides one of Goody's main claims to be making a contribution to further research: the field worker, whether anthropologist, historian, social psychologist or whatever, can ask of a specific culture why literacy did not fulfil its potential there, and what were the factors that 'restricted' its development. Since most societies would appear not to match up to Goody's ideal, there would seem to be few studies that can avoid the question. Goody cites a range of examples where factors in the society itself or intrinsic to literacy 'restrict' its potential: the secrecy of the Koranic tradition in Africa and the Middle East; the ceremonial texts of Egypt and Mesopotamia; Brahminic uses of the Veda; the 'guru' tradition; the educational system of Europe in the Middle Ages; the religious uses of alphabetic literacy in Tibet; the uses of literacy by the Io Dagaa and Gonja in northern Ghana, where Goody himself did field work (1968, 1977, p. 20). The concept is taken up by Meggitt in relation to Melanesia where he refers to 'ritualised' literacy (Goody, 1968) and more recently Clammer has allowed it to influence his study of *Literacy and Social Change in Fiji* (1976).

Goody himself seems to suggest that 'restricted' literacy is indeed the norm in all societies except later classical Greece, thereby undermining somewhat the significance of these general applications of the term: 'Nowhere was the impact of literacy as radical as it has been in classical Greece. Indeed the kind of situation which so often arose elsewhere seems more akin to the "restricted" literacy that characterised pre-alphabetic scripts. In other words, the potentialities of the medium were not explored to anything like the same extent' (1968, p. 4). This argument is of course open to the same criticisms as were levelled against the distinction originally drawn between 'literate' and 'non-literate' societies. The categories 'restricted' and 'full' realisation of potential cannot be so clearly distinguished. They in fact shade into each other, even more obviously so where the distinction is between different forms of literate practice; and the distinction, if it is based on supposed differences in cognitive processes, in 'logic' and the development of 'science', is open to the criticisms that Goody himself, along with Lévi-Strauss and others, levels against the theory of a 'great divide'.

But there is a further problem: classical Greece it transpires, is a less than perfect model of 'full' literacy and certain periods and uses, even there, have to be termed 'restricted'. Pythagorean uses of literacy, for instance, did not fit the criteria and Goody had to cite them as exceptions; they did not 'typify' Greek uses of literacy or 'the Greek reaction to the growth of learning' (1968, p. 11). Moreover, Greek historians appear to have not always distinguished as clearly between myth and history as their adoption of literacy would lead Goody to expect. And Greek script was less 'easy' and 'unambiguous' than the consequences assumed to arise from it would require. In addition Havelock has pointed out that the Greek concern with metaphysics did not, in fact, develop simultaneously with the growth of alphabetic literacy but only much later. The pre-Socratics, he explains, were 'essentially oral thinkers, prophets of the concrete linked by habit to the past, and to forms of expression which were also forms of experience' (quoted by Goody, 1968, pp. 3–4). Havelock is here, of course, giving authority to Goody's distinction between 'oral' and 'literate' thinkers and their connection respectively with the concrete and experience as opposed to the abstract and impersonal. But he is also posing the problem of how subscribers to that view accommodate examples where 'oral' thinking is found in literate societies. Goody's answer is simple: these uses represent 'restricted' literacy. However, although early Greek literacy must therefore also be labelled 'restricted', the foundation was nevertheless being laid for future developments of the 'full' potential of literacy: 'It was only by the time of Plato that the language had changed sufficiently to express new ideas' (ibid.). Havelock, like Goody, sees these changes as 'generated by changes in the technology of the intellect, or what he calls the "technology of preserved communication'" (ibid. p. 4). But since literacy was already present in early Greece, at a time when the ideal consequences of literacy (such as logic, metaphysics and objectivity) had not yet developed, it is impossible to test the extent to which these developments were due to literacy itself. What happened between early and later Greek society to generate these developments must have been something other than the 'intrinsic' qualities of literacy alone since literacy was present in both periods. To argue that the early period represents a situation of 'restricted' literacy is simply to beg the question.

There is a circularity in these arguments about the consequences of literacy that makes it difficult to test them out or to apply them fruitfully elsewhere. As we have traced them so far, Goody's arguments and my counter-arguments seem to go something like this.

Oral communications, being face-to-face and immediate, are more limited than those in literate cultures, where meaning can be held and validated in impersonal ways. However, many of the examples of literate societies that are available for study suggest that this is not the case: in fact these societies continue to practice what Goody has defined as 'oral' modes of communication, with all its limitations. So he labels them 're-stricted' and continues to pursue his ideal by identifying it with a specific culture, that of classical Greece, where the 'potentialities' of literacy were fully realised. Unfortunately classical Greece as a whole does not live up to these ideals either, and he is forced to recognise certain periods and sectors of that society as having 'restricted' literacy. The search becomes desperate and one begins to get the impression that Aristotle alone is going to fit the bill. The constant narrowing down, redefinition and drawing of ever more refined distinctions lead to a position where the argument has no general significance at all: Greek society, defined in a particular way, represents the advantages of a form of literacy defined in the same way. Greek society developed 'logic', 'scepticism' etc. Literacy, too, has the potential to generate logic and scepticism – but not literacy in general, only that form of it which developed in classical Greece. What one is left with, then, is a particular correlation: alphabetic literacy, of the kind that facilitates unambiguous communication, is first found diffused throughout a whole society in that period of late classical Greece when the idea of 'logic' and other aspects of 'unambiguous' communication also first developed.

If this were all that Goody claimed he was saying there would still be problems of definition but it might provide some insight into the specific nature of classical Greece and the specific forms of literacy developed there. However, he often appears to be saying much more than this and he has certainly been taken as making significant generalisations about the nature of literacy as such. The way in which the argument has been couched in Goody's work over the years has been to construct an apparatus of grand distinctions on which discussion of literacy could be based. He distinguishes between literate and non-literate societies; between 'restricted' literacy and the 'full' realisation of the 'potentialities' of literacy. And, in describing the consequences of what he defines as literacy, he distinguishes between societies which employ the notion of 'logic' and those which do not, between societies with 'historical sensibility' and those with only myth, and between societies where 'scepticism' is present involving 'deliberate rejection and reinterpretation of social dogma' and those limited to 'semi-automatic readjustment of belief'. The relationship of literacy to these supposed changes from limited to more developed states is described in terms which implicitly tend towards determinism, despite explicit denials: literacy 'fosters' a 'spirit of enquiry' (1968, p. 14); it 'cannot but enforce' a more 'objective definition of what was and what is' (ibid. p. 34); historical sensibility 'can hardly begin to operate without permanent written records' (ibid.); the existence of an elite group 'followed from the difficulty of the writing system' (ibid. p. 37); 'logic' seemed to be 'a function of writing' (1977, p. 11) etc.

The contradictions between these implicit tendencies and Goody's explicit rejection of them can be explained by the framework of distinctions on which the inquiry is based in the first place. By making such distinctions Goody is constructing a model in which literacy is conceived of as 'autonomous' and which has a built-in tendency to determinism.

I would argue that it is possible to consider both literacy and social change from a perspective which avoids such distinctions and such determinism and which allows us to develop a model from which new and interesting research questions can emerge. The nature of scientific endeavour and achievement, for instance, can be analysed in terms of a framework which does not require a rigid dichotomy between science and mysticism. As I have emphasised above, what we think of as 'scientific' endeavour takes place in a social context, within institutions and ideologies which are not themselves necessarily committed to 'scientific' thought or logic. The development by the Pythagoreans, for instance, of important mathematical theories out of organisations concerned with mystical cosmologies and shamanistic practices is no more an exception to the way in which scientific progress has been made or to the 'spirit of enquiry' than the fact that many modern scientific achievements arise out of arcane political interests or commercial ethics. These intellectual developments, and the apparent contradictions within them, can be more satisfactorily explained in terms of models which stress their political and ideological character than by the dualistic, cognitive models proposed by Goody. This alternative approach, instead of looking for polarities and constructing rigid distinctions in intellectual development with which to correlate similarly reified literacy practices, recognises these literacy practices as themselves social products, no more isolable from the political and ideological context than are the 'scientific' achievements that Goody would associate with them.

The arguments concerning the social nature of scientific progress relate also to the product of that progress – technology. This includes what Goody calls the 'technology of the intellect'– literacy. Technology is, however, not a neutral 'thing' that arises out of disinterested scientific inquiry and which must then be accommodated, responded to, decided about in the society. It is itself a social product that has arisen as a result of political and ideological processes and institutions and its particular form has to be explained in terms of such processes. Literacy, then, is not, as Goody appears to be arguing, a 'neutral' technology, with 'potentialities' and 'restrictions' depending simply on how it is used. Rather it is a socially constructed form whose 'influence' depends on how it was shaped in the first place. This shaping depends on political and ideological formations and it is these which are responsible for its 'consequences' too.

Before I examine some of the ways in which recent analyses of literacy practices in a number of disciplines have taken account of these political and ideological factors, and have implicitly challenged the model of literacy put forward by Goody, it is important to recognise the extent to which many of Goody's arguments and those of the 'autonomous' model of literacy have derived support from assumptions within the specific field of linguistics. In the next chapter, I consider these assumptions in the light of recent developments within that discipline and I shall attempt to demonstrate that they do not, in fact, justify the claims made for literacy by Goody and others. Many linguists in recent years have questioned the early assumptions of the discipline with regard to literacy and their work now serves to undermine rather than to support those arguments regarding literacy that I have referred to as the 'autonomous' model.

3

LITERACY AND LINGUISTICS

Many of the claims for literacy examined above rest upon theories developed within the discipline of linguistics. If, however, we look at recent developments in this area, we find that there is little justification for such claims. Those linguists who have paid explicit attention to literacy, and they are as yet few, have been forced to question the early assumptions of the discipline with regard to literacy and to cast doubt on what I have termed the 'autonomous' model. Writers in other areas, however, as well as many linguists, have gone on using these assumptions as though they were secure and certain. It is important, then, to establish what linguists have had to say and are now saying about literacy.

Many influential linguists of an earlier generation, such as Bloomfield, and grammarians and educators deriving their practice from linguistic theory, assumed that there was little significant difference between speech and writing. Given that speech is primary, in that all peoples have speech but only some have writing, they assumed that the main function of writing must be to represent speech. They did not recognise that writing is multifunctional and has characteristics which may be different from and independent of speech. Despite this view of the dependence of writing on speech, some linguists and educators have, apparently paradoxically, used written forms as models for spoken forms. It was assumed that spoken forms which failed to observe the rules of morphology and syntax considered appropriate to written forms were 'incorrect' and 'ungrammatical'. In fact there was no paradox, for it was the theoretical assumption that speech and writing were fulfilling the same functions and the inability to recognise their separate characters that made it possible to use one as the model for the other.

This perspective is now being made more explicit amongst linguists. Deuchar, for instance, offers a social rather than 'pure linguistic' explanation for the dominance of written language in both linguistic theory and general belief. In many literate cultures, written language 'has greater social prestige than the spoken language, and most official recognition' on account of the important functions which writing fulfils in those societies. As a result of these specific, socially constructed functions: 'Speech is often evaluated socially according to its closeness to the written language, which explains why standard spoken English is probably closer to written English than is any other spoken variety. Written language is often viewed as more "correct" than spoken language, and as more worthy of study' (Leech et al. 1982, p. 8/3). However, she points out that 'from a linguistic point of view we can only say that speech and writing are different: we cannot say that one is superior to the other' (ibid.).

Linguists have not always, however, made this point clear and, indeed, many of them have, often implicitly, taken their models of language from their own experience of written forms. The issue has recently been pursued in greater detail by Per Linell in Sweden. In *The Written Language Bias in Linguistics* (1982) he lays out for fellow linguists the detailed ways in which that bias has, he believes, affected their theory. He writes: 'It seems to me that a great number of our explicit or implicit theories, our methods and preferences are heavily influenced by the very long traditions of analyzing mainly, or only, certain kinds of written language. Even when we are in fact focussing on spoken language, we seem to approach it with a theoretical apparatus which is more apt for the analysis of written language' (1982, p. III). As we shall see, there is some question as to whether that apparatus is really 'apt' for written language either. Linell, however, provides a basis for pursuing both questions by indicating 'the extent to which linguistics, like most other sciences, is still dependent on important events of the past, both technological inventions ... and practical political goals and social concerns that have motivated the practice of linguistic science since antiquity' (ibid. p. 1).

Crystal has shown how this bias in linguistics carries over into lay views of language. Many educators and non-linguists, for instance, have criticised such spoken uses as 'you know', which they have taken as signs of 'sloppy' speech or 'imprecise' thinking. In fact, he says, they are rule governed and functional: 'In informal conversation they have a proper role, as they are one of the main means language has of expressing the various alterations in the force and direction of argument that we find ourselves using' (Crystal, 1976, p. 24). They facilitate syntactic flexibility in conversation. Furthermore: 'They are governed by rules of usage, as any other area of grammar. These rules may not much resemble the traditional grammatical rules of school textbooks but rules they are none the less.' (ibid.) The interpellation 'you know' is not considered appropriate in standard written styles of the kind taught in schools and used in the 'essayist tradition' nor in certain formal situations, for example in a television interview. But Crystal points out that most language use does not occur in such contexts: language is generally used in informal, everyday, conversational ways and writing or formal utterances are special cases of language use, with their own conventions and rules.

The problem has been that descriptions of language in general tended to be based on these special cases. It was from these that the 'grammatical rules of school textbooks' were derived, at least until the work of descriptive linguistics in this century, and perhaps still despite it in some cases. This was partly because of methodological difficulties in recording 'natural' everyday speech and partly because early grammarians tended to privilege the conventions and prestige associated with their own practice of academic writing. Advances in technology and methodology as well as in linguistic theory have now enabled researchers to gather sufficient evidence of conversational speech for its significance, grammaticality, and difference from such special cases as the literary standard and other writing styles to be recognised.

The argument has not, however, been resolved in linguistics and many prominent writers, notably Chomsky and, as we shall see below, to some extent John Lyons, have argued that linguists have to study idealised 'system sentences' because much of everyday speech is ungrammatical. These idealised sentences often turn out to be based, in fact, on the conventions of written language in the academic sub-culture and these linguists could be seen to be perpetuating, albeit in more sophisticated terms, the older, ideological conception of writing as the model for speech.

Chomsky's work has also encouraged another set of assumptions in linguistics that have consequences for the models of literacy with which we are here concerned. These have been loosely termed 'universalist' theories of language, since the basic tenet is that there are universal structures of grammar and especially of syntax, in which all people have 'competence' and which underly and make possible the different utterances that we observe in the actual practice of language. Criticising this development, Lyons says: 'Linguists have been very much concerned in recent years with the postulation of universals of language structure and have all too often discounted the differences among languages' (1982).

Recently ethnolinguists, deriving their inspiration in England from the work of J. R. Firth and his disciples at SOAS (The School of Oriental and African Studies), have also challenged 'universalism' and have argued for more attention to 'language-specific' descriptions before more general claims about language can be made. Fought, for instance, writing of attempts to analyse traditional Mexican languages, argues:

> traditional grammatical structures ... are not appropriate to Mayan structures: they can be applied only with violence to their common usage or to the structural features they are intended to fit ... If the pattern of formal equivalences and differences of a language cuts across the categorical distinctions as they are usually interpreted, the result of using the traditional categories will be a confusing description, despite careful redefinition of the familiar terms to suit the unfamiliar forms. I think it is fair to say

that the tradition of structuralist and transformational descriptive grammar contains many examples of this kind. (Fought, 1973, p. 64; see also Hymes and Fought, 1975.)

Lourdes de Léon (1982) similarly points out how many Amerindian languages were studied and described by Catholic missionaries who, despite their undeniable achievements, fell into this ethnocentric trap by using Latin grammar as their model and then forcing native data into it. She cites a number of linguists working on non-European languages who, recognising this problem, have argued for 'language-specific descriptions adequate to the particular structure of those languages' (1982, p. 9).

This challenge to 'universalism' need not pose in its place a simple relativism or a mere piling up of empirical descriptions. Rather, as in social anthropology, it is possible to develop a dynamic model in which the student begins from the acute self-consciousness that his or her own concepts may be culture-specific at depths so far unexamined, and so starts out tentatively from them, being ready to revise them in the light of new ethnography. He or she then constructs new, cross-cultural models for further work, recognising that these too may have to be revised. Moreover, members of other cultures are understood to be themselves active participants in such model building and so their social and linguistic 'grammars' have to be taken into account also.

In the work of most linguists today, then, speech is not overtly seen as dependent on the rules of written language, while for many the 'universalism' of some approaches is being closely questioned. However, the theoretical advances that these views represent do not seem to have significantly affected statements about literacy, which appear at times to remain in a pre-Saussurian world. The special cases of literacy usage represented by the analysts' own academic experience, by the literary forms of their own culture and other specific social conventions are still taken by many, often implicitly, as the appropriate models for describing the 'universal' qualities of literacy and for testing other groups' or societies' conventions of literacy usage.

John Lyons, for instance, while complaining that 'much linguistic theorising is vitiated by the uncritical transference by linguists and philosophers of attitudes which derive from the cultural peculiarities of English and a few other so-called world languages' (1982), himself goes on to rest part of his view of literacy, implicitly, on exactly such 'cultural peculiarities' of written English. Rather than giving the same recognition to differences among literacies which he proposes to be differences among languages, he uses what is in fact the 'autonomous' model of literacy as the basis for arguments about the specific nature of the English language.

His argument begins with a rejection of 'universalism' and a claim that different varieties of language can be associated with different levels of such general qualities as 'objectivity': 'there are gross differences among languages, such that it does seem reasonable to say of some that they allow their users to approximate to neutral, objective description'. 'Languages can', he maintains, 'legitimately be analysed in terms of their greater or lesser context-dependence and culture-dependence.' (ibid.)

He substantiates these claims with reference to his own language: 'it is possible to address someone, or talk about someone, in English without indicating one's relative social status or attitude etc., whereas in many languages this is not possible. Again it is possible to make categorical assertions in English without giving any indication of the evidence that one has for making them or of one's attitude towards what one is saying: there are languages that cannot do this.' (ibid.)

The similarity of these claims to those made by Olson, Hildyard and others for literacy is striking. Indeed, as we shall see below, Lyons' general arguments about language differences can be claimed to rest to some extent on implicit assumptions about literacy of the kind that they make. These arguments are subject to the same criticisms, regarding ethnocentrism and academic-centredness that were levelled at these writers, both in terms of their assumptions regarding literacy and those regarding 'objectivity'. Within linguistics, then, as we have seen within other disciplines, these two concepts are closely linked. Before investigating further what Lyons has to say about literacy, then, it is important to analyse what he means by 'objectivity' and what force arguments about it have within his own discipline.

The argument that in English one can theoretically address others without revealing status, on which some of Lyons' claims for the 'objectivity' of the language rest, is not in fact readily subscribed to by linguists. Testing these claims against how a language actually operates in practice, Pulgrum, for instance, points out:

> We can recognise a person by his speech quite apart from the intelligence or intelligibility of his utterance. The mere physical features of his speech, conditioned anatomically and by habits, suffice for identification. If, in addition, what he says and how he says it, in other words his style, provide further clues, all the better. The what and how are socially conditioned, however, by the speaker's education, surroundings, profession etc. Directors and actors of radio plays who cannot convey any part of the contents of the performance visually, are very skilful in the art of voice characterisation. Even the psyche, the temperament of a person finds expression in his speech, to say nothing of his temporary moods and *every hearer makes a certain value judgement*

of a speaker simply on the basis of 'what he talks like' (Pulgrum, 1951, p. 17). (My emphasis.)

The point is not simply that we can identify status from speech if we wish to, such as with the clever elaborations developed on radio; rather, that it is difficult to conceive of an utterance in English in which this is not the case. Whatever formal characteristics Lyons might attribute to English in theory, in practice it would be difficult for him to sustain the claim that 'it is possible to address someone or talk about someone in English without indicating one's relative social status or attitude'. It would certainly be unsafe to generalise from a quality that is so difficult to establish, that English therefore 'allows its users to approximate to neutral, objective description'.

More precisely, in linguistic terms, it has been suggested that it is not as straightforward as Lyons implies to attribute the possibility of 'neutrality' to English grammar; some aspects, such as pronoun usage, are more context-dependent than he allows. The use of 'one', for instance, is frequently a device for indicating status or attitude, as when a politician attempts to establish neutrality or objectivity for his or her own opinions, through such phrases as 'one knows ...'. Similarly, the use of 'we' to express solidarity and 'institutional voice' may invoke power and status through, amongst other things, lending oneself the strength of numbers. 'We' may be used in a number of status-embedded ways, as when a doctor addresses a patient with 'How are *we* feeling?' or an adult says to a child 'Have *we* lost our voice, then?'. Although, as Lyons says, English does not *oblige* speakers to classify the addressee with regard to status, an analysis of the actual uses of pronouns demonstrates that it is, in practice, almost impossible to avoid.

Dialect, accent, lexical choice and grammatical structures are all interpreted by speakers and addressees as signifying status. One might, perhaps, break this down further by maintaining a distinction between 'grammatical' and paralinguistic ways of indicating status. In these terms one might argue that some languages 'give away' more about the status of a speaker (and the relationship with an interlocutor) through their grammatical structure, while others do so through paralinguistic features. The T/V distinction found in every European language except English provides the classic example of this, while English is, according to Lyons, a particularly clear example of how status, while clearly indicated in paralinguistic ways as Pulgrum indicates, need not be indicated in the grammar (Lyons, 1977). Within this framework, Lyons' emphasis on the particular demands made on English by its international functions might provide some partial explanation for its greater use of paralinguistic features rather than grammatical ones for indicating status, although more comparative and historical research would be necessary. Lyons, however, is attempting to say more than this. He is attempting to link these differences in ways of indicating status, as between grammatical and paralinguistic forms, with the concept of 'objectivity'. There is, however, no necessary reason to suppose that languages which indicate status only in paralinguistic ways offer their users more possibility of 'approximating to neutral, objective descriptions' than those which oblige their users to do so through grammatical structures.

Lyons would argue that his statements are only about 'language-systems' (Lyons, 1977) and that the paralinguistic aspects are by definition not included in these and so are irrelevant to the point about 'objectivity'. The idealised language-system encodes meaning through grammar, phonology and the lexicon and the question of how this system is used differs from that of how linguists analyse and describe it. The relationship of the language-system to other things, such as culture, psychological mechanisms etc. is, he maintains, a separate problem. When he says that 'English' relates to such cultural characteristics as 'objectivity' in specific ways, he is referring to a language-system, not to English in the loose everyday sense. What the utterer commits himself to is all encoded in the language-system. Within any particular language-system that English users subscribe to, and these may include different dialects, different phonological relationships and different lexical choices, it is possible, argues Lyons, to make statements without qualification of the speaker's commitment to their truth. That such qualification may occur outside the language-system, through paralinguistic means and in the observation of and judgement on which language-system, dialect etc. is operating in a given context, is irrelevant, Lyons would claim, to his central point. There are language-systems, he points out, within which that characteristic of English whereby the utterer is not obliged to commit himself as to the truth of his utterance is not to be found; in such systems the utterer is obliged to commit himself, within the language-system itself, to some judgement as to the truth of the utterance. The grammar and lexicon oblige him to do this. It is more difficult, according to Lyons, for users of such language-systems to approximate to neutral, objective statements since they must always comment on and judge the truth value of what they say (Lyons, 1982).

The problem with this argument, however, is that it is impossible to discover, in practice, a 'pure' use of English syntax that does not, also, similarly oblige its users to indicate a view on what is uttered. As we saw above, and Lyons would not disagree, it is mostly in the paralinguistic features that English performs this function. But Lyons cannot simply shrug off such features as irrelevant and somehow 'impure', for no use of English occurs without them. Utterances are always coloured by their context. The meaning of any spoken language is not simply altered but actually determined by dialect, accent, facial expression etc., while written communication derives much of its meaning from the format, layout, institutional context etc. If such features are to be separated, for purposes of the division of academic labour, from the language-system itself, then one wonders quite what is left at the core and what uses it can be put to. Whatever uses it may serve within descriptive linguistics, and there is clearly some advantage in dividing up and abstracting fields of study for specific purposes, it is quite a different matter to then take such abstract categories as 'language-systems' rather than language uses as the basis for cross-cultural comparison, particularly when what is being compared is such a socially charged concept as 'objectivity'.

As soon as the language-system is related to concepts such as 'objectivity' then it is located within the social and ideological domain and concepts in that domain have political and evaluative implications, whether the user wishes to make them or not. Once he introduces them, the linguist cannot simply retreat into claiming that he is only dealing with the abstractions of descriptive linguistics. The concept of 'objectivity' is not neutral in English culture nor in international affairs in the modern world; the appeal to it has significant implications not only for status but, more crucially, for power and control of resources. If it could be demonstrated that English facilitated 'objectivity' more than other languages, then users of it would have a powerful weapon for affirming and legitimating their rights to certain positions of authority in relation to cultures or subcultures in which language use lacked this quality. Members of those cultures might, with some justification, argue that the distinction between language-systems and the state of the world is not simply a neutral, theoretical tool but itself an ideological weapon constructed within a dominant culture and serving the purposes of cultural and linguistic imperialism. Once the linguist 'brings over' his formal abstract concepts into the cultural domain then, however much he protests that no ranking is intended, the attribution of such qualities as 'objectivity' to some languages and not others cannot but have implications for ranking and for power. There are also powerful economic implications in this attribution of 'objectivity' to the English language.

The provision of English language teaching is already a major source of revenue to Britain, from the language schools that yearly bring literally millions of foreign students to the country, to the British Council exports of English language and culture across the world and the institutional supports for such practices provided by publishing houses, printers and writers of textbooks. In Third World countries, in particular, where governments are seeking efficient ways of adopting scientific and technological know-how, the characteristics of English as an international language already give it considerable advantage over others in the commercial competition to 'sell' such language training. In addition, the hidden advantages for the host country of other nations using its language, such as ease of commercial interaction, cultural ties etc., are well enough known and indeed provide one of the justifications for the continuation of such institutions as the British Council. In the hard sell of this linguistic and cultural economy, claims are made for English, not unlike those formerly made for Latin or for certain styles of French, that it is better suited to particular intellectual and scientific purposes, notably in the current situation, those for which consumers want to buy languages. If scholars in the host country can establish with authority that English really can facilitate neutral, objective statements then its value on the world market is correspondingly increased. To attribute these characteristics to English is not, then, 'neutral', even if it may have derived from a genuinely detached 'academic' inquiry.

These arguments are given some strength when we realise that the claims being made for English language by Lyons are remarkably similar to those being made for other aspects of English in general, or of English class culture in particular, by other writers. Bernstein, for instance, in his attempt to attribute less 'context-dependence' and greater 'objectivity' to certain language uses, correlated these characteristics with certain 'codes' which he identifies with certain social classes (1971). Greenfield has attempted to apply this to other cultures, using questionnaires given to Wolof children to establish an empirical basis for the distinction (1972). Hildyard and Olson have restricted the claim to written modes of communication, arguing that speech forms are 'context-dependent' while written forms, in which English is particularly developed, facilitate 'objectivity' (1978).

The same attempt is being made by all of these writers to distinguish 'objective' and 'context-independent' uses from 'subjective' and 'context-dependent' uses: in one case the difference is couched in terms of 'differences among languages', in another in terms of differences within a language (elaborated and restricted codes), and in yet another in terms of differences between language modes, namely speech and writing. Claims made for the differences between speech and writing, then, are put into perspective by the fact that the same claims are attributed to other variables. One is led to ask whether it is the attention to and general nature of such claims that first needs explaining, especially when it appears that they derive from such a specific social group, namely those in a western academic sub-culture who could arguably be said to have their own interests at stake.

I would suggest that this attention to differences between context-dependent and objective description can be explained as a product of the specific academic tradition to which these writers are the heirs. Some description of that tradition, in terms of its linguistic and literacy conventions, may help to put into perspective the claims for language and literacy made by exponents within it. The academic tradition in which Lyons, Olson, Hildyard, Bernstein and others work has developed, over time, specific aims, one of which is indeed 'approximation to dispassionate, neutral, objective description'. In fulfilling these aims, specific use of the potential of different aspects of language and of literacy has been instrumental. The organisation of seminars, lectures, essay writing, journal articles and books in academic institutions makes use of a number of different 'forms, characteristics and functions' (Leech et al. 1982) of speech and writing. Seminars make use of the speech function of instant feed-back, and of quick and direct communication, with the help of such speech forms as intonation, stress etc. Lectures make less use of the feedback function of speech but depend heavily on the speech characteristic of needing less explicitness. The lecturer can point to objects, diagrams etc. and the context of the lecture means that he or she does not need to make explicit statements about why everyone is there and for what. The essays required of students make use of the writing function of 'visibility' (ibid.), which enables re-reading and planning, while the publication of articles employs both this function of writing and its ability to facilitate communication over distance and to large numbers. With articles and books the distance between addresser and addressee is theoretically at a maximum, and communication is at its most impersonal. Indeed, these qualities are frequently the ones cited as crucial in identifying writing as 'neutral' and 'objective'. However, in practice, these forms of communication belong, like the other aspects of the academic tradition, to a specific culture, or sub-culture, in which assumptions are shared and meaning remains dependent on context. Such articles and books will make little sense, for instance, to an untutored reader: this, in fact, is the major justification for organising learning in specific institutions where such readers can learn how to make sense of 'the words on the page'. Students are taught, for instance, to 'read' in a different way from that of everyday practice: rather than reading a text from beginning to end in the sequence in which the publisher has ordered it, they are urged to select what they want for particular purposes from different parts of the text, using the contents page, index, chapter headings etc. and moving backwards and forwards within that text and to other texts. They also learn to plan and edit their own writing in a way which is not common to most everyday uses of written language.

The unusual nature of this process can be seen through a comparison of these academic practices with those conventionally associated with the most common uses of reading and writing in this culture, such as reading adverts, notices in factories, magazines, popular newspapers etc., and the writing of lists for shopping, writing letters and filling in forms. Academic tutors not surprisingly experience considerable difficulty in attempting to teach their particular forms of reading and writing to students acculturated in the conventions of these popular uses of literacy. The use of tape recordings and videos adds further elaborations of form and function which are just being recognised and incorporated into this traditional complex of language use. All of these processes combine to produce a particular form of language, what we can loosely call 'academic language'. It is clearly a product of specific circumstances and needs, and it makes variable and often distinctive use of particular language forms, functions and characteristics.

It is often this particular language to which academics are referring when they make general claims about the nature of English or of literacy. They tend to privilege their own language, to make claims for it which derive from the requirements which brought it into being in the first place. Popper, for instance, makes it quite clear that his 'World Three' is a world of academics. He argues, for instance, that the evolutionary emergence of 'our self transcendence by means of selection and rational criticism' depends upon developments that have taken place in academic language: 'It is only within a language thus enriched that critical argument and knowledge in the objective sense become possible.' (Popper, 1979, p. 122.) Similarly, Olson's claims for literacy, that it for instance 'unambiguously represents meanings', turn out to rest on descriptions of the 'British essayists' of the seventeenth and eighteenth centuries. They were 'among the first to exploit writing for the purpose of formulating original theoretical knowledge ... Knowledge was taken to be the product of an extended logical essay – the output of the repeated application in a single coherent text of the technique of examining an assertion to determine all of its implications.' (Olson, 1977, pp. 268–9.)

Olson, indeed, recognises the historical specificity of the development of scientific institutions and of distinctly academic forms of language and literacy in England and he notes that these were not general in the society as a whole: 'Locke's essayist technique differed notably from the predominant writing style of the time' (ibid.). But Olson nevertheless slides from these precise comments into grander generalisation and appears to attribute the characteristics associated with specific exponents of the essay technique to writing as such and to the whole culture. He claims, for instance, that Locke's 'intellectual bias' characterises 'our present use of language', presumably using 'our' to refer to himself and fellow academics but failing to make the restriction clear. 'The essayist technique', he admits, 'was not an ordinary language, not a mother tongue, but rather a form of language specialised to serve the requirements of autonomous, written, formalised text.' (ibid. 1977, p. 270.) This might be better put as follows: that the specialist language and the written formalised text alike served the purposes of the particular sub-culture. By attributing the specialisation to the 'requirements of autonomous ... text', he inverts the historical process and reifies the text.

These writers, then, derive doubtful generalisations, often implicitly rather than explicitly, from the specific character of 'academic language'. They assert, for example, by implication that non-academics in their own culture and members of other cultures, particularly illiterate 'primitives', cannot have the skills of 'objectivity', 'neutrality' and 'logic' which their own academic language is specifically designed to facilitate. The fact, however, that they have designed a language to fulfil these functions does not necessarily mean that these functions could not be fulfilled in other ways, nor that their language is intrinsically connected with them, nor that the language has necessarily been proven to succeed in achieving these ideals. Anthropologists and others have produced evidence of the range of languages and institutions within which 'scientific progress' has been made, as in the mix of mathematics and astrology in ancient Greece (Goody, 1977, p. 17), and of geometry and the building of sacred altars in ancient India (Parry, 1982, p. 23), while in Europe developments can be traced through a number of traditions, of which the essayist tradition is only one.

Attention to differences between context-dependent and objective language may arise, to some extent, from this particular essayist tradition. However, this does not mean that people do not act upon or make some such distinction, in everyday life and in other cultures. The distinction may, though, be conceptualised in different ways than those familiar to English academic usage, and the means employed to attain 'objectivity' may be different. To privilege one of these ways of attaining objectivity, particularly when that way happens to be one's own, is fraught with difficulty, not least because the assessment is likely to be circular, depending on the very standards that the proponents are trying to verify. To put such an effort into perspective, it is necessary first to investigate cross-culturally the various different conceptions of 'objectivity' and different means of attaining it. This involves, in the first instance, taking the concept of 'objectivity' as itself an object of study, rather than as a known and secure starting point.

It is, in fact, relatively obvious and uncontentious to argue that in some societies or sub-cultures the distinction between 'objective' and 'context-dependent' is more consciously drawn and given more weight than in others (cf. Karp and Bird, 1980; Finnegan and Horton, 1973; Wilson, 1974). The explanation for the differences is, however, more problematic. One way of explaining them is by reference to institutional features of these societies. For example, the existence of educational institutions specifically directed to this task can clearly be a causal factor.

John Lyons could be taken to be offering such an analysis when he says that the English language is different from other languages in that it 'extends' the meaning of particular words beyond the culture-specific because of the international demands made on it (Lyons, 1982). Lyons attempts to put this into perspective by pointing out that 'the value set upon objectivity varies from society to society: indeed, that the concept itself may be given no recognition at all in some societies'. However, he says, 'our own society – at least the academic sub-society within it [a significant qualification in view of the current argument] – sets great store by what it calls, and thinks to be, objectivity and has certain standards of dispassionate, scientific investigation, to which at least lip service is paid and which may, of course, be distorted by unrecognised prejudice of one kind or another' (ibid.).

He is not content, however, to leave it at that: to recognise that the perception of and attention to objectivity varies culturally while claims to objectivity itself are often more biased than is realised. He wants to go beyond this testable assertion and maintain that there is a real difference, not simply one of perception, between different languages in their ability to 'allow their users to approximate to neutral, objective description' and that English has this ability. This would seem to imply that some, at least, of the terms developed by academics within the English tradition are really 'universal', 'culture-free' and 'analytic' as their proponents claim them to be. This, however, remains problematic and unproven, if not unprovable. Whether, for instance, concepts such as 'ethnicity', 'class', 'politics' are 'culture-free', that is whether academics have succeeded in freeing them from their narrow everyday cultural uses and made them available for cross-cultural use, is a question of judgement and, ultimately, of ontology. Yet, in the cultural and specifically academic world within which Lyons is making claims for 'objectivity', this is what the term is taken to imply. Whatever claims for the English language he may wish to make from a supposedly technical, linguistic perspective, he cannot assume that attributing 'objectivity' to it is unproblematic, or that the meaning attributed to it within that sub-culture can safely be carried over into cross-cultural correlations with the features of certain languages and grammars.

Romaine (1982) suggests an alternative framework to the 'objective/ subjective' dichotomy that Lyons' argument seems to rest on. She 'would prefer to think of different languages as having the potential to exploit differing degrees of subjectivity' but she does not think there is 'any neutral ontology or world view which is objective and can serve as a universal yardstick. The most we can get is some idea of the world view our own language commits us to by virtue of what it is possible to say on the one hand, impossible to say on the other and most importantly, what it is *not* possible *not* to say or avoid saying/implying' (personal communication). She adds that we 'only realise this by learning other languages' (ibid.).

Anthropologists, who attempt to answer precisely such questions by the learning of other languages, can provide ethnographic substance for Romaine's study of 'differing degrees of subjectivity'. Lienhardt, writing of the Dinka of the southern Sudan, provides support for Romaine's view but also suggests a further elaboration of it, impinging as he does so on a number of the issues raised here. He compares Dinka representations of the 'self' with those common in certain English usage and concludes:

> It seems to me that the Dinka language, unlike modern, educated, and for the most part metropolitan English, compels its speakers to integrate the moral and physical attributes of persons together within the physical matrix of the human body. In modern English, moral and mental conditions are spoken of in more or less abstract terms (anger, suspicion, forcefulness and so on) cut off for the most part, from their etymological roots ... It may be that the disjunction, for most modern English speakers, between abstract terms and concrete imagery has something to do with the complex foreign origins of the English language. Non-literate Africans can explain the etymology of words as non-literate English-speakers cannot ... The difference is ... consistent with the absence, among (in this case) the Dinka, of the mind–body dichotomy which many writers of this century have wished to resolve. (1980, pp. 77–8.)

Lienhardt is not, however, being quite as Whorfian as this may sound. He is not denying the possibility of the English language overcoming the mind–body dichotomy nor of the Dinka language expressing it. But he sees such expression as running contrary to the dominant idiom and cultural meaning in which users of the language are socialised and as therefore not what the anthropologist is trying to make sense of. With regard to English, he suggests that what he sees as the limitations of 'metropolitan' use of the language may not be present in other registers: 'still an integration of thought and feeling in metaphor and imagery is what we seek to have recreated for us in the best literature' (ibid. p. 78). As regards the Dinka, he suggests that it may be possible to persuade users of the language to reply to questions about the mind–body dichotomy: it is not that the language is incapable, at a formal level, of making such a distinction, but that such usage would be unrepresentative in cultural terms. He writes: 'among [the Dinka] I had that experience of daily conversation which enables one to discriminate, as we take for granted in the language into which we were born, between what people mean and what they say. Then one learns what kinds of questions, formulated in an alien mode of thought, might receive answers – but answers which, though grammatically, syntactically and even semantically plausible, do not represent, and may positively misrepresent, indigenous and spontaneous interests and ideas' (ibid. p. 74).

The general implications of Lienhardt's argument are that all languages have the potential to make abstract, relatively neutral statements, if called upon to do so. (The ability to make statements without indicating status, which Lyons attributes to English, is not, of course, the only or even the major way in which abstract and neutral meanings can be formulated.) Hence, in terms of what they can 'say', it would be wrong to argue that there are distinctions between languages according to their approximation to neutral, abstract description. However, in terms of what they 'mean', their use in a specific cultural context, it is reasonable to maintain that some languages pay less explicit attention to abstract formulations. This cultural, as opposed to linguistic, distinction does not, however, necessarily tell us very much about 'objectivity', as Lyons claims. Even if these differences did tell us something about differences in *attention to* 'objectivity', this would not necessarily be the same as attainment of 'objectivity', as we saw above in relation to 'academic language'. Lienhardt, as an anthropologist, leaves that question alone and is concerned simply with the different ways in which people in different cultures make sense of their worlds, without attempting to attribute greater truth to any one way as, by definition, the attribution of 'objectivity' does. His work would, I think, support Romaine's general concern with studying 'differing degrees of subjectivity' rather than assuming and searching for ontologically neutral 'objectivity'.

Lyons, in fact, concedes this point, although I feel that he does not follow through fully its implications for the rest of his argument. He admits that he cannot appeal to some absolute conception of 'objectivity' in claiming that some languages 'allow their users to approximate to neutral, objective description'. He maintains, instead, that there are differences between languages as regards their *relative* 'objectivity'. However, he couches his explanation for these differences not simply at the level of what actual language users 'mean', that is in relation to particular cultural practice and institutions (within which the concept of 'relative objectivity' might make some sense), but instead at the level of what they 'say', that is in relation to 'the lexical and grammatical structure of languages', at the level of 'language-systems', which appears to assume again the notion of absolute 'objectivity', since, as we have seen, it offers no cultural context in which to make sense of such systems. When Lyons attempts to specify differences between 'language-systems', such as in the example of English pronouns, or in that of the lack of status marking in English grammar, it becomes virtually impossible to keep the formal 'lexical and grammatical' features separate from the cultural context. This methodological problem generates a crucial theoretical problem since, as Lienhardt demonstrates, whatever formal 'grammatical' features a language may exhibit, they do not make much 'sense' apart from the context in which they are used.

One way in which some writers have attempted to avoid this problem has been by appealing to literacy, as a case where the formal features of language can be claimed to make sense apart from context. With writing, at least, they believe, what is said can be taken to be what is meant. Lexical and grammatical structures, when represented in written form, can be isolated from the context-dependence of oral modes of communication. 'Objectivity', then, is more possible in English because it has a highly developed form of writing. It can be argued that it is on the strength of these supposed qualities of writing, as identified by Hildyard, Olson and other exponents of the 'autonomous' model of literacy, that Lyons rests some at least of his more general claims for 'differences among languages'. The 'objectivity' and neutrality that these authors discover in certain uses of writing correspond to the 'objectivity' that Lyons identifies in the English language.

Moreover, Lyons himself does make explicit appeal to the characteristics of literacy in his description of 'objectivity'. He suggests that the *perception* of objectivity to be observed in some areas of English culture may stem from the 'real' objectivity provided by writing: 'The intrinsically greater objectivity of written language (or, alternatively, the intrinsically lesser subjectivity) could', he argues, 'have encouraged the development of an institutionalised greater respect for written evidence' (1982).

There is, however, powerful ethnographic evidence to challenge this explanation and to suggest that the 'institutionalised greater respect' for written language in England can be better explained in terms of political and ideological practices in the real history of that country. Clanchy shows that, between 1066 and 1307 in England, the criteria for validation of land rights and other significant social facts, and the relative weight given to written and oral criteria in such validation changed as a direct result of political pressures (1979). The Norman conquerors, in attempting to establish rights to land in England, undermined indigenous oral criteria for proof of ownership, by which they as newcomers were on weaker ground than native land owners, and set up centralised, bureaucratic procedures with emphasis on written documentation, records, cross-referencing etc. over which they could exercise greater control. As a result of the 'literate mentality' that these institutions helped to form in England, and to which Lyons and fellow academics now subscribe, later historians, looking back to records of eleventh century England, tended to discard medallions, seals and other material objects that had been major criteria of validation in the oral culture of that period. They retained and emphasised, instead, the written documents deliberately produced by a centralised Chancery and other Norman offices and institutions. Clanchy points out the anachronistic nature of the historians' practice. The knights of the eleventh century, not being socialised in the 'literate mentality' of these later historians, knew well enough that such institutions were not simply a 'neutral' bureaucracy guaranteeing the 'objectivity' of written documents, and they knew well enough, too, how these documents were untrustworthy. Both the institutions and the documents were the product of deliberate political manipulation to deprive them of their rights to land. Written documents could be and were easily forged whereas seals, crosses, medallions etc. were, in the way in which they had been developed and used in pre-Norman Britain, distinctive individual objects, which were less easily forged, more identifiable and more obviously linked to particular individuals. Moreover, these material objects were 'known' to generations of those for whom the land rights that they validated were important. They were thus more reliable guarantees of 'truth' than written documents. To both later historians and eleventh century knights it appeared that 'truth' was intrinsic to the kind of evidence that they had both, in their different ways, been socialised into respecting. To us it is clear that it was the forms of social organisation in which such evidence was carried that gave them this quality and not the intrinsic nature of the evidence itself.

The same, of course, is true of the written records of the present period. In contemporary England written language takes precedence, for instance, in a legal context – a written contract being more binding than a spoken agreement – while in Scotland verbal contracts are binding in some cases. These differences are to be explained in terms of those contexts and the socially agreed constructions of how these institutions should operate rather than in terms of any supposed intrinsic qualities of writing.

It is, then, unsafe to generalise as Lyons does that: 'until modern methods of sound recording were developed (a) the inscription of language utterances on durable materials provided a more reliable means of transmission than memory and oral reproduction' and (b) that this was 'recognised to be so in the western tradition in which literacy developed in the first instance for this purpose' (1982). Not only was literacy not necessarily recognised as more 'reliable', but we would be bound to say that it really was not more reliable. Lyons, in fact, concedes (b): 'I am only too prepared to accept that in other traditions scribal records either are not or are not seen to be intrinsically more reliable than memory and oral transmission.' But he still wishes to maintain (a), that writing is intrinsically more reliable. This appears to be contradictory. In conceding (b) he recognises that scribal records actually were unreliable, as well as being seen to be. There is, then, no intrinsic reason why 'the inscription of language utterances on durable materials provides more reliable means of transmission than memory and oral reproduction' and there is empirical evidence to the contrary. Moreover, the criterion for 'reliability' is itself culture-dependent. In some cultures, scribes do not record texts with word-for-word fidelity, while in others one is not free to alter anything in the process of re-recording.

Lyons could legitimately maintain that scribal records have some potential, according to the institutions in which they are developed and used, for 'reliability' as defined in that culture or even as defined by him. But, as we have seen, other products of social organisation, such as seals and medallions, can have this quality too and, in the right conditions, may be aptly considered more reliable, as they were by the medieval knights. So writing is not unique in this respect. However, like Olson, Hildyard and Greenfield, Lyons does not allow such qualifications to impinge on the general claims he is making for literacy.

Olson, for instance, does admit at one point that all we can really be sure of is that some academics have made claims for objectivity while the question of assessing those claims is a different matter:

> Whether or not all meaning can be made explicit in the text is perhaps less critical than the belief that it can and that making it so is a valid scientific enterprise. This was clearly the assumption of the [eighteenth century] essayists, and it continues in our use of language for science and philosophy. Explicitness of meaning, in other words, may be better thought of as a goal rather than an achievement. But it is a goal appropriate only for the particular, specialised use of language that I have called text. (Olson, 1977, p. 275.)

If that were all Olson were saying, then it would be reasonable enough and would provide an interesting basis for historical study of the reasons for specific literacy practices in specific cultures. But, throughout his essay, his use of language suggests that he is making more general claims. Like Lyons, he links cultural interest in 'objectivity' with the supposed 'real' objectivity to be found in writing. Olson says, for instance, that:

> the invention of the alphabetic writing system gave to Western culture many of its predominant features including an altered conception of language and an altered conception of rational man. These effects came about, in part, from the creation of

explicit, autonomous statements – statements dependent upon an explicit writing system, the alphabet, and an explicit form of argument, the essay. In a word, these effects resulted from putting the meaning into the text. (ibid. p. 262.)

He also says that 'the decoding of sentence meaning should be treated as the end point of development' as though the universal superiority of the essayist technique had been firmly established.

Amidst these grand claims for the 'effects' of writing, Olson suppresses the qualification cited above that 'whether meaning can be made explicit in text is perhaps less critical than the belief that it can' and proceeds as though it were agreed and verifiable that writing can and does have such effects because of its intrinsic qualities. According to Olson, it was not the beliefs of the eighteenth century essayists that led to changes in the conception of language and rationality, an assertion that could be tested against the historical evidence, but the forms they used, the alphabet and the essay. Yet the only evidence that he brings forward turns out to be, in fact, the essayists' own belief that this was what literacy could achieve. Both they and Olson use the fact that claims for 'objectivity' are made as proof of their veracity.

Similarly, Lyons presents in universalistic asocial terms an argument that elsewhere he admits is culture-dependent. He recognises at one point that claims for the 'intrinsically greater objectivity of written language' in literate culture may derive from socially constructed beliefs about what literacy can achieve (1982). But he then proceeds to write as though those claims were really 'true' and uses this 'fact' to 'explain' the beliefs. With all of these writers the technical, and apparently neutral, quality of their specialist language is used to give greater weight and universality to arguments about literacy and objectivity which, when analysed closely, can be demonstrated to rest upon social and ideological presuppositions.

Ragnar Rommetveit has provided a powerful challenge to this positivist tendency (1982). He identifies the attempt by some linguists to discover 'literal meanings' with the belief that there can be a 'natural science' approach to language. He notes, for instance, that linguists have attempted to apply some of the terminology of natural science inappropriately to language, often through such metaphors as 'cohesion', 'balance' etc., which fix and reify what is in fact a more flexible and dynamic phenomenon. He opposes to this a hermeneutic approach which asks always what a particular utterance is for and where it is located. From this viewpoint, meaning is seen as relative and truth as negotiable. Rommetveit does not believe that we can understand meaning by paring an utterance down to its 'core meaning' and then following up variations on it, as the formal linguists are attempting to do. They build idealised models but then carry them over into real usage as though they really existed, forgetting that they had initially involved 'bracketing' certain assumptions. Rommetveit quotes Hilary Putnam as saying 'we cannot know ourselves as we understand hydrogen' (ibid.); linguistics, in contrast, must always take into account contextuality. This involves 'redrawing the boundaries of semantics/pragmatics', in other words recognising that meaning cannot be understood by addressing ourselves only to formal, syntactic processes: 'pragmatics', the study of why and how utterances are used, has to be included within the study of what the utterances mean, and how their semantic load is constructed and regularised. We are concerned, then, with more than simply linguistic competence. There is never only a 'core meaning' of an utterance but rather there are always alternative models; novel contexts are being re-created with each utterance; language users are continually establishing and transforming social reality in their communications. The social system is dynamic and our models of language must take account of this and not be restricted to idealised models of 'literal meaning'. The ambiguity of the social system is present in the semantic system too.

This involves, in Rommetveit's opinion, rejecting 'pre-theoretical notions' such as the belief that language functions as a 'conduit', simply passing on feelings and transferring literal meanings. Rather, he prefers to view language as a 'circular' process of inter-communication in which speakers take account of the view of their listeners in constructing the utterance in a continual interaction. Language is activity and we will not understand it by trying to put a static model of a complete language-system into the head of an individual user. Meaning is not simply in an utterance, irrespective of the participants: to understand it we must take into account the inter-subjectivity of the participants, addressing ourselves to such questions as who controls the meaning and the nature of the reference. Rather than looking for formal 'truth conditions' in an utterance, Rommetveit prefers to start from H. James' point 'we trade on each other's truths' (Rommetveit, 1982). The ambiguity of layman's oral language should not be lost in specialised technical language. Calling upon Wittgenstein's writings on aspect theory, 'possible worlds' and pluralism, Rommetveit proposes that the meanings of an utterance can be analysed in terms of their 'aspects' (ibid.). There are always referential alternatives possible to the speaker and addressee and to the observer in relation to any utterance. Knowledge is not storage but activity and making sense of it will be very impoverished if this involves looking for only one account of it, the so-called 'literal meaning', at the expense of all the other 'potential' meanings. Even if Popper's claims for 'World Three' and Olson's for 'autonomous text' were valid – and Rommetveit's work casts further doubt on them – the world which they are striving for would be an impoverished one and the 'knowledge' which could be stored in it would be narrow and limited.

Linguistics, according to Rommetveit, can provide an experimental study of the process represented by 'knowledge as activity', showing, for instance, the different possible worlds, perspectives, aspects and referential alternatives embedded in any speech act. This is not a matter of adding information to an assumed 'real world' on which any communication is based, but of recognising that there is no unequivocal, neutral description of a situation: once verbalised, communication involves many possible worlds. As a language user you may start from a position of 'innocent egotism', whereby you assume that others are like you and share your assumptions, or you can start by trying to assume what the addressee's terms of reference are and continue in a circular process of mutual discovery. Although many of us in our social use of language may begin from the ideologically narrow position of 'innocent egotism', this position is not a fruitful one for the student of language to begin from. The social reality of language use always involves the latter, interactive process even though the participants may act 'as if' it does not. Indeed, that 'as if' model is an important part of the act of communication and must itself be treated as an object of study.

In a communicative act all possible worlds are not, in practice 'dragged in', even though they are potentially available. In order to communicate, some agreement has to be reached by the participants as to what worlds, out of all possible ones, are being referred to. This commitment to shared worlds is in fact socially contingent and will vary from time to time and between different communicators. Although it may be represented by the participants themselves as 'real' and 'literal', the analyst should not be taken in by appearance which, while necessary for the act of communication, is only an 'as if' state. This perspective, says Rommetveit (1982), makes arguments about the 'truth conditions' of utterances sterile, since what we should really be looking at is how the participants themselves constructed such an appearance. Analysts, however, have taken the concept of 'literal meaning' as a 'neutral' and 'universal' tool of study rather than treating it as an object of study in itself, as a part of the 'social construction of reality' which they are trying to describe and to explain.

For instance, one explanation for the emphasis on 'truth conditions' in linguistics, Rommetveit claims, could be the beliefs associated with literacy. Popper has claimed that the possibility of understanding meaning as in the sentence alone, independent of its social context, increased with the growth of literacy. He cites Luther's ability to claim that truth was 'immanent' in the text of the Bible as being associated with the growth of printing in his time (Rommetveit, 1982). This, says Rommetveit, might have been all well and good for religions, but it should hardly be taken as axiomatic in the rational study of society. The belief that 'meaning is in the text', which represents a particular and currently powerful aspect of the search for 'literal meaning', should be treated with the same scepticism with which we confront Luther's claims. We need, then, to 'demystify' the authority given in our society to written texts. Lawyers in Norway, he suggests, are doing this with regard to legal concepts and linguists have to do the same with regard to linguistic concepts and theories (ibid.).

Sociolinguists in this new, pluralist tradition, of which Rommetveit is perhaps an extreme exponent, have recently begun to challenge the 'mystification' of writing and of 'literal meaning' and to apply to literacy the more culturally relative, anthropological perspective that Rommetveit is proposing for language in general. Stubbs, for instance, presents arguments that seriously challenge Olson's belief that the 'meaning is in the text' (1980). Stubbs points out that, in order to analyse how readers:

> make sense of written material we need to know more than simply the 'linguistic' characteristics of the text: in addition to these characteristics we need to recognise that any writing system is deeply embedded in attitudinal, cultural, economic and technological constraints ... reading and writing are therefore also sociolinguistic activities. People speak, listen, read and write in different social situations for different purposes ... If a coherent theory of literacy is to be developed, it will have to account for the place of written language, both in relation to the forms of spoken language and also in relation to the communicative functions served by different types of language in different social settings. (1980, pp. 15–16.)

Until recently, he complains, theories of literacy have tended to be based on instructional techniques rather than linguistic theory: research on reading has been dominated by experimental psychology, with the kinds of results we saw above (Chapter 1). He urges, instead, emphasis on literacy as a mode of language and on its social functions. As a sociolinguist Stubbs sees reading, for instance, as more than simply a mechanism for decoding written into spoken words: he prefers to concern himself with understanding meaning, pointing out that 'we do not normally read meaningless material' (ibid. p. 15).

Emphasis on the different communicative functions of speech and writing involves Stubbs, and others he cites such as Vachek and Basso, in seeing the complementarity of the two modes of language. As with the freeing of the study of speech from 'universalism', this approach to speech and writing can lead to value judgements: 'this view therefore allows us to make controlled value judgements about the appropriateness of written and spoken language for different functions ... written language clearly serves various functions which spoken language never could and is therefore superior from that point of view. Conversely, written language has clear disadvantages in other situations' (ibid. p. 17). Such value judgements must, however, be controlled and at the level of functions: this might lead to precise descriptions of particular skills appropriate to one or the other but would not justify the grandiose claims for 'logic', 'objectivity' and 'culture-free neutrality' which we have been examining. In relation, for instance, to Clanchy's material on medieval England, Stubbs' 'controlled value judgements' might lead to an examination of the relative advantages of seals, medallions, the swearing of oaths and the use of writing for the 'reliability' of claims to land rights, according to the interests of the different groups involved. In order to do this one would need to know about the nature of land rights in that particular society and about the organisation of writing within central bureaucracy, and not just about the different functions of written and spoken language in general. The various functions that different language modes serve are closely integrated with the institutions, structure and conventions of the society in question.

The sociolinguist and the anthropologist, then, in studying the various functions of spoken and written language, begin from the social data of the conventions in which they are acted out and through which members of that culture are socialised into their use. Stubbs points out, for instance, that many of the confusions for children acquiring literacy arise because these children are not yet familiar with some of the purposes for which writing is used and the conventions through which these purposes are articulated in their culture: 'many of its functions are often so specialised and particular' that they are 'mostly quite beyond children's experience' and 'many of the situations which conventionally require writing are of a fairly specialised and restricted kind' (ibid. p. 108). There is no simple free variation in the choice of written or spoken modes for particular purposes: 'the choice of medium is normally determined by the social function of the communication. In our society, there are conventions, usually quite clear cut, which determine whether messages are relayed orally or in writing and little choice is possible.' (ibid.) Committee meetings, for instance, are conventionally recorded in writing not on tape; certain forms of legal contract must be written down to have the 'force of law' (a practice whose specific historical and ideological origins have been well described by Clanchy amongst others). A child is often unacquainted with the precise and specialised social functions which are conventionally ascribed to either speech or writing and thus may be confused when asked to acquire 'skills' whose functions he or she cannot see or act upon.

Stubbs makes some effort to link the conventions for the use of writing to general linguistic characteristics of writing, but finds it difficult to establish any hard and fast rules since different cultures see different characteristics as significant and so a variety of literacies has been developed. For instance, the fact that the addressee is often unknown in written language cannot be cited as a general 'characteristic' of writing, since it is relative to the social use of the medium (ibid. pp. 108–9). In personal correspondence the addressee is known and some feed-back is expected; in institutional writing, on the other hand, the addressee is usually unknown, as with the bulk of published material, books etc. and feed-back, therefore, is at most only indirect. There are, then, different conventions for these forms of writing that relate directly to the differences of function and context. Where the addressee is unknown and feed-back is indirect, as with much institutional writing, the writer has to supply contextual information unnecessary in speech or in letters. Certain forms of writing, such as academic articles, extend this even further and writers are required to develop skills in explicitness, and in being aware of hidden assumptions, so that readers who have not directly had the writer's experience may understand it. For Chipewyan literates, on the other hand, in situations where the relationship between the addresser and the addressee is unknown, the norm is to keep silent (Scollen and Scollen, 1979).

The differences in these forms of writing, and the different skills required of writer and reader in relation to them, are more appropriately understood as different social practices related to, amongst other things, different functions they are attempting to fulfil. They are explicable, therefore, in terms of different social structures, rather than in terms of the supposed 'intrinsic' qualities of writing *per se*. Exponents of the 'autonomous' model of literacy, by searching for absolutes, especially in what is currently limited data, run the danger of having to change their supposition concerning the 'intrinsic' qualities of writing every time a new form of literacy practice is identified, which undermines their claims to 'universality'. The problems of such an approach can be easily identified in relation to Stubbs' description above of the varied functions of literacy.

To extrapolate from the fact that some forms of literacy practice develop explicitness to a theory that literacy is intrinsically capable of being culture-free and therefore represents an evolutionary advance in intellectual power, as some of the writers we have been examining do, is to take literacy out of the very context that enabled it to develop explicitness. It is to reify the technical aspects of a more complex and integrated practice. As Stubbs says: 'Although institutionalised writing is decontextualised in these ways, it nevertheless has some firm points of contact with social situations and social purposes, even if these are indirect and heavily conventionalised' (Stubbs, 1980, p. 109). One point of contact between institutionalised writing and the social situation, for instance, is that the 'text' has a communicative function and so one can 'talk meaningfully of a sender/addressee, a message, a receiver/addressee, and a purpose' (ibid.), even if the communication is not face-to-face and the audience is attenuated over time and space. Also, the writers always write as incumbents of 'known social roles: academic, journalist, newspaper editor, lawyer, "expert", and others' (ibid.).

Moreover, the very form of the text itself is important to its meaning. Whether the words are printed, typed or handwritten; whether they appear on a screen or on different types and qualities of paper; whether a 'text' occurs as a separate item, as part of an academic journal, or in a book or an encyclopaedia; how the page is laid out, the extent to which it is broken up by illustrations, headings, and the use of different typefaces. All of these aspects of the production of the text affect its meaning, both from the point of view of the author's intention and of the most probable interpretation, even before we consider the wider social situations in which it may be encountered. Researchers in the adult literacy campaigns in England have devoted considerable attention to these features of writing and have pointed out the possible practical consequences of imprecise layouts and unconsidered presentation of text. In 'Understanding Labels', for instance, an article in the ALBSU (Adult Literacy and Basic Skills Unit) Newsletter, it is pointed out that many of the subjects questioned about their 'reading' of a label on a bottle of pills would have given their children the wrong dosage as a direct result of the interpretation of the layout of the instructions. The writers of the article recommend that typeface, size, colour of print and label background be taken into account by those responsible for the production of such labels, since these factors are also significant for 'meaning' and not just the actual words themselves (ALBSU, 1980b).

Olson, then, is claiming too much for academic texts when he says 'an explicit writing system unambiguously represents meanings – the meaning is in the text' (1977, p. 264). The meaning of a text cannot, in fact, be derived only by 'decoding written words and knowing their linguistic characteristics', as Stubbs points out (1980, p. 15). Texts are always ambiguous since their meaning depends not only on the lexical and syntactical structure, in which ambiguity, according to Olson and others, can be reduced to a minimum, but also on paralinguistic, contextual structures, of which interpretation can never be exhaustive. Even the academics of Popper's 'World Three', then, do not work with 'literal meanings' but only with relatively more or less ambiguous languages, texts and contexts.

Lyons, in fact, would support this view and, whatever other characteristics he might attribute to literacy, or to specific language-systems such as English, he would not associate them with lack of ambiguity, as do Hildyard, Olson and Greenfield. Indeed, as regards literacy, he has argued that 'there is *more* ambiguity in written texts – though possibly in certain styles greater explicitness – because of the absence of disambiguating prosodic information' (1981c, p. 95).

Recent studies of literacy by sociolinguists have also suggested that, even with regard to syntactical and lexical structures, the case for the unambiguity of writing has been overstated. Stubbs gives some examples of how written English is seen, in linguistic terms, to reduce ambiguity. He notes that 'there are many more homophones (words which sound alike but differ in meaning) in spoken English than there are homographs (words which look alike but differ in meaning) in written English'. 'It follows', he says, 'that the written language pays more attention to disambiguating word meanings than the spoken language does' (1980, p. 56). He is referring here to the way in which written language may make the difference between structures clear, rather than to 'ambiguity' in the sense that a word may be taken as having two or more meanings. However, even in the structural sense, written English does not always clearly 'disambiguate' units such as words, sentences, morphemes etc. One cannot read English unambiguously, he says, unless one has competence in the phonology and morphology of the language, a source of difficulty for foreigners and a problem even for competent native speakers:

> In English writing, word boundaries are marked by spaces, but morpheme boundaries are generally not marked at all. So it is a problem for readers to know where to put them. For example, nothing indicates that the word structure differs in 'finger' and 'singer'. One simply has to know that 'sing' is a word but *'fing' happens not to be one. Similarly one has to decide whether to read 'misled' as 'mis-led' or as 'misl-ed', assuming a verb to 'misle' ... Fluent readers do occasionally have problems with this. For example, I recently came across the word 'homerun' and tried for several seconds to read it as 'homer-un', until I saw the correct morpheme structure. It is only relatively rarely then, that morpheme boundaries can be inferred unambiguously from the spelling alone (Stubbs, 1980, p. 56).

Stubbs cites many other examples of how written language may involve structural ambiguity so that making grammatical sense of it depends on context and the knowledge the reader brings to the text (e.g. ibid. p. 59). In this sense writing is not necessarily 'better' or 'worse' than speech, it simply involves further variations in the relationship of structure to meaning. Both writing and speech require context to make sense of what might formally be ambiguous.

Deuchar notes that: 'In spontaneous speech, sentences are often difficult to delimit: they may simply be unfinished, because the knowledge of the addressee makes completion unnecessary, or they may not be discernible as units at all.' However: 'In context, the absence of clear sentence boundaries does not mean that conversation is difficult to follow: it just shows that conversation is organised in a different way from writing' (Leech et al., p. 8/7).

One such difference for English users can be discerned in conventions for punctuation. In written English, says Deuchar, 'a grammatical sentence is expected to begin with a capital letter and end with a full stop and people are expected to write in sentences' (ibid.). This does not, however, mean that the written form is necessarily easier to make sense of or to follow than speech, nor that this particular set of conventions necessarily advantages English users.

Meaning does not, of course, depend upon the representation of utterance in the form of separate words or sentences. This, in fact, is why Lyons has proposed the concept of a 'system-sentence'. He would distinguish the various forms in which meaning may be actualised from the underlying structures on which meaning rests. I would simply add that such analysis remains partial if it excludes, as his does by definition, paralinguistic features of communication. The ways of constructing and understanding meaning, both within the lexical and grammatical structure and in paralinguistic features, vary across cultures and in different mediums and styles, and the attribution of general value, such as objectivity, logic, or lack of ambiguity to any one system, medium or feature is both impossible and fruitless. The English conventions for punctuation, for instance, may have some advantages for some purposes, although disambiguating 'sentence' units should not necessarily be taken as a significant one. Other literacies make use of different conventions and may, for instance, without any loss of clarity for those who know the rules, not mark sentence boundaries at all. In Persian uses of Arabic script, for instance, words are distinguished from each other by the forms the letter takes at the beginning, middle or end of a word but there are no particular conventions for indicating where a sentence begins and ends. The sentence unit must be inferred from the context, to some extent as with speech. However, this does not necessarily create problems for understanding any greater than those present in speech, as Deuchar suggests. In Vai script there are no spaces between either words or sentences and the reader has to become practised at separating out units of meaning without visual guides. Cole and Scribner point out that the specific skill developed for this purpose can be transferred to other tasks: they tested literates and illiterates in the Vai script for their ability to distinguish and reproduce units of meaning when heard as a continuous flow, and discovered that the literates were better at this task (1981).

There are, then, many different varieties of literacy practice whose characteristics, advantages and disadvantages for various purposes have scarcely yet been investigated. Far more cross-cultural research, of the type suggested by Cole and Scribner for instance (ibid.), would be necessary before any useful generalisations could be made even about the relative functions and worth of the various parts of these different systems (such as their punctuation conventions). This is even more true if we wish to make generalisations of the kind I examined above with regard to the relative logic, objectivity and neutrality of whole systems.

Olson, at least, does appear to accept such qualifications, although like others attempting to make general claims for literacy, he does not always follow through the implications of this for these claims. He writes: 'The faithful transcription of the sound patterns of speech by a fully developed alphabet has freed writing from some of the ambiguities of oral language. Many sentences that are ambiguous when spoken are unambiguous when written.' (1977, p. 265.) As we have seen, such claims require more precise demonstration before they can be readily accepted and Olson would not be justified in using the facility of written English to 'disambiguate' some units of structure, such as sentences and words, as proof of its overcoming ambiguity. One might, for instance, add that if 'many sentences that are ambiguous when spoken are unambiguous when written', the opposite is also true. Olson does, in fact, recognise that writing alone will not in itself provide the clarity he wants and he continues: 'However, a fully developed alphabet does not exhaust the possibilities for explicitness of a writing system. According to Bloomfield (1939) and Kneale and Kneale (1962), the remaining lack of explicitness necessitated the invention of formal languages of logic and mathematics' (ibid.). It is not, then, writing *per se* that has the qualities of explicitness and lack of ambiguity which Olson is attempting to locate, but rather the languages specifically designed for this purpose, of which certain aspects of literacy are a part. 'Written language can only become *relatively* free from judgement or interpretation' and higher standards of certainty require more precise tools.

Despite these important qualifications, Olson still implies elsewhere in that and other articles (1977; Hildyard and Olson, 1978) that writing itself can be unambiguous and that this is what facilitates objective knowledge. Referring to the English essayists, he says: 'A sentence was written to have only one meaning': and the writer's 'task was now to create autonomous text – to write in such a manner that the sentence was an adequate, explicit representation of the meaning, relying on no implicit premises or personal interpretations' (1977, p. 268). As we have seen, this is an impossible task and at times Olson himself seems prepared to admit as much. But the tenor of his claims, and those of others, for the lack of ambiguity of literacy, and of Lyons' claims for its 'objectivity', are, as we have seen, such as to imply that not only can the goal be achieved, but that it has been uniquely achieved in the form of writing developed in their own culture or sub-culture.

A more appropriate model of academic goals, one which does not construct or require a 'great divide' between an 'objective', written, academic language and a 'context-dependent', oral, lay language, is offered by Godfrey Lienhardt, in his attempts to find a language for describing concepts of 'self' in different cultures. He cites a distinguished, contemporary English descendant of the eighteenth century essayists, Gilbert Ryle, whose account of 'self' corresponds in both mode of thought and expression to that of the non-literate Dinka people of the southern Sudan, amongst whom Lienhardt did field work. Ryle says of 'the elusive concept of I': 'Like the shadow of one's own head, it will not wait to be jumped on. And yet it is never very far ahead, indeed sometimes seems not to be ahead of the pursuer at all. It evades capture by lodging itself inside the very muscles of the pursuer. It is too near even to be within arm's reach.' (Quoted in Lienhardt, 1980, p. 79.)

Lienhardt says of the similar Dinka way of conceptualising 'self': 'Thus in the use of bodily imagery, the Dinka (and probably other African peoples), and one of the most reformist of modern English philosophers, come together – the Dinka never having been entangled in the "entities and quidities" of European metaphysics, the Waynflete Professor of Metaphysical Philosophy in Oxford having determined to get rid of them.' (ibid.)

The 'objective' language which Olson, Lyons and others are so concerned to identify, and which they incorrectly associate with written language, turns out not to be so functional after all. The representation and classification of complex concepts may, perhaps, be achieved equally well in other ways that do not, whether explicitly or implicitly, pose a 'great divide' between European philosophy and primitive thought. To Lienhardt, oral Dinka language can be as effective for intellectual purposes as academic, written English: 'at almost every point the Dinka language allows for a wide range of moral and intellectual discriminations without leading into a seemingly autonomous world of abstractions. Words, as it were, must return to base.' (ibid. p. 78.)

4

THE 'IDEOLOGICAL' MODEL

There have recently appeared some works on literacy that have challenged elements of the 'autonomous' model: they have attempted to understand literacy in terms of concrete social practices and to theorise it in terms of the ideologies in which different literacies are embedded. I would now like to use some of this work in order to explore more explicitly than perhaps these writers themselves have done the theoretical foundations for a description of literacy, and to put together the elements of an alternative 'ideological' model.

I begin with the work of Ruth Finnegan, who has put forward an explicit and complex programme for future research in this field (1981). She has argued against the concept of a 'great divide' and in favour of detailed study of 'specific characteristics or consequences likely to be associated with orality and literacy' (1981, p. 12). She writes that when we look beyond grand propositions and generalisations to specific literacies then we find:

> the contrasts between non-industrial cultures themselves may be as striking as those between industrial and non-industrial, and the same can be said of contrasts between cultures (and historical periods) that, on the 'pure types' model ought to fall together on one side of the great divide. Once the idea of this kind of basic division is challenged it is no surprise to see the interaction between written and oral modes of communication not as something strange – representing, as it were, two radically different types or even 'evolutionary stages' of human development – but as a normal and frequently occurring aspect of human culture. It is true that differing cultures lay different emphases on, say, written learning and that the specific uses and purposes of oral media vary at different times and places – but this is the kind of situation that demands detailed investigation rather than defining out of existence (ibid. p. 6).

She takes each of the specific consequences attributed to literacy by the kinds of writers we have been discussing above and challenges each in turn, concluding that 'many of the generalisations that have been put forward about the consequences of literacy do not really hold as causal relationships: literacy being seen as the sufficient or necessary condition for some further state of affairs. There are enough exceptions or – at best

– qualifications to each of the possible generalisations to make them (even if they do sometimes apply) very doubtful as definitive guides to constantly occurring associations' (ibid. p. 31).

She does not, however, want to be simply negative but rather to suggest positive directions for research. Firstly, adopting Gough's notion of literacy as an 'enabling factor' (Goody, 1968, p. 153) Finnegan notes that this implies studying also 'a large number of *other* factors – the current political and economic conditions, social structure or local ideologies become arguably of equal relevance with the technology of communication' (Finnegan, 1981, p. 7). Nor does she mind that this means that 'the enticing simplicity of the strong model is lost' (ibid. p. 32). Secondly, she would concentrate on the uses of literacy rather than on the technology: 'Focussing on the uses of literacy and orality means shifting attention away from the search for universals, ideal types or human development in general terms to more detailed investigation into actual choices in specific societies.' (ibid. p. 34.) This is clearly an important corrective to the universalistic and technological determinist arguments of the 'autonomous' model, but I would suggest that the point needs to be taken further. Before we can look at the 'choices' made between different technologies and their different uses and consequences, we have first to recognise that what constitutes a particular technology and how it came to be available for choice is itself problematic. The technology of communication can involve many things, themselves the outcome of previous social processes and 'choices', and in order to study these we have to examine the structural, political and ideological features of the society in question.

Raymond Williams' analysis of the development of television technology (1974) suggests how this can be done. The requirements of profit, he argues, directed technological inquiry in the early part of this century into efforts to produce individual viewing units for sale to each household rather than large screens for use in communal halls. He would maintain that it is false, then, to dwell on the 'influence' or 'consequences' of television as though it were a neutral technology that had just appeared due to the disinterested work of scientists. Rather, the 'influence' of television depends upon the particular form its development has taken and thus on the commercial practices involved in the production and distribution of that form – in this instance, the nature and context of the individual 'set'. The material that is transmitted through the set depends, in the first instance, on the purposes for which that technology has been shaped. In western societies, the content is controlled, produced and distributed by the same commercial interests that determined the form in the first place and has thus to be explained in terms of that larger perspective. Technology, then, is a cultural form, a social product whose shape and influence depend upon prior political and ideological factors.

A similar argument can be used in relation to literacy. The particular technologies associated with different literacy forms have been varied and rich. They include, for instance, the use of manuscripts, print and telescreen: alphabets, ideographs, syllabaries and various combinations of them: slate and chalk, quills and biros, typewriters and word processors; parchment, linen, computer paper etc. Each has its own specific history and is connected with particular social institutions and functions. Social control has often been exercised by means of control of the materials associated with it. Clanchy, for instance, suggests that the sheer expense of quills in medieval England was a major factor in restricting writing to the wealthy or to those organised to pool resources as in the monasteries. In nineteenth century Fiji the importation and control of printing presses by missionaries helped them to control also the dissemination of knowledge and the power associated with it. But literacy, of course, is more than just the 'technology' in which it is manifest. No one material feature serves to define literacy itself. It is a social process, in which particular socially constructed technologies are used within particular institutional frameworks for specific social purposes. We cannot predict the social concomitants of a given literacy practice from a description of the particular technological concomitants. Goody, then, is misleading when he refers to literacy as 'the technology of the intellect' (1977). Finnegan points out that studies are available which in fact illustrate the *differing* ways in which certain media can be used adding 'this is particularly striking in the case of writing, when its actual use is not totally predictable on the basis of the established generalisations' concerning its supposed technological nature and consequences. Something more is involved, she says, 'than the mere adoption of writing in itself' (1981, pp. 35–6).

Research into literacy and orality must take account of this complexity and eschew the determinism exemplified by writers like Goody.

> One cannot just pick out one variable – say, printed media – and draw consequences from that, but one must also take into account the whole organisation that lies behind this (the organisation of writers or printers, say, the oppositions between those who control different media, the distribution and marketing, the constraints of particular materials, the costs and benefits of new technological processes ...) not to speak of the way print media are used by various sections of the community in particular places for various purposes at various times, or the interaction between, say, the use of printed books and papers and of other media such as music, sermons, public addresses, pictures or word of mouth communication. (ibid. p. 34.)

It is towards an understanding of these aspects of literacy that a number of writers in different disciplines are currently working and it is this that I am arguing can be taken as the basis for a new 'ideological' model of literacy. A summary of what they have achieved so far will help both to clarify what such research involves and to discover what generalisations are possible at this stage.

Within anthropology, and apparently independently of Finnegan, John Parry has recently provided both a detailed analysis of the kind she demands of specific aspects of literacy and orality and a general statement of theory. He explicitly challenges Goody's approach and implicitly, I would argue, the 'autonomous' model. Using his own field work in Benares plus his knowledge of Indian tradition, Parry concludes: 'None of Goody's predictions hold unambiguously good for traditional India' (1982, p. 4). Challenging particularly Goody's technological determinism, he says: 'It seems to me that it is not so much in terms of literacy, but in terms of a wider ideological framework that the transformation of mental life to which Goody alludes must be understood' (ibid. p. 25).

Parry looks in particular at the ideological framework within which Brahmins in India control powerful knowledge, both of ancient texts and of current practice. He suggests that Brahmin culture is a culture of the spoken word, despite what one might be led to expect from its emphasis on texts. Domination over others is achieved verbally, by 'rendering others speechless by the force of one's own speech and erudition' (ibid. p. 11). This process can be seen in the institution of the *shastrath* – 'a kind of formalised verbal battle over the interpretation of the texts' (ibid.). This emphasis is exemplified by the history of the Veda themselves. There was a millennium between the composition of the Veda and their being written down, although literacy skills had been available during that period. The transmission had been assured by rules for accuracy and precision of the kind which Goody would associate with literacy. Each verse had to be endlessly repeated by a pupil until he had completely mastered it and 'an elaborate system of mnemonic checks and phonetic rules (*vyasa siksa*) was designed to ensure the exact replication of the proper sound' (ibid. p. 12). This leads Parry to challenge Goody's generalisations about literacy: 'rather than the essential character of oral discourse being modified by intellectual procedures inseparable from literacy, as Goody predicts for literate cultures, it would be nearer the mark to say that in traditional India it was literary expression which was subordinated to the demands of oral transmission' (ibid.).

As Clanchy suggests with regard to medieval England, the development of writing takes place within an oral framework of thought and this may continue to dominate the uses of literacy. Parry suggests that 'much of the sacred literature of India was composed in a form and with a redundancy which was clearly intended to facilitate memorisation and faithful replication' (ibid.) and it has been these oral traditions which have continued to dominate the uses of texts. There is a belief in the power of words 'once they are materialised in speech' and 'for that power to become manifest they must be pronounced with precision and exactly the right inflexion. Wrongly accentuated, they may have an effect opposite to the one intended.' (ibid.) The words on the page, then, do not in themselves constitute the 'text' or its meaning. If Popper were to discover such literature in his 'World Three', it would remain meaningless without the accompanying rules of pronunciation and social use and these are oral rules that, without tape recording, could not be stored. For the scholar to 'translate' such texts in the study would not be the unpacking of ancient knowledge that Popper suggests literacy allows in a way that oral cultures do not. Without the oral tradition in which they are embedded, the writing alone is not 'knowledge': it does not have 'universal' meaning but only that given it by the context. The scholar's 'meaning' would be quite different from that described by Parry as belonging to indigenous uses of such sacred texts.

The spread of literacy in modern India does not, then, threaten the power of the Brahmins over the sacred texts since 'without the guidance of a guru book learning is said to be without value and even an obstacle to the acquisition of knowledge' (ibid. p. 14). The Brahmins maintain control of the system through 'the stress on oral transmission and correct pronunciation' (ibid.) and this depends upon individual tuition which they monopolise. Such control, however, is not that of a secret society maintaining esoteric knowledge for itself: the Brahmins have an obligation, within what Parry calls a 'transactional code' (ibid. p. 15) to disseminate this knowledge and if they do not then serious penalties will follow.

The broad communication of knowledge that this entails means that against the tendency for 'experts' to preserve the 'text' in immutable form is the counter pressure for each one to offer his own interpretation. This situation, Parry suggests, is the exact opposite of that posited by Goody. Goody maintains that oral knowledge is volatile and malleable while literate knowledge is resilient and 'restricts spontaneity'. Parry points out that, for traditional India at least, oral knowledge is resilient while the literate tradition allows for a range of interpretation and 'spontaneity'. Ironically, this variety rests upon the very characteristics of 'texts' that Goody thinks leads to their being 'fixed'. It is the fact that a guru can appeal to a text as though it were immutable which allows him to dress up his own interpretation as *the* authoritative one. With regard to the Veda, for instance, Parry points out that they are the ultimate authority on 'right conduct' and yet in practice they have little to say about the practical, everyday world. This immunity from the 'corrosive' effects of the mundane world is precisely what guarantees their authority; it is also precisely what allows, indeed requires, each guru to offer his own interpretation of how it is relevant to everyday life: 'It is knowledge of texts that have nothing to say about dharma ("right conduct") that authorises him to rule on it. The way would seem to be open for him to say what he likes.' (ibid. p. 16.)

This malleability of literacy is, according to Parry, true not only of the Veda, where the 'content is fixed but its direct application to practical life is minimal' but also of texts where the opposite is the case. The Garuda Purana for instance, a much later text than the Veda, is the last word on matters relating to death, mourning and the conduct of mortuary rites, providing detailed practical guidance on these everyday matters in a way that the Veda do not. There are, in practice, many written versions of this book each under the same title but with different content. Yet each version claims the same ultimate authority that Parry showed was associated with texts where the content did not change (although, as he points out, even in that case interpretation varied). Parry compared an English translation of the Garuda Purana with its Indian source and found that 'virtually the only thing that the two versions have in common is the claim that unsurpassable benefits accrue to those who hear them, and the exhortation to give liberally to the Brahmin who recites them' (ibid. p. 17). Otherwise the content is quite different. Moreover, 'it is dubious whether either of them bears any relationship to the ancient texts of the same name since the contents of none of the existing versions conform to what is said about the Garuda Purana in better authenticated Puranas' (ibid.). Parry also came across a trust in Benares set up to produce 'authorised' versions of the classical texts, which is now using western scholarship to restore the Puranas to their 'original' form. The western techniques employed to this end had, he points out, been developed with relation to different kinds of 'text', where a single author could be identified and different versions of his or her text were to be compared. In the case of the Puranas, however, 'it is very doubtful that there ever was a single original written text – the probability being that we are dealing with a number of quite different recensions which evolved out of the oral traditions of the regions from which each comes' (ibid. p. 18).

Apart, then, from Parry's point that written discourse is as likely to be as 'malleable' and 'volatile' as oral discourse, we might also note here the way in which the conventions associated with one particular literate tradition are applied to another where the original aims were quite different. The comparison highlights the extent to which the uses of literacy reside in conventions rather than being 'universal', 'technical skills', as exponents of the 'autonomous' model would have us believe.

One can, however, take Parry's point regarding western scholarship further in the light of recent internal critiques. While Indian students are currently applying western conventions to traditional Hindu texts, some students in Europe are rethinking those conventions and proposing ways of 'reading' texts that are more akin to those of the Indian tradition, at least as described by Parry. Recently structuralists have attempted to pose the relationship between literacy and literature in terms of 'malleability' and reader construction rather than of 'fixity', single versions and author's authority. They argue that our particular education and political systems make use of the written forms in such a way as to promote the 'literising' of experience. This has implied that a literary text represents a 'real' world which we can have concrete knowledge of. The written form has been taken simply as an external dress of speech, a reduced 'coded' version of the voice. The reality according to such critics as Derrida is that writing is not a transparent window onto an established reality: writing in our society has certain structured properties which are employed in such a way as to provide an illusion of a real 'whole' world. An analysis of writing in structuralist terms leads to a break-up of the limited view of meaning inherited in our culture and offers an extension of the potential meanings (Derrida, 1978). The idea, for instance, that an individual reader relates to an individual author is in fact a construction derived from our 'literising' of experience. Derrida is saying something similar to Lévi-Strauss' famous contention that he does not read myth but myth reads him (1968), but Derrida, unlike Lévi-Strauss, believes that this interpretation holds for written forms as well as oral (ibid.).

The emphasis on the 'structured properties' of writing does not, however, lead to claims for 'autonomy' of the kind discussed above. Rather Derrida and others are led by this emphasis to recognise even more acutely the ideological and political nature of our use of written forms. Like the sociolinguists cited above (Chapter 3) they recognise that any independent analysis of the properties of writing, as distinct from those of oral language, must avoid the reification apparent in what I have termed the 'autonomous' model of literacy. In recognising as problematic the relationship between the analysis of such properties and the analysis of the ideological and political context in which written forms are produced and used, they are helping to develop, I would argue, an alternative 'ideological' model of literacy.

They are, then, challenging the concept of the 'original text' even in contexts where a single author can be identified. They suggest that we should be as sceptical of claims regarding single 'authoritative' texts in our own culture as we tend to be in relation to the more apparent 'mythologies' of other cultures. In the Indian case these claims took the form of accounts of mythical heroes and gods. The 'original' version of the

Garuda Purana, for instance, is held to have been handed down by the god, Siva, to a mythical hero, Vyasa, and thence to the current reciter. Parry comments: 'the whole apparatus of the critical edition is directed ... to the essentially religious purpose of recovering as nearly as possible the divine inspiration of a purely mythical character. The objective result, however, is a completely new recension of the work.' (ibid.) The application of this comment to the interests of western scholars in 'original' texts might well lead us to some important insights into western literary production. We might, for instance, apply to it something like the account given by Parry, for traditional India, of different 'versions' and 'interpretations' of a 'text' in different contexts. The text is, says Parry, 'like an empty box into which an enormous range of possible contents might be poured' (ibid.). Such an account, as we have seen, applies to oral and literate 'texts' alike and indicates what is the predominant social practice: a 'mix' of the two and continual reworking of material in them.

All of this, of course, represents a challenge to the view of literacy proposed by Popper which, as we have seen, assumes an association between written texts and 'objective knowledge'. In fact the 'objective' features of the text reside not in their content but in the social facts of their use in specific contexts: the 'new recensions' to which Parry refers. If there is any universal pattern to be discerned, it is that both oral and written traditions combine the continual reworking of key 'texts' with the continual assertion that each new version is fixed, immutable and thereby authoritative. In both modes a variety of devices is employed, ranging from mnemonics to print, to preserve the 'accuracy' of a purported 'original' while at the same time altering that original to suit current interests without appearing to do so. It would seem, from the kind of evidence now being produced by anthropologists, literary critics and others, that we should not expect the acquisition of writing, nor its application in a given context, to take any one direction. In particular, we should not expect it to result in greater 'fixity', 'objectivity' or 'truth'.

It is not only within social anthropology, then, that a challenge is being mounted to Goody's view of literacy and to the 'autonomous' model in general. Indeed, recently a number of writers, though identified with specific disciplines, have deliberately attempted to cross disciplinary boundaries in posing alternative views of literacy. Since much of the work on the 'cognitive' consequences of literacy, to which writers in other disciplines often appeal for more grandiose claims, has come from within various branches of psychology, it is significant that one of the most powerful challenges in recent years has come from the psychologists Cole and Scribner. Their book *The Psychology of Literacy* (1981) consolidates research that they and others have been engaged in over a number of years, only some of which has been available in England. They point out that the assumptions made about changes in a culture's thinking due to the introduction of literacy require evidence of changes in the thinking of individuals in that culture. Their challenge, as psychologists, is to provide such evidence which has been notably lacking – to 'turn other social scientists' hypothetical mechanisms into demonstrated mechanisms' (ibid. p. 5). They conclude that there is little evidence to support the grander claims that we have been considering.

The problem they encountered was that which we have seen as integral to all questions about the 'consequences' of literacy: namely, how to isolate literacy in order to test whether it was a significant variable. Since the introduction of literacy is always accompanied by the introduction of new forms of social organisation, differences in thinking processes cannot, as we have seen, be attributed to literacy *per se*. Cole and Scribner point out that most attempts to test for the 'cognitive consequences' (or even just 'implications') of literacy have foundered at this hurdle. The leaders in the field (from Luria and Vygotsky to Greenfield, Olson and Bruner) have all tested schooled as opposed to unschooled subjects rather than literate/non-literate ones. Their findings, however, have not infrequently been used to make generalisations about literacy itself.

Cole and Scribner, nonetheless, believe that they may have found a situation where literacy can be isolated from schooling and where, therefore, all the grand theories (and Unesco expenditure) can be tested as 'in the laboratory'. The Vai people of Liberia have developed an indigenous writing system which is learnt through individual teaching not in schools. So Cole and Scribner, along with a number of colleagues and students, set up an elaborate project, which ran from 1974–9, in order to investigate it as an independent variable. They engaged in the team members of the Vai themselves, anthropologists and experts in questionnaires, data processing and computers. The story of the enterprise itself is worthy of sociological inquiry and, indeed, they invite such consideration by the form in which they present their material. They summarise grandiose theory, and set up against it the specifics of their own thorough investigation, down to such details as personalised descriptions of the team's experience, precise accounts of ethnography, how the questionnaires were constructed and the definitions of specific 'cognitive skills' that were tested for. One can thus set out to check their findings in a way that, I have suggested, is often not possible with the work done by exponents of the 'autonomous' model. In any case, their conclusion is more modest and more precise than much of the literature we have been considering. Specific uses of literacy, they conclude, have specific implications: 'particular practices promote particular skills'. Resisting the poles of 'no difference, all thought is the same' and 'the Great Cognitive Divide', they opt instead for a framework which they call 'a practice account of literacy' and which, in fact, provides a basis for the application of the 'ideological' model of literacy to the particular interests of psychologists (1981, p. 12).

Comparing Vai, Arabic and English literacy, all of which are found amongst the Vai, they found that some 'cognitive skills' were enhanced by practice in specific scripts. What they mean by such 'skills' is precise and not lodged at general levels of human logic etc. It approximates more to what I have been describing as 'social practice'. Knowledge of Vai script, they suggest, facilitated explicit verbalisation skills, as tested by an exercise in explaining the rules of a board game to another person. The level of skill demonstrated by Vai literates on this test, however, was not the same as that indicated by schooling, where Vai literacy was not a significant variable. Script associated skills, then, were more localised than those developed by schooling, which contributed more to performance on most tasks. Schooling, rather than literacy, they conclude is the significant cause of any major changes in 'cognitive skills'.

The main body of their research findings consists of numbers of such tests, with similarly precise conclusions drawn from them. Those who knew Arabic script, for instance, were tested for certain kinds of memory skill. They performed better than others on 'incremental recall' but on 'free recall' they had no significant advantage despite the characteristics often attributed to the experience of rote learning of the Koran.

This work, then, provides an important development in literacy studies within the discipline of psychology and will, hopefully, check the proponents of the more grandiose and sententious claims for literacy.

Such claims and associated hopes for the practical 'success' and consequences of literacy have formed the basis for much of the theoretical work in this area. As we saw in relation to the researches of Hildyard and Olson, the 'consequences' of literacy are seen as the major justification for expenditure on education programmes in general. Where Cole and Scribner's work forces us to rethink the basic concepts whereby such 'consequences' have been described, much of the recent challenge has been pitched at a more explicitly 'political' level. Harvey J. Graff, a social historian, has recently put forward a powerful and explicit challenge to such claims for literacy in a book provocatively called *The Literacy Myth* (1979). He questions the 'myth' that the acquisition of literacy leads to social mobility, overcoming poverty and 'self-fulfilment'. Making use of data and methods from a number of fields, Graff argues that such claims are not supported by the evidence which he examined in relation to nineteenth century Canada and he suggests that this may be the case more generally too. While examples could be found from his detailed statistics that some individuals had gained by acquiring literacy, he demonstrates that deprived classes and ethnic groups as a whole were, if anything, further oppressed through it.

Analysing the processes of schooling and of literacy acquisition for different ethnic and occupational groups in Canadian cities in the nineteenth century, he argues that greater literacy does not correlate with increased equality and democracy nor with better conditions for the working class. Rather it correlates with continuing social stratification. Literacy was bound up with the ideology of the educators in the sense that it was used as part of the elaboration of the moral bases of behaviour and of social control. Particular approved forms of literacy were employed by a particular class as socialising agents for particular oppressed groups and as a means of imparting to them a specific moral code. Graff argues that the analysis of literacy entails, then, a politically sensitive analysis of the social structure within which it is embedded.

In nineteenth century Canada, the concept of a 'literate' or 'illiterate' person was seldom an independent, neutral one. It was a normative one which 'can only be understood in the specific context of social structural processes' (1979, p. 52). Isolated from its social relations, literacy takes on a reified and symbolic significance unwarranted by its own, more restricted influences. Thus, to the middle class, 'illiterates' were conceived as dangerous to the social order, as alien to the dominant culture, inferior and bound up in a culture of poverty. As such they represented a threat to the established order and the effort to increase literacy rates was a political move to maintain the position of the ruling group. However, the teaching of literacy involved contradictions. The potentialities of reading and writing for an under-class could well, they feared, be radical and inflammatory, so the framework for the teaching of literacy had to be severely controlled and only those consequences of its acquisition that the ruling class were concerned with were to be allowed. This involved specific forms of control of the pedagogic process itself and specific ideological associations of the literacy being purveyed. The workers had to be convinced that it was in their interests to learn the kind of literacy on offer, in the kinds of institutions in which it was taught, but had to be restrained from taking control of it for themselves or developing their own alternative conceptions of it. Although the consequences of the kind of literacy being provided were not, according to the figures Graff produces, in reality advantageous to the poorer groups in terms of either income or power, they had to be persuaded that they were. It is in this sense that the concrete forms and practices of literacy are bound up with an ideology, with the construction and dissemination of conceptions as to what literacy is in relation to the interests of different classes and groups. Indeed, the power of the conception of literacy that was successfully conveyed in contexts of the kind Graff is describing is such that many sociologists and writers have themselves accepted it as the starting point for their analyses.

Graff argues that, as a result of the contemporary acceptance of such conceptions of literacy, the initial view of literacy in nineteenth century Canada tends to be that it was necessary for the development of individuals and for the collective good. A superficial look at the facts seems to support this since they demonstrate that those who were 'illiterate' were also most commonly impoverished. A closer look, however, undermines the myth and demonstrates its ideological nature. Comparing levels of literacy achievement, as defined at the time, with such factors as migration patterns, social origins, wealth, ownership and family formation, Graff concludes that literacy is not an independent nor a determining factor but served rather to mediate these primary processes and interacted with them.

The figures can be read, for instance, as they were at the time, to indicate that literacy improved an individual's chances of acquiring skilled jobs. In fact, however, literacy itself, as learnt in State schools, proved not to be sufficient to overcome ascribed characteristics rooted in age, gender and race. Certain ethnic groups were disadvantaged, whatever their literacy rates, while others maintained disproportionate claims on skilled jobs, despite higher 'illiteracy' rates. Irish Catholics did badly, regardless of their education: of 'illiterate' Irish Catholics 63% were in unskilled jobs whereas only 50% of 'illiterate' English Protestants were similarly 'underachieving' (1979, p. 60). Amongst black people, those who were 'illiterate' did relatively less badly than those from other ethnic groups, but 'literate' black people did relatively less well than others. In other words, the extent to which literacy was an advantage or disadvantage in relation to job opportunities depended on ethnicity. It was not because you were 'illiterate' that you finished up in the worst jobs but because of your background.

The pattern is confused by the fact that most jobs, even lower unskilled ones, had a majority of 'literates' working in them: 75% of labourers and 93% of semi-skilled workers were 'literate' (ibid. p. 72). Despite these high literacy levels, not all skilled jobs were filled by 'literates'. The work of artisans, blacksmiths, tailors, carpenters and even some higher commercial positions could be taken by 'illiterates' if they came from the 'right' background. Literacy, then, was not as intrinsically necessary for such jobs as the ideology through which literacy attainment was being encouraged was suggesting. As in medieval England, quite significant positions that would appear to us to require literacy skills can actually be filled by 'illiterates' in certain conditions. In medieval England (Clanchy, 1979), hired scribes could perform the task of writing and reading documents for the lord of the manor, authors could 'write' by dictating aloud, and students could 'read' degrees by listening in lecture halls. In contemporary England, blind people, with different literacy skills than those assumed to be prerequisite for administrative tasks, can hold posts such as the leader of a city council. In nineteenth century Canada, many rewarding commercial posts could be held by an 'illiterate' person if he could get the bureaucracy performed by someone else: the skills expected for such posts were social skills, of the kind imparted by particular socialisation processes such as private education and middle-class value training. In the Iranian village similarly (see Section 2), entrepreneurs could run complex business enterprises, record transactions, and make profits without having reached levels of literacy that could be guaranteed, via formal testing, to figure in the national statistics. Literacy, then, is only important for specific positions if that is how they are defined in the particular society: burghers, kings and councillors have, in many societies, managed perfectly well without it. If many tasks do not intrinsically require literacy, then we must search other than in utilitarian job descriptions for explanations as to why it is believed that literacy will lead to better job opportunities. Graff claims that, with regard to nineteenth century Canada, the answer lies in the ideological interests and constructions of the middle class.

The same, he argues, is true of beliefs about the relationship of literacy to wealth and poverty. He attempts to demonstrate that the acquisition of literacy was not correlated with improved wealth, any more than with improved job opportunities. For instance, of all the poor in Hamilton in the 1861 census, only 13% were 'illiterate' (1979, p. 84). If most of the poor were 'literate', one could hardly attribute poverty to 'illiteracy'. The main cause of poverty was, in fact, ethnic origin. Stratification, likewise, varied with age, gender and ethnicity rather than with levels of literacy. Amongst Irish Catholics, literacy produced very little material advantage: 65% of those who were 'literate' were poor and only 11% more of 'illiterates', 76%, were poor (ibid. p. 77). For them the pursuit of education would appear to have been practically irrelevant.

Where literacy did make a difference was within groups already advantaged on other indices. Thus, English 'illiterates', while gaining greater rewards than other 'illiterates', received less rewards than English 'literates'. Amongst semi-skilled workers the advantages of literacy, however, were negligible: 45% of 'literates' in this category were poor and 47% of 'illiterates' (ibid. p. 72). The evident success of white Protestants could, however, be used to persuade others to attend school and thereby acquire the skills they supposedly had.

What actually went on in the classrooms supports Graff's view that the educators were concerned with literacy as a means of social control rather than as offering any real prospect of 'improvement'. In Kingston in the 1850s, for instance, reports tell of bad, crowded conditions, poorly-paid teachers, large undivided classes and irregular attendance partly caused by understandably high truancy rates. Teaching methods further militated against the general quality of learning: emphasis was put on reading aloud rather than understanding texts; the differences between styles and conventions of written and speech forms were not understood; the exigencies of keeping order in crowded classrooms meant that there was no scope for students to ask questions or for any real interaction. As a result of these and other factors the products of the schools were deemed to be generally 'imperfectly skilled'. In the 1870s, some 'modernisation' was introduced: activity replaced disciplined inactivity in the classroom, although according to Graff it 'took the equally useless form of recitation, drills etc.' (ibid. p. 277) fulfilling the management role of the teacher rather than the pedagogic one. School inspectors, presumably with some professional commitment to the pedagogic role, complained that only small proportions of school pupils reached even minimum standards, by their criteria, and that many who had soon lost it. Their reports make interesting comparison with the recent HMI (Her Majesty's Inspectorate) reports in the UK, where similar contradictions between the stated and the latent functions of schooling have surfaced.

Graff argues that the inspectors' reports do not simply indicate 'failure' on the part of the schools. In fact, the practices that they highlighted corresponded precisely to the schools' functions of social control and hegemony. This is particularly clearly brought out in the emphasis on reading aloud as a major process in the learning of literacy. Students from different ethnic groups, when reading aloud, would be 'corrected' for pronunciation, stress and fluency. Training in literacy was, in fact, used to train speech habits, which are a different matter, and to homogenise language use. Differences of class and culture were to be eradicated by this means and all pupils would be assimilated to one dominant order. The pronunciation demanded to accompany written forms was that of the white, Protestant minority. Stubbs (1980) points out that a given written form can represent a variety of pronunciations and that reading aloud fails to capitalise on the potentialities of silent reading, such as scanning backwards and forwards, repetition for meaning etc. These potentialities (still missed in many schools today, cf. Section 3 below) were not drawn upon because the dominant emphasis of the education system itself, if not always of individual teachers, was on the political functions of literacy. Members of subjugated minorities were taught that their very patterns of speech were inferior and were in some way connected with their deprivation. What literacy meant for them, then, at the explicit level was 'school reading', while at more hidden levels it was associated with specific social and political assumptions. Far from being taught to develop logical and critical skills, which Goody and others see as the prime outcome of literacy, pupils in schools in nineteenth century Canada were being offered a narrowing experience aimed at inculcating the moral norms and disciplines of the ruling class.

Associated with this hidden curriculum went such apparently 'neutral', technical concerns as a stress on libraries and on the appearance of books. Graff discusses the way in which learning to adopt a particular attitude to book bindings, illustrations, covers etc., and to the placing of books in specialised locations, was also part of the moral, socialising function of literacy teaching. 'Training in literacy involved more than understanding all that was read. The moral bases could be transmitted and reinforced in a number of ways, symbolically and orally, in conjunction with literacy.' (1979, p. 289.) Thus students were taught certain verbal skills and an ability to handle institutional settings which were important not to the intrinsic performance of job skills but to the social management of them. Lower-class 'illiterates' might not, for instance, be disadvantaged in terms of the intrinsic skills necessary for a particular job, but they might be disadvantaged in terms of the hidden norms and values associated with, for instance, handling the social context and its underlying framework of rules and meanings. Hence middle-class 'illiterates' may be found in 'high' positions, because they have learnt these skills through their background, while working-class 'literates' may still not achieve these positions because they have not learnt the appropriate social skills.

Schools were designed to impart some of these social skills – they were, in a sense, middle-class training camps – so there was scope for individuals to use this as a stepping-stone to 'success' and the example of the few reinforced the claim that it could happen to all. Graff concludes, then, that the meaning of literacy is context-dependent: 'It can be established neither arbitrarily nor abstractly for all members of the population' (ibid. p. 292). The structures of demands, needs and uses for literacy, and thereby the definitions of it, vary according to context. In nineteenth century Canada the needs and uses of literacy were constructed in relation to class and ethnicity and to their relative power positions in the context of specific social and economic structures.

Graff addresses himself mainly to the social consequences and definitions of literacy and emphasises its cultural relativity. His material, however, also has significance for the arguments about the 'cognitive consequences' of literacy. Goody, for instance, argued that ideally literacy would improve the logical and critical faculties but that if it did not do so then this was because what was being displayed was 'restricted' literacy. As we noted above, most empirical examples of literacy appear, by Goody's standards, to fit into this 'restricted' category, which casts doubt on the usefulness of the term. Certainly, by his standards, nineteenth century Canada would have to be an example of 'restricted' literacy as would much of what passes for literacy in England today. To ask why this form of literacy failed to raise 'consciousness' or to develop critical faculties would be to misunderstand the reason why it was constructed and conveyed in the first place. Clearly what is being described as 'literacy' in nineteenth century Canada is not so much a 'restricted' technical skill but rather a form of political and ideological practice: the reference to 're-stricted' literacy disguises this larger framework and the fact that the writer is making a judgement based on his or her own beliefs.

Graff believes that the difficulties of transcending the limited and con-straining form of literacy being purveyed in nineteenth century Canada stemmed from the relative position of class and ethnic groups in the social structure. The ideology itself was directly opposed to such transcendence. Nor was it seen as relevant to daily needs. These were not dominated by print and writing: work and information did not require literacy, even at higher levels, and even clerkly jobs required simply rules of thumb rather than critical thought (ibid. p. 302). The emphasis on the need for literacy was placed on status, culture and power. Accepting exaggerated claims for literacy in itself, and the concomitant need to describe most literacy practices as 'restricted', fails to ask, Graff says, 'how important and in what ways is literacy related or central to different aspects of life and culture' (ibid. p. 303). In this sense, then, Graff is contributing to what I term an 'ideological' model of literacy and his critique of the literacy 'myth' is a contribution to the more general challenge to the 'autono-mous' model of literacy which I am identifying.

Graff also indicates a further direction in which that critique may be developed. The claims made for literacy tend to overstate the difference between literacy and orality and to hide the fact that in most societies there is an overlap and a 'mix' of modes of communication. Graff points out that people learnt to find their way around the growing nineteenth century Canadian cities, for instance, through a 'mix' of oral and literate modes. Icons and symbols as well as print were significant for 'reading the city streets' (ibid. p. 309). Visual signs, adverts and decorations themselves were as important as the letters and written words engraved on them when it came to finding one's way around. For many, in this context, hearing and seeing were more important than the new 'literate' culture. The road signs agreed as international conventions recognise this feature of our modern 'literate' society and use written words as little as possible, as do most adverts. This is not merely a gesture towards those labelled 'illiterate' but rather a recognition that communication operates through 'mixed' modes for all, whether 'literate' or not. Such analyses demonstrate the limited value of either/or designations of literacy and demand that researchers look more closely at 'non-literate' aspects of 'literate' society and vice versa as well as at the way those labelled 'illiterate' actually manage in a 'literate' society.

One such analysis of 'mixed' modes is to be found in the book by Michael Clanchy *From Memory to Written Record 1066–1307* which has already been discussed briefly in Chapter 2 above. The book represents a further contribution to elaborating our 'ideological' model of literacy. He argues that the shift from oral to literate modes which took place for certain purposes in medieval England was facilitated by the continuing 'mix' of modes, and by the gradualness of the transition whereby written forms could be adapted to oral practice rather than immediately undermining or radically altering it. The analysis recognises the importance of the social meaning of these practices for the participants, the political imperatives that generated the change, and the 'ideological' rather than 'technical' nature of reading and writing.

Clanchy describes: how the shift entailed the production of records on an unprecedented scale; the growth of trust in writing and what could or could not be done with these particular forms of it; the development of the habitual use of written as opposed to oral procedures for certain purposes; the appeal to written record rather than oral memory or seals and symbols in order to establish land rights; the development of literacy for day to day business through the setting up of a centralised bureaucracy. The emphasis was particularly on claims to land and buildings at this time, as a result of the Norman invasion and the conquerors' interest in establishing and legitimising control. The Normans appear to have become eager bureaucrats, insisting on minute and detailed records of the land they were attempting to control and thereby contributing to a change from oral to literate forms of legitimation. Formerly, rights to land and property had been legitimised through such socially verifiable and integral means as the swearing on oath of twelve good men and true, or the passing over of land with seals and symbols that represented the right to it.

The Normans had no place in these customs and practices and instead instigated a system which required claimants to produce documentation before a court of law, and which established verification through the centralisation of records. They could, of course, exercise control over this new system in a way that they could not have done over the old system. If a Norman wished to give land to a faithful knight in return for services rendered, he would do so by constructing a written document and appealing to the courts. Even though such documentation had not existed when the land had originally passed hands, the present owner was obliged to defend his rights on these new grounds. The indigenous material and social practices had been, by their very nature, less easy to forge than written documents: a single seal or a sword that symbolised a piece of land would be so distinctive and well known that forgery was almost impossible. It was quite apparent to the natives both that the new system disadvantaged them since it was controlled by aliens, and that it was more subject to forgery. The 'literate mentality', then, to which Clanchy refers was a deliberate construction for political and economic purposes rather than the intrinsic good which both the Normans and those who currently promote the 'autonomous' model of literacy would suggest. Literacy was a terrain over which the struggles between colonised and conqueror crucially took place, as in many Third World countries today. The natives found themselves having to produce and even forge written records that were embedded in an alien system in order to maintain holdings that provided their livelihood, while the conquerors became dependent on rolls, records and written laws in order to acquire and control the knowledge that gave political power and legitimacy.

The change only happened slowly and through the interaction of a number of factors. Clanchy suggests that the Domesday Book on its own did not have such a significant influence on the process as subsequent writers have believed: 'Literate modes could not be imposed by royal decree' (1979, p. 12). He suggests that writers in later periods looking back to the Norman Conquest had their own interest in promulgating a myth that the Normans had brought the conquered people under the rule of written law and that the Domesday Book had been the primary instrument. In reality, he says, the Domesday Book suffered from difficulties which face all forms of bureaucracy: it could not record absolutely everything and it rapidly became out of date, particularly when recording livestock and individual ownership. Only gradually, with the spread of ongoing records and their acceptance across different classes, did the habit of consulting documents and eventually of depending on them become established. The Domesday Book, in fact, only became regularly consulted at a later period – in the fourteenth century – when the practice of such consultation had become established and when it could be used retrospectively where long-held rights were in dispute. Its application to such cases depended less on its intrinsic value as a 'real' record of landholding than on the place which was now ascribed to it within a 'literate' ideology. The gradual process to which Clanchy refers, and which took over two centuries to come to fruition, involves, then, a number of aspects, notably the development of forms of government organisation and bureaucracy, the adaptation to such needs of specific forms of literacy, and the construction and spread of a 'literate mentality' – an ideology within which writing could be trusted and understood by users in relation to its specific functions for them and placed within the wider philosophy and belief system to which they subscribed.

The Normans, in fact, demanded such detailed surveys that, as Clanchy points out, they were often too ambitious for the limited level of clerical services available: the only surviving surveys are from Oxford and Cambridge, an area where there were enough clerks to undertake the task. Making records was a product of the distrust that followed the Conquest.

New ways of keeping financial accounts, the organisation of an Exchequer and the elaboration of legal procedures were all responses to the political and organisational problems faced by the invaders. Clanchy, however, points out that they were not simply crude impositions from above but adaptations of existing practice to serve new interests. He cites such pre-Conquest Anglo-Saxon traditions as the division of land into shires and hundreds, the binding nature of oaths on the community and the existence of centres of learning in monasteries. The development of literate forms was a product of the interaction of these specific social conditions.

These bureaucratic and organisational needs required particular forms of writing and reading and these were themselves both constrained and developed in relation to the contemporary technology of literacy. Clanchy argues: 'A particular technology of writing shapes and defines the uses of literacy in a region or culture' (ibid. p. 88). I would add simply that the 'technology' is itself shaped and defined within the culture. The technology of literacy in medieval England resulted from a combination of skills and processes geared to the production of written records. The tanner, tally cutter, book illuminator, master in school and quill maker were all parts of the system that produced and constrained both traditional and new forms of literacy. This interaction between material constraints and social practices is apparent in the way in which the development of literate modes in twelfth and thirteenth century England was not effected by a 'technological revolution' but, according to Clanchy, by the modification of traditional materials.

For example, parchment paper continued to be used as it was cheap and available in sufficient quantity to be readily adaptable to the increased demand. A new style of script was developed – 'cursive' – that enabled scribes to write faster (ibid. p. 99). Clanchy argues that this new script was, in fact, an adaptation of book hand and glosses already in use and did not constitute a new 'invention'. Its significance lay in the fact that the largest expense in producing written documents was the scribe's labour time. Enabling him to work faster saved money as well as time and facilitated the greater use made of writing. Similarly, new layouts, lists and business documents evolved and new formats for keeping records were developed. Pipe rolls, for instance, which were already familiar to scholars through their association with Old Testament and Jewish sacred texts, were adapted to the needs of centralised, bureaucratic storage of records. It was, according to Clanchy, their association with previous familiar forms that enabled many of the new developments to be accepted and so become institutionalised in a way that radical change and invention would not have facilitated. Charters, for instance, were laid out in the way traditionally used for Bibles. The Domesday Book assumed authority by association with religious texts. Scribes were familiar with something like cursive script in the glosses written in the margins of sacred texts.

The initial and most difficult task was to make the laity, typically knights in the countryside, accustomed to writing. Traditionally monasteries had symbolised gifts of land with Bibles and illuminated manuscripts where the knights were concerned more with the form and context than with the content. The new government forms of documentation could become legitimate in their eyes, then, by association with this practice and we find land charters during this transition period presented with all the decoration and trappings of monastic forms of writing. The changes were, in many ways, relatively small and often went unnoticed at the time, but they set in motion and facilitated fundamental changes.

This process is similar to that which I describe in Chapters 5 and 6 in relation to an Iranian village: familiarity with sacred Islamic texts and documents facilitated the use of written records by a small literate class and the gradual spread of what I term 'commercial' forms of literacy. By adapting written forms and technology that were legitimised through association with sacred texts and made familiar through daily use in a common community, entrepreneurs were able to make use of new developments of literacy without alienating or confusing fellow villagers. It was in a similar way, according to Clanchy, that the knights of the countryside in medieval England came to accept government documentary practices because they were produced in forms and materials already familiar and legitimised through association with the monasteries. Many contemporary literacy programmes tend to fail because their exponents eschew such 'gradualism' and assume that radically new technology and practices must be introduced in order to stimulate a shift to the 'literate' mentality that they are aiming for.

In every case the shift is a complex matter. New forms challenge existing deeply-held convictions or create new problems and new contradictions. In medieval England the development of literate habits and assumptions, comprising what Clanchy calls a 'literate mentality', had to take root in diverse social groups and areas of activity. The prejudices of such groups had to be overcome and previous orthodoxies revised. These changes came about gradually, as with changes in materials and practices, and more often adapted rather than radically altered deeply-rooted belief. The complexity of the process demonstrates the extent to which literacy is bound up with ideology and why analysis of the uses and consequences of literacy must take into account quite profound levels of belief and the fundamental concepts through which a society creates order and design in its world. Clanchy provides a particularly clear example of this in relation to medieval concepts of time and space and how changes in literacy related to them.

In medieval England fundamental templates for the division of time and space were constructed within a Christian theology. The writing and dating of documents, which became intrinsic to the new literacy with its emphasis on record-keeping and on resolving disputes over land that hinged on recorded claims, had grave implications for this belief system. Dating a document (ibid. p. 236) placed its maker in temporal and geographical perspective: it involved expressing an opinion about the writer's place in the world. The framework for this had been established through the Church's history of the Creation and its use of the birth of Christ as a reference point. It would have been sacrilegious for a secular document to appeal to such sacred matters. Faced with these theological constraints on the one hand and the practical ones on the other, writers adopted the practice of placing documents in time by reference to important historical events rather than to theological time. In any case, the time span considered necessary for many documents was generally shorter than the Church's reference point, although this was not a powerful pressure since contemporary practice was to use the Gregorian calendar as a reference for quite short spans of time. Clanchy, nevertheless, argues that the years of a king's reign were in some ways more immediately relevant to a knight obliged to date a charter than was the Christian calendar. This, however, had its own problems since the political and secular power implied by such a term of reference might be objected to by the clergy. A compromise, which became standardised, was for the king's reign to be used to date years while the Church calendar of feast days was used to name days. This reminds us that the modes of validation of written forms depend, amongst other things, on agreed systems of dating to which they can be referred, and such systems are neither given nor 'natural' but are themselves socially constructed and deeply embedded in prevailing ideologies. The compromises and conflicting pressures described by Clanchy are what literacy practice is composed of in all societies, even in such apparently 'neutral' areas of activity as record-keeping and dating.

Nor was the development of literate practices a simple matter of writing down the language that was spoken. There were a variety of languages in use, while Latin had special status as the literary language. Indeed, to be 'literate' meant to know Latin rather than to be able to read and write. This tradition had to be overcome if a 'literate mentality' of the new kind were to extend beyond a small minority. As with the uses of writing with regard to land rights and to dating records, so the shift in court practice regarding language and writing require analysis of such fundamental concepts as indigenous means of asserting and validating truth and explication of the conceptual system in which such ideas were rooted.

In medieval England a variety of institutionalised and culturally specific criteria for validating claims to truth in general and to land rights in particular were used. These represent a 'mix' of oral and literate modes, involving autographs, seals, witnesses, symbols, ceremonial acts, oaths etc. The attachment of a seal or a symbolic object such as a knife to a document that established the owner's title to land or property often bore more meaning than the words written on the document. Even as late as the thirteenth century, Earl Warenne is represented as claiming rights to land on his family sword as more concrete proof than a written record. Learning to trust documentary proof is a social process and for it to be acceptable its advantages must be clear to those being taught. To people in the Middle Ages it was not obvious that a written document could be trusted more than a person's word. Indeed, those involved had ample cause to be sceptical since the pressure for written documentation made it more susceptible to forgery than traditional forms of validation. Title to land owned by a family over generations was traditionally vested in a symbolic gift passed over by the original owner. A Bible, a knife or a sword, as in Earl Warenne's case, were common symbols of such a heritage. Under the Normans, however, the claimant was required to produce evidence before the courts in written form, even though none such had existed before. If this was the only way to establish rights that to the owners were clearly established by oral forms of validation, then written documents would have to be, and were, produced to suit the purpose. Those who fabricated these documents, however, would have little faith in them while general trust was undermined by the fact that the courts were constantly challenging them for the forgeries that indeed they were. The credibility of written documentation was, then, in these circumstances, quite reasonably held in greater doubt than traditional forms of validation.

In Europe at that time the development of notarial practice to some extent counteracted the ease of forgery by providing a bureaucratic infrastructure for validating written forms. A public notary would state his name and his authority on a document and either sign it or impose a 'signum' that could be checked against a register which contained examples of his style and seal. In England, however, the institutional forms that could have facilitated such a spread of literate practice developed more slowly. Clanchy argues that the reason for this was that there was already a well-established practice of using seals for this purpose.

Seals provided an easy device that non-literates could use to authenticate documents written by their scribes: they provided a bridge from non-literate to literate, a mass-produced form of authentication in the tradition of the use of symbols, swords etc. A seal with a central symbol and a name around the outside would be attached to the bottom of a document: it could be seen and touched and gave the 'feel' of the donor's wishes to a charter. It was thought to be more durable than parchment and therefore a more secure form of validation. It also represented the donor himself rather than an intermediary such as a scribe or a notary and was therefore a more direct form of validation. Abstract documentary proof was considered inadequate without such material reinforcement through symbolic objects.

In later periods, however, archivists versed in a 'literate mentality' saw the survival of the knives and seals attached to documents as just so much medieval paraphernalia. Indeed, many such relics were thrown away and attention was paid only to the written document, an anachronistic practice since to the people at the time it had often been the document that was of secondary importance. These archivists were trained in specific literate ways of ensuring the effectiveness of a document for establishing proof – by dating, signing, copying into registers etc. They used professional standardised rules and depended on a notarial system for the cross-checking of manuscripts. In the earlier period a variety of different criteria had been used for validating claims, both literate and non-literate – criteria that had similarly been learnt according to particular ideological assumptions. Clanchy warns us against applying the standards of proof embedded in one ideology to another different one, as the archivists were doing.

His criticism of such anachronisms also puts into perspective the grander claims for literate standards which I examined earlier. Goody, for instance, claimed that literacy engenders a 'critical' mentality because it makes it possible to place two written texts side by side and to check one against the other for accuracy. He associates this with 'open' rather than 'closed' thinking and with 'rationality' and logic, in the manner of Hildyard and Olson. Clanchy's account makes it clear that the faith of these writers in the written text is a product of their own society's ideology of literacy. In early medieval England it was written texts that were suspect, for good reason, while material seals and symbols could be fully checked for accuracy and so were more trustworthy. The technology for establishing 'accuracy' and 'trustworthiness' does not necessarily have intrinsic consequences for the quality of truth standards. Oral as well as literate modes involve critical judgement, disputation of criteria for truth and the challenge of forgery and misrepresentation.

Clanchy provides useful source material from which to elicit the advantages of such oral modes of validation. The requirement in medieval England that twelve witnesses should affirm the passing over of a charter must have made it difficult for later claimants to forge or misrepresent. During their lifetime witnesses could be brought back to court and asked to recall, on oath, what had taken place. The numbers alone would have made deception difficult (though not, of course, impossible) apart from the power of belief in oaths. If you can put two documents together, as

Goody suggests, to check for their accuracy, then you can also put two or more witnesses together as a similar check on each other. Where knowledge of the handing over and witnessing of a charter would become part of collective history it would be difficult to alter such knowledge, certainly for an individual. When witnesses had died, their families might be called to affirm that for instance 'father told us that he had witnessed the gift of this land to X'. In these social conditions the community itself is a living form of validation and of security against forgery. When validation became impersonal such integral checks were lost: in this sense impersonal and disembedded written forms could be said to be more, not less, subject to forgery.

This was indeed the case during the transition, in medieval England, from oral to literate forms. Forgery was rife until means were devised to secure written documents against misrepresentation. That such means (a notarial system, bureaucracy etc.) were necessary demonstrates that written forms are not intrinsically more capable of 'accuracy' than oral forms. Their use for purposes of accuracy and validation depend upon the social construction of systems that fit them for such purposes.

Many people at the time of the transition to written forms of validating claims were aware of the advantages of contemporary oral forms and the disadvantages of the new modes. St Francis, for instance, argued that the word was inscribed spiritually in men's hearts, whereas letters on parchment were separated and less trustworthy (Clanchy, 1979, p. 210). He denigrated the mere learning of literacy. Similarly when messengers from Anselm, the Archbishop of Canterbury, to the Pope brought back oral records of what the Pope had said, they were represented by Anselm as more credible and valid than the written records of the event brought back by King Henry's messengers. Henry's representatives had brought back reports which favoured his position in a dispute with the Archbishop. The conflict between the two parties was thus enacted in terms of a debate between the advantages and disadvantages of literacy. Anselm's messengers brought the whole weight of Christian theology to bear on the defence of oral ideology and the denigration of the value of the written record, which they represented as 'mere sheepskin with blackening and lumps of lead' (ibid. p. 209). The material form of writing is represented as less trustworthy than the words inscribed in men's hearts and minds (to which, of course, clerics could claim privileged access). The detachment of the written form from its originator makes it less, not more, testable for accuracy. These are clearly loaded arguments but they put into perspective the claims of academics like Popper, Goody and others who likewise select those culturally developed characteristics of literacy or orality which suit their purpose and then claim that these are intrinsic to the medium.

Clanchy puts the case for the advantages of oral forms in medieval conditions with equal force. For business purposes oral forms of commerce had the advantage of secrecy – only the parties to a deal need know of it. Oral discourse was (and is) convenient since it can be conducted directly and immediately, whereas engaging in written communication involves expenditure on scribes and parchment and a great deal more time. In social conditions where documents were rare, the occasional use of them was cumbersome and inconvenient. Again, their advantages depend upon the specific social conditions of use, notably in later times the construction of generalised bureaucratic institutions.

The written forms of proof which Goody elevates to a higher plane of logic turn out to be specific cultural forms of authentication that are neither proven to be more 'critical' or 'rational' than the oral forms described above nor necessarily owe any advantage they may have to literacy itself rather than to the social institutions in which they are embedded.

Clearly the social construction of bureaucracy and of a notarial system has some social and political advantages. It enables the development of larger-scale commercial transactions and facilitates centralised political control. In this sense it is possible to describe literacy, as Gough has done, as an 'enabling factor' (in Goody, 1978). But these are political judgements – indeed their advantages and disadvantages are still a matter of dispute today. Literate systems such as bureaucracy develop, then, in relation to specific conditions where such judgements and decisions based on them are being made.

In the Middle Ages, the social and intellectual strengths of forms of authentication associated with, for instance, seals meant that there was no obvious necessity or pressure for the development of a notarial system and the accompanying form of literacy practice. This only occurred when a conquering power's need for a centralising bureaucracy and the political pressure it exerted on the natives to adopt literate forms of authentication led to the provision of resources and manpower for the development of such a system. Anglo-Saxon groups in pre-Conquest England had been under less pressure from the social conditions to spread literacy practices beyond the contemporary monastic forms and local record-keeping, while the accompanying quasi-literate forms of seals and symbols adequately functioned to validate land rights.

Clanchy provides other examples from medieval England of the 'mix' of oral and literate modes. Letters, for instance, were not always used in newly literate times to impart the message written in them. In the medieval period they often served as a means of validating the bearer who would then deliver the message in person. Letters in this role served as symbols in the way that rings had often done before (and, indeed, were still represented as doing so by Dumas in his *Three Musketeers*). Proclamations might be written in Latin but were read aloud by town criers in the vernacular: their posting on the doors of village halls represented the gradual nature of the transition to literate practices for the majority and shows how the 'literate mentality' was ushered in through familiar forms. In medieval times the receiver of a message would still expect to listen rather than to read: indeed, the word 'reading' meant hearing not seeing, a form that persists in contemporary descriptions of students as 'reading' for a degree where this originally referred to their attendance at lectures as hearers. Authors addressed hearers, accounts were literally 'audited', a judge inspected a document in court by having it read aloud rather than reading it silently to himself. Writing was conceived as an extension of speaking rather than in terms of any independent qualities it might have. It referred to composition, as it does in one meaning today when we refer to someone as 'writing' a book or a letter. In either case the actual material process of recording the composition may be done by someone else, such as a secretary. In medieval times writing of this kind, the task of the scribe, was a minor and not very prestigious activity. Reading and writing in the sense used in medieval England were, then, not inseparably coupled together as they are sometimes thought to be today. The association was with 'mouth and ear rather than hand and eye' according to Clanchy (ibid. p. 219). People whom we would classify as 'non-literate' were able to participate in 'literate' practice either by listening/'reading' or by composing/'writing'.

The visual aspect of 'writing', on the other hand, was associated not with function nor with the meaning of 'words on the page' but with display and connotation. Manuscripts were elaborately decorated, bibles were illuminated, and these skills were of higher status than those of the scribe. The written text of a bible was seen as the Word of God displayed and the book was thus a symbolic and sacred object.

This emphasis on the visual presentation continued in the more bureaucratic secular documents which began to proliferate, thus providing some degree of access for those not able to read for themselves the words on the page. 'Reading', then, was understood to involve understanding of the context, format, layout and general presentation of a text rather than simply understanding the relationship of sounds to letters as in much contemporary pedagogy. Officials learnt only as much as was necessary to do their jobs – scribes could be hired to do the task of writing so that officials could often read but not write. There was no clear division between 'literates' and 'illiterates' and none of the status associations that are currently built on top of the distinction. Clanchy maintains that it was precisely because of such a 'mix', the persistence of oral alongside written modes and the use in literate modes of oral forms, that the shift from memory to written record was enabled to take place: the fears, judgements of status and prejudices that might have impaired acceptance of a 'literate mentality' were allayed. This contrasts with the domineering and absolutist nature of many literacy programmes today and of the associated theoretical work of many contemporary researchers.

Clanchy's material, then, confirms that in talking about literacy we are referring to the ideology and concrete social forms and institutions that give meaning to any particular practice of reading and writing. The material on medieval England indicates the kind of forms, institutions and ideology that go to make up any such literate practice and raises questions that can usefully be applied to other literacies.

Such insights into literacy have been developed, for a variety of reasons, in relation to cultures distant in either time or space from our present circumstances. They have been applied only recently to contemporary western societies. I conclude this chapter with an important example from America of the application of the 'ideological' model to more familiar situations. Shirley Brice Heath has been developing in a number of works many of the elements of this model (1982; 1983). I will consider, for the moment, her article entitled 'What no bedtime story means: Narrative skills at home and at school' (1982). In this she rejects the conception of reading as a 'technical skill' and describes it instead as 'a way of taking' meaning from the environment (ibid. p. 49). Taking meaning from books is but one 'way of taking' though it is often interpreted as 'neutral' rather than learnt. In fact 'ways of taking' from books are 'as much part of learnt behaviour as are ways of eating, sitting, playing games and building houses' (ibid.). These 'ways' vary both across and within cultures according to ideology in general and specifically in relation to parent–child interactions and socialisation patterns.

Her main concern is to compare the 'ways of taking' evident in pre-school, Mainstream families (and which complemented those which the children would be exposed to in Mainstream schools) with those evident in other communities (and which in these cases might lead to conflicts for the children when they entered Mainstream schools). Following the analysis of Mainstream literacy and associated values, she asks: 'Are there ways of behaving which achieve other social and cognitive aims in other sociocultural groups?' (ibid. p. 57). Comparison of Mainstream 'ways of taking' with those Heath describes for Roadville and Trackton, white and black working-class communities respectively, provides some positive answers that are of relevance to the analysis here of different literacies and 'ways of taking from books' .

She describes, for instance, how pre-school children in Mainstream families learnt attention to books from a very early age. They learnt through bedtime stories an infrastructure of pedagogical practices and cultural assumptions which match, to a great extent, those they encounter in schools. They learn 'initiation–reply–evaluation' sequences, for instance, with their parents that replicate those used later by teachers. They become practised in labelling, through learning to answer 'what-explanation' questions posed by parents in relation to pictures in books. They also learn to build book knowledge onto their experience of the real world and to use it to frame and express that experience. Even before they enter school, this home training has enabled them to 'use their knowledge of what books do to legitimise their departure from the truth' (ibid. p. 52); an interesting reminder, after Clanchy's material, that the relationship of literacy to 'truth' is as equivocal as that of orality. They learn to suspend reality 'telling stories which are not true and ascribing fiction-like features to everyday objects' (ibid.). When they are a little older, however, these children are discouraged from the 'highly interactive, participatory role in bookreading' that they have learnt up until now and are encouraged instead to 'listen and wait' as an audience to adult-read stories and to store up questions until appropriate breaks. This, again, prepares them for the pedagogical way of using books which they will experience for most of their schooling. These learnt features of literacy practice derive from the specific ideology of their parents, which is school-oriented and based on a conscious desire to prepare their children for school and subsequent middle-class careers.

What, however, Heath is particularly interested in is 'the variety of ways in which children from *non-Mainstream* homes learn about reading, writing and using oral language to display knowledge' and how these differ from the better-known, middle-class experience. 'Little is actually known', she complains, 'about what goes on in story-reading and other literacy-related interactions between adults and preschoolers in communities around the world' (ibid. p. 50). Her attempt to redress the balance by describing two 'non-Mainstream' communities in America brings out the cultural nature of literacy practices that many would otherwise assume to be 'natural' and provides useful questions for the more general project I am attempting to outline within the terms of the 'ideological' model of literacy. As Heath argues, the 'literacy events' to which people are exposed and the meanings they 'take' from them 'require a broad framework of socio-cultural analysis' for sense to be made of them (ibid.).

Roadville children, for instance, learn a different way of relating literacy to 'truth'. Their working-class, committed Christian parents use literacy for instruction and moral improvement in which 'fiction' is rejected in favour of 'real' events that tell a message. The reading of a book in this community was a performance, not an inter-participatory event as it was in the early years of a Mainstream child's upbringing. It was used to 'entertain, inform and instruct' an effectively passive audience (ibid. p. 61). Heath sees great differences between Mainstream and Roadville literacy that make clear how far literacies differ even within a country as well as between countries, thus making such concepts as 'western' literacy unhelpful for cross-cultural comparison. These differences stem directly from differences in ideology: 'Roadville adults do not extend either the context or the habits of literacy events beyond bookreading. They do not, upon seeing an item or event in the real world, remind children of a similar event in a book and launch a running commentary on similarities and differences' as Mainstream parents do (ibid.). As with Clanchy's account of literacy in medieval England, we find ourselves having to give an account of fundamental moral and conceptual principles in order to understand the particular form that literacy takes. Conversely an account of literacy in terms of an 'ideological' model provides a lead into the understanding of such principles. Heath's comparison of Roadville and Mainstream uses of literacy is pitched at this level. She writes, for instance:

> Neither Roadville adults nor children shift the context of items in their talk. They do not tell stories which fictionalise themselves or familiar events. They reject Sunday school materials which attempt to translate Biblical events into a modern day setting. In Roadville, a story must be invited or announced by someone other than the storyteller, and only certain community members are designated good storytellers. A story is recognised by the group as a story about one and all. It is a true story, an actual event which occurred to either the storyteller or to someone else present. The marked behaviour of the storyteller and audience alike is seen as exemplifying the weaknesses of all and the need for persistence in overcoming such weaknesses. The sources of stories are personal experience. They are tales of transgressions which make the point of reiterating the expected norms of behaviour of man, woman, fisherman, worker and Christian. They are true to the facts of an event (ibid. pp. 62–3.)

Thus in Roadville children come to know a story as either an accounting from a book, or a factual account of a real event in which some type of marked behaviour occurred and there is a lesson to be learnt. Any fictionalised account of a real event is viewed as a lie: reality is better than fiction. Roadville's church and community life admit no story other than that which meets the definition internal to that group. Thus children cannot 'decontextualise their knowledge nor fictionalise events known to them and shift into other frames' (ibid. p. 63).

The children from these different communities were, then, socialised into fundamentally different world views by means, amongst other things, of the specific ways in which literacy was taught and in which, in their daily interaction with adults, certain practices were reinforced and others discouraged. Mainstream children, on the one hand, were encouraged and rewarded for developing 'book talk' and for experimenting in suspensions of reality modelled on those found in books their parents read to them. Thus when they were away from books they continued to use book knowledge and conventions to frame and describe experience, such as by ascribing fiction-like features to everyday objects. Roadville children, on the other hand, were encouraged and rewarded for telling stories that derived a moral message from 'real' experience. The books to which they were exposed, reinforced these normative, 'naturalistic' rules. They did not learn to use them as a flexible and always available resource for experiments with reality but rather they learnt, from their contact with books as well as from oral experience, that story-telling was a culturally-framed event distinguished by specific learnt conventions regarding who could tell stories, how they could be called upon to do so, when and in what way.

The differences between Mainstream and Roadville ideologies which these differences in literate practice represent, lead their children to respond differently to formal schooling. They also lead them to respond differently to other aspects of the wider culture which members of different communities are invited or obliged to share. Heath suggests that such an analysis can help to account for differences in 'success' and 'failure' at school of children from different communities. Avoiding the implications in Bernstein's work, that cultural differences can be associated with differences at deep cognitive levels, Heath instead asks for more detailed research on how such differences work in context and how they might be incorporated into general education for all. She proposes that students be exposed to aspects of literacy and pedagogy from a variety of cultural backgrounds: 'Knowing more about how these alternatives are learnt at early ages in different sociocultural conditions can help the school to provide opportunities for *all* students to avail themselves of these alternatives ... For example, Mainstream children can benefit from early exposure to Trackton's creative, highly analogical styles of telling stories and giving explanations and they can add the Roadville true story with strict chronicity and explicit moral to their repertoire of narrative types.' (ibid. p. 73.)

She concludes with a statement that makes explicit some of the fundamental tenets of the 'ideological' model of literacy and which has remained implicit in many of the writers being examined:

> if we want to understand the place of literacy in human societies
> and the ways children acquire the literacy orientations of their
> communities, we must recognise two postulates of literacy and

language development: (1) Strict dichotomization between oral and literate traditions is a construct of researchers, not an accurate portrayal of reality across cultures. (2) A unilinear model of development in the acquisition of language structures and uses cannot adequately account for culturally diverse ways of acquiring knowledge or developing cognitive styles. (ibid.)

She goes on to say:

Literacy events must ... be interpreted in relation to the *larger sociocultural patterns* which they may exemplify or reflect. For example, ethnography must describe literacy events in their sociocultural contexts, so we may come to understand how such patterns as time and space usage, caregiving roles, and age and sex segregation are interdependent with the types and features of literacy events a community develops. It is only on the basis of such thorough-going ethnography that further progress is possible towards understanding cross-cultural patterns of oral and written language uses. (ibid. p. 74.)

SECTION 2

Literacy in Theory and Practice

INTRODUCTION

In this section I will attempt to apply some of the ideas concerning literacy that were worked out at a more general level above to specific situations in both rural and urban Iran during the 1970s. My knowledge of these situations derives, to a large extent, from field work visits to villages in the hinterland of Mashad, North East Iran during that decade. I also spent a period teaching at the University, the British Council and the Iran America Society in Mashad. The 1970s saw a dramatic expansion and then equally dramatic decline in the Iranian economy, and an upheaval in the political order culminating in the fall of the Shah and the coming to power of Ayatollah Khomeini. It is against this background that I will consider the nature and significance of different literacies in specific rural areas where I did field work and more generally in relation to urban educational developments at that time. I shall attempt to test against these specific situations both what I have called the 'ideological' model of literacy and also those aspects of the 'autonomous' model that are subject to empirical examination. I shall then consider general proposals for further research into literacy that might be developed from such an analysis.

In Chapter 5, I shall describe the literacy that was taught in the Islamic school in Cheshmeh, a mountain fruit-growing village above Mashad, and then consider some of the developments that were taking place in this 'maktab' literacy as it adapted to the pressures of change during the 1970s. One strand of this development can be traced in the specific arguments and concepts used by teachers and students of the Islamic school to confront and encapsulate what they perceived as the scientific achievements of the west. I shall examine the intellectual framework constructed to confront western ideology as they encountered it. A further development of 'maktab' literacy was its adaptation, by a number of village entrepreneurs, to the needs of the new large-scale, fruit marketing system generated by the economic growth and infrastructural developments of the early 1970s in Iran. I refer to this adaptation as 'commercial' literacy and I shall consider it further in Chapter 6. The relationship of both 'maktab' literacy and this new 'commercial' literacy to the kind of literacy that began to be taught when a State school or 'dabestan' was built in the village in 1960 adds a further complexity. Finally Cheshmehis, like many prosperous fruit-growing mountain villagers in this period, were beginning to invest their new wealth in urban advantages, including winter off-season housing and city schooling for their children. The forms of literacy taught in these city schools differed in significant ways from those of either the 'maktab' or the village 'dabestan'. When the youths who were exposed to this urban literacy returned to the village, as they frequently did both for leisure and to look after orchard interests, the differences between the various forms of literacy and their accompanying ideologies became acutely apparent.

One problem with attempting to test the 'autonomous' model of literacy against situations such as this is that it tends to set up polarised absolutist concepts which can result in overstatements on either side. It tends to force one, for instance, to judge any particular literacy as either 'restricted' or as having the full, rational qualities of the essay-text ideal. Anthropologists, because of their familiarity and identification with the culture they have spent some time living within, are often inclined to 'defend' the practices they find there against ethnocentric judgements. In the case of literacy, an attempt to redress the balance of culture-bound assumptions regarding 'restricted' literacy could lead to an overemphasis on the 'rational' qualities of the particular practices described. Each pole towards which the 'autonomous' model of literacy forces both its supporters and its critics can be misleading and detracts from the attempt to understand the specific form of literacy in its own right and in relation to the culture and ideology in which it is embedded. That attempt need not involve an untheoretical, empiricist listing of different literacies but it does, at this stage of our knowledge, require more limited and cautious hypotheses than exponents of the 'autonomous' model have put forward. I will, then, attempt to resist the pressure to represent the literacy of the traditional Islamic school in the Iranian villages I am describing as either 'restricted' or as a model of intellectual development.

Some of the concepts being developed within what I have called the 'ideological' model of literacy can, I believe, be helpful in avoiding this dilemma and in making sense of the complex overlapping of literacies and ideologies. I will use, for instance, the notion that there is a 'mix' of oral and literate modes of communication, rather than searching for 'pure types' of either. I shall describe different literacies rather than assuming a single, autonomous literacy; I shall consider these literacies as they are embedded in specific ideologies and cultural practices rather than attempting to separate out literacy as such or treat it simply as a technology; and I shall describe how the specific ideologies and literacies of village Iran related to and interacted with alternative ideologies and literacies to which their exponents were being exposed at this time. This leads me to propose two specific areas of literacy practice around which to focus the account. These are the traditional, religious literacy as taught in an Islamic school and which I refer to as 'maktab' literacy and the 'commercial' literacy being developed particularly in mountain, fruit-growing villages like Cheshmeh in the 1970s. I shall refer more briefly to State school or 'dabestan' literacy as taught in these and other villages and to urban school literacy.

5

'MAKTAB' LITERACY

When I arrived at the village of Cheshmeh in the mountains above Mashad in North East Iran in 1970, modern school learning had ostensibly supplanted the traditional religious schools or 'maktab', in which mullahs had imparted Koranic learning. However, the Ministry of Education school was a relatively recent incursion and it was earlier generations of students from the 'maktab' who still dominated village social life and institutions. The literacy which they had acquired there was still significant for their religious dominance and, I argue, contributed in important ways to their social and commercial dominance. One 'maktab' in particular seems to have provided most of the leaders of the village and the two mullahs who ran it, who were brothers, still occupied an important position in the village while I was there. The literacy and ideology imparted by such mullahs constitute, I argue, a specific form of literacy practice which I term 'maktab' literacy. To describe and analyse this particular literacy we need first to consider some of the general characteristics of Islam as well as the specific form it took in the villages I am describing.

To translate the Farsi term 'mullah' as 'priest' would be misleading since this would imply a western model of priestship that does not properly exist in Islam. Mullahs do undergo some training at a theological college, but they are not appointed to 'parishes' as are western priests and they do not fit into a formal framework of dioceses nor into a hierarchy of priestly offices. They have to make their own living and usually combine teaching for payment and the performance of religious services with participation in local forms of labour. In Cheshmeh, the two brothers who ran the 'maktab' owned and worked considerable orchard holdings, just like their fellow villagers. Some mullahs travel from village to village offering classes to children or adults and there were usually enough students in Cheshmeh to warrant one such itinerant pedagogue at any one time. Besides offering classes, the mullahs also provide ritual services such as at death, marriage and birth and will lead the congregation in the prayers and ceremonials that play a significant part in Shiite Islam, especially in the area of Mashad which is a holy city of pilgrimage. While many mullahs are respected for their learning and their work, others are frequently scorned and laughed at because, for instance, they are seen to be 'hypocritical', too 'serious' or simply 'lazy'. I was frequently in the company of a group of villagers who, while clearly 'religious' in my experience of them, would satirise some visiting mullah unmercifully for such reasons. The status and credibility of a mullah, then, is contingent on how they are judged as individuals in a variety of both religious and mundane practices and they do not receive the automatic respect due to an office holder.

The knowledge that is imparted in the 'maktab' is primarily that of the Koran, although in some cases, as in Cheshmeh, mullahs may add knowledge of commentaries and also teach vernacular literacy and numeracy. For some students their experience of the 'maktab' may involve no more than learning to recite by rote whole passages of the Koran, often without 'reading' in the sense of 'cracking the phonemic code'. They would not necessarily be able to relate letters or clusters of letters to sounds if they encountered them in new contexts. They might become so familiar with the appearance of the book from which they had been taught passages that they could recognise and recite sections according to such mnemonics as the position of the passage on the page, the layout and style of the book and the use of headings, rather as students of Latin used to revise for 'set books' in the English examination system. Since, however, they have had even this minimal encounter with literacy, and have of course seen how others such as their teachers and fellow students were employing more elaborate literacy skills for powerful purposes, it would be wrong to ascribe these students to a 'pure type' of oral tradition, in contrast with a 'pure type' of literacy. They represent, in fact, a particularly interesting example of what, throughout this book, I have referred to as the 'mix' of oral and literate modes which I see as the major reality in terms of modes of communication.

Their acquaintance with literacy in this way means, for instance, that they will perceive the kind of literacy being thrust upon them and their children through modern education systems, through new forms of commerce or even just in their experience of the organisation and layout of a modern city in a way that is different from those who have not been to the 'maktab' or from those who take their 'maktab' literacy further. They are aware, for instance, of the way in which meaning is dependent on the layout of a page as well as on the content of the words so they will have some sense of what is involved when they are shown forms by officials. As we shall see below, when Cheshmehi entrepreneurs adapt their 'maktab' literacy to commercial purposes they are helped by the fact that fellow villagers are familiar with the use of pieces of paper to signify lists, contracts etc. and so are able to participate in their use in such ways as 'signing' with their thumbs papers of which they cannot read the verbal content. Similarly, when modern literacy campaigns are brought to such individuals, they do not come to minds that are *tabula rasa*, as many of the officials who bring them seem to think. Those involved in such campaigns have perhaps underestimated the significance of such local acquaintance with literate forms for understanding the different ways in which subjects respond to literacy programmes and for assessing their 'success'.

Other students in the 'maktab' may develop their literacy to the extent that they can 'read' the Arabic letters and do more than simply recite recognisable passages. Since the Arabic alphabet is largely the same as the Persian, with only a few minor differences in letters and diacritics, this development virtually means that they have acquired indigenous literacy. A number of the students of the 'maktab' at Cheshmeh learnt to read Farsi in this way. The development was enhanced by the fact that the mullah there also made use of commentaries in Farsi and had Farsi versions of the Koran even though, according to some theological positions, 'translation' of the Word of God would be sacrilege. What they derived from such commentaries was both facility in reading the script of their own alphabet and an intellectual framework and ideology which gave meaning to their particular literacy and, as I shall argue below, facilitated the adaptation of it to new purposes and a different ideology.

Approaching these practices in terms of an 'ideological' model of literacy involves, then, attempting to elaborate on the specific contexts which give meaning to literacy for those learning and using it. In the case of 'maktab' literacy, this necessitates some account of the particular variety of the 'Islamic Tradition' to be found in Iranian mountain villages in the 1970s, of the ways in which that tradition was responding to western ideas and concepts, notably those regarding science and history, and of the particular uses to which such literacy and the ideas associated with it were put by different groups of people who had been exposed to it.

The Islamic Tradition

Although what is loosely called the 'Islamic Tradition' does have some defining unity, there is, in fact, more variety and more scope for interpretation than is often recognised. Marshall Hodgson makes this point central to his account of Islam:

> When we look at Islam historically, then, the integral unity of life it seemed to display when we looked at it as the working out of the act of Islam (submission) almost vanishes ... We can no longer say that Islam eternally teaches a given thing, or that another thing is necessarily a corruption of Islam. Such judgements a believer may feel able to make, but not an historian as such. At a given time, in a limited milieu perhaps, Islam may form a relatively delimited and inviolable pattern. But over time

and especially on a world scale, any particular formulation of thought or practice is to be seen as the result of how the ever-changing setting formed by the Islamic Tradition is reflected in particular circumstances and in relation to the other cultural traditions present. (Hodgson, 1974, Vol. 1, p. 85.)

It is important to bear these remarks in mind when dealing with Islam as it manifests itself in Iran, particularly since the events of the Khomeini revolution there might appear to suggest to western observers the existence of a single, monolithic and fixed tradition. The Islamic belief and practice that I am describing in the mountain fruit-growing villages of the Mashad hinterland represent a particular formulation of the tradition, one which is different in significant ways from even the nearby plains villages and from the formulations characteristic of other parts of the country. It is a variation which may already have changed as a result of the revolution. The variation to which Hodgson refers can be found not only across 'time' and on a 'world scale' but also within specific milieux.

I do not make any claim to be an Islamic scholar or an 'Orientalist'. My approach to these variations is that of the anthropologist – the 'historian of the present', as it were, attempting to understand how the participants conceptualise these different world views and religious interpretations and how these are 'reflected in particular circumstances'.This involves rejecting the notions both of a single, monolithic, autonomous Islam and of a single, 'autonomous' and 'restricted' literacy that many have taken to correspond to it.

One source of this 'autonomous' view of both Islam and literacy has been the apparent fixity and lack of interpretation which many associate with religions of the Book. As Muslims would themselves say, the Koran is the Word of God and so there is no need for interpretation. To many students in 'maktabs' over the ages, recitation by rote of the Holy Word was itself sufficient. However, there is more to the transmission of knowledge in Islam than this, as indeed there is to all religions of the Book. As Parry (1982) says, in describing similar views of the Hindu tradition, the authority and apparent fixity of the written tradition in such religions is the very characteristic that provides scope for individual mediators to offer their own interpretation as the authoritative one. Literacy appears to deny different interpretations while at the same time, in reality, facilitating them.

In the Hindu tradition, Parry suggests, the Veda is taken as the ultimate guide to behaviour and yet, since it has virtually nothing to say about everyday life, it can in fact be used to validate each guru's own interpretation. Parry (1982, p. 15) cites this in order to criticise Goody's claim that knowledge associated with a 'literate' tradition is relatively immutable, while that of an 'oral' tradition is volatile and malleable. In fact, it is the very belief that this is the case which allows for the degree of variation that Parry observes in practice. For each interpretation can claim to be more than just individual perception and can therefore dissociate itself from supposedly volatile oral usage, by claiming authority from the written text.

The situation with regard to interpretation and 'malleability' of texts in that variety of the Islamic tradition to be found in Cheshmeh and similar villages in Iran is not unlike that described by Parry. The Koran is a fixed text, immutable since it is the Word of God. Unlike the Veda it does pronounce on daily life and offers detailed rules for behaviour, but like the Veda this apparent fixity disguises and in fact facilitates a variety of interpretation in practice. Moreover, as in the Hindu tradition, the central book of Islam is supplemented by commentaries and other texts. The most important of these in Islam are the 'Hadith', which transmit the 'sunna', the body of reported actions and sayings of the Prophet and his Companions and which correspond roughly to what the New Testament is to Christianity.

The 'Hadith', according to J. A. Williams, 'reflect the religious opinions of the first generations of pious Muslim scholars and relay the values which earlier generations of experts pronounced "Islamic", whether or not they relate to an historical event ... It follows that not even "Hadiths" of dubious authenticity may be rejected out of hand' (Williams, 1972, p. 45). 'Hadith', therefore, may vary from one sect to another and may be selected by a teacher according to his own interests. They often persist in the oral tradition alongside written versions, particularly in the form of stories about Mohammed and Ali. In that variety of the Islamic tradition which I experienced in Cheshmeh and similar mountain villages in North East Iran, such stories were regularly adapted to contemporary issues and problems, notably the impact of western science and ideas, as we shall see in more detail below. My experience, then, supports Parry's emphasis on the malleability of sacred traditions, whether oral or written.

The Shari'a or Sacred Law in Islam is derived from both the Koran, 'in which God appears as commanding and forbidding, rewarding and punishing' (ibid. p. 78) and from the 'Hadith', in which the actions of the Prophet and his Companions provide a model for right action. Understanding (*fiqh*) of these rules was, according to J. A. Williams, the major activity of Islamic scholarship: 'The most characteristic activity of Islamic scholarship has not been, as in other religions, theology, but the study and explication of the Law.' (ibid.) Although the boundaries of Islamic Law were laid down during the first four centuries following Mohammed's death, the custodians of the Law today may still decide what is an 'official position' (Rizvi, 1980, p. 345).

Such scope for interpretation is particularly evident in Shiite Islam, the sect to which over 90% of Iranians belong. For Shiites guidance has also been provided by God through the Imams, the rightful successors of Mohammed, and the story of their lives and in particular their dramatic deaths form a crucial basis for religious instruction. Shiite mullahs, in the 'maktabs', use these accounts to provide commentary on the history of Islam and on the messages it bears for present behaviour, and have therefore further scope for offering their own interpretation of the sacred texts. In the village of Cheshmeh, in addition, the mullahs made use of more recent commentaries, one of which 'Tosi ol Mosa'el' had been employed in the theological college attended by one of the mullahs and brought by him to the village to provide interpretations relevant to the situation in a rapidly westernising Iran.

Although each of the texts cited above may be appealed to as an ultimate authority, the range of texts available and the ability of the mullah to select according to his own interests and beliefs suggests that the mullahs, like the gurus in India, had scope in practice to say what they liked. Goody's belief in the immutability of sacred texts turns out to be simply an acceptance of what many of the participants might themselves believe or claim. But, as Parry says, it does not provide an accurate account of how the texts are used in practice nor a useful theoretical framework for making sense of the uses of literacy in religions of the Book.

Ruth Finnegan suggests a more tentative model than Goody for describing the processes whereby belief and knowledge are transmitted in such circumstances. Her suggestions can, perhaps, illuminate the material I am considering rather more than traditional theories concerning literacy and transmission, of the type I have termed the 'autonomous' model. Proposing constructive alternatives to Goody's position, she outlines 'some of the recurrent patterns that I think it can often be helpful to distinguish in the study of transmission in oral and written traditions – even though they are not ones which could be assumed to apply in particular cases in advance of the detailed research' (Finnegan, 1981, p. 46). She offers a distinction between the content and the mode of transmission and a warning against the tendency to ethnocentrism in current conceptions of literacy: 'Because of our socialisation into the traditions of western culture as established over the last few centuries and also more specifically, for most of us at least, into a literary and academic ethos, it is easy for us to assume when we discuss transmission that what is actually transmitted is quintessentially a text; either a text in the sense of something which appears in a fixed documentary form, or as the product of an oral performance which is, at least in principle, "writable", even if variable.' (ibid.) But, she points out, some examples of such oral performance that are turned into 'texts' may be very different from 'texts' in the literary and academic sense. 'What is transmitted is more a storehouse of known formulae and themes and the performer's skill and experience in using these, rather than a text as such even though there may be elements of verbal recurrence and fixity.' (ibid.)

She has in mind specific traditions of oral literature where the amount of 'verbal crystallisation' that is subsequently written down as text will vary, but the principle she is enunciating may also be developed in relation to the uses of literacy that I am considering here. Phillips' comments on Mandinka poetry, to which Finnegan alludes, provide a hint of these possibilities. As Mandinka poets become more experienced they gradually 'rely less heavily on memorization and word-for-word repetition and instead exploit their ability to express the same meaning in varied form' (quoted in Finnegan, 1981, p. 48).

Intelligent mullahs and their students in Iran could be said to be doing something like this in their conversational play on variations in the meaning of the sacred Islamic texts. They may not do so in the self-conscious, literary manner of the poets described by Finnegan and Phillips, but they do play upon the basic themes and formulae of the Islamic creed and create new ways of expressing old meanings: 'what oft was thought but ne'er so well expressed'. A man who attempted to explain to me about pollution with the aid of a metaphor of mud and dust, for example (see below p. 149) was both expressing old meanings in new ways and attempting to work out for himself in doing so what those meanings were. In this sense, the acquisition of literacy in the Koranic school does not simply 'fix' for ever sacred rules and beliefs, but provides a particular development of the malleability that Goody would associate only with an oral tradition. The scholars of the 'maktab' exemplify a 'mix' of oral and literate modes of communication in which malleability and fixity are likewise 'mixed'.

Finnegan describes in more general terms the process whereby a variety of oral statements may become written at different times and warns against the assumption that any version becomes final once this has happened: 'what looks like a single text on the page once it has been recorded and published may represent a number of starting points in its initial realization – a fixed and memorized text, a unique, perhaps once-off performance never repeated in similar form, a version by an experienced specialist who, despite minor verbal variations, has gone through many similar performances often in his career ... or a gallant try by a willing but inexperienced non-specialist in response to a foreign researcher's prodding' (Finnegan, 1981, p. 48). Although she is referring here again to creative literature, her conclusion can be applied also to the uses and representations of sacred texts and commentaries that I am describing in

Iran. She advises: 'We would do well not to assume from the similar-looking transcriptions on a printed page that the kind of transmission that lies behind it was always of an already frozen text.' (ibid.)

We can apply this insight fruitfully to, for instance, the historical process within Islam whereby the 'Hadith' were transmitted first through word of mouth and then in written versions alongside a continuing oral tradition. In the early days of Islam, anyone who had come into contact with the Prophet and his Companions might pass on anecdotes and stories, some of which became established and assumed moral significance. As J. A. Williams notes, even 'Hadith' which are:

> themselves false may have a certain historical and moral value for later generations if they are accepted in the early collections: they reflect the religious opinions of the first generations of pious Muslim scholars, the 'Consensus' which has been so vital in the formulation of law and doctrine. They thus relay values which earlier generations of experts pronounced 'Islamic', whether or not they relate a historical event. It follows, then, that not even 'Hadith' of dubious authenticity may be rejected out of hand. (1972, p. 45.)

The corpus represents, then, a range of sayings and interpretations that were not necessarily equivalent in their original form. Although they are represented in the form of 'true historical' stories, they are in fact, as J. A. Williams' comments imply, exemplary moral tales with a refractory relationship to actual events. The process of writing down 'acceptable' 'Hadith' depended on the moral and, one may add, political decisions of early scholars. Some versions may have been passing on anecdotes that happened to be available to those with the authority to decide what was to be included as sacred text and to have it written down; others may have become relatively 'fixed' over time by constant repetition and so were already 'writable' texts; some may have been represented in many different versions and that which came to be written down and transmitted was only one. What we have now is not, then, uniformly the written representation of an already 'frozen' text.

Nor were they necessarily 'frozen' once they became written down. The process gives ample scope for modern 'experts' to continue to use stories of the Prophet and his Companions in order to relay values which they consider appropriate to current circumstances, with all the authority of the past sages. Mullahs and their students in Cheshmeh, for instance, recount tales of Ali and his Companions in order to demonstrate that the founders of Islam had knowledge, even at that time, of 'modern' scientific principles and in order to draw from this implications for moral behaviour today.

From this perspective it is possible to see that those who attended the mullah's school in Cheshmeh had learnt more than just the content of the Koran and of fixed sacred texts, despite the appearance of rote learning and memorisation. One is led, instead, to look for evidence that they had developed skills, of the kind which Finnegan describes, in playing upon basic 'formulae and themes'. Those who became more experienced could, perhaps, be described, as Phillips describes Mandinka poets, as relying 'less heavily on memorisation and word-for-word repetition' and instead as exploiting their ability to 'express the same meaning in varied form' (cf. p. 138 above). 'Maktab' literacy, then, may involve skills as well as content and the texts that are learnt in this way may not be simply 'fossilised'.

In the Shiite tradition which we are considering there is further scope for the exploitation of such skills. Apart from the Koran, the 'Hadith' and the Law Schools of orthodox Sunnite tradition, Shiite Islam has a rich corpus of stories about the twelve Imams. Central to these are accounts of their martyrdom at the hands of their religious enemies and in particular the dramatic murder of the third Imam, Hossein, the youngest son of Ali. These events form the basis of a passion play or 'tazi'eh' that is performed on the tenth of Moharram, and which provides scope for the kinds of elaborations to which Finnegan refers.

After the death of Hassan, Ali's eldest son, Hossein became his successor as head of the Prophet's family and leader of the growing Muslim world. However, he was challenged for the position of Caliph by Yazid, a descendant of a rival clan, the Umawis. The inhabitants of Kufa, Ali's former capital, countered these claims with an offer to make Hossein Caliph and he set out from Medina in AD 680 across the desert in Iraq. However, Yazid's viceroy in the meanwhile put down this insurrection in Kufa and set patrols at the approaches to the city. Hossein walked into the trap with his family and a few retainers at Kerbala, some twenty-five miles from Kufa. J. A. Williams writes:

> As the Prophet's favourite and only surviving grandson, he apparently did not expect to be seriously harmed and refused to surrender, although surrounded and cut off from water. After ten days the little band was cut down to the last man and Hossein's head sent to Yazid in Damascus. Muslims everywhere were appalled and the 'Martyrdom of Kerbala' became the rallying point of all who distrusted the Umawis. With many moving and pitiful details, the story forms the basis of the passion plays ... originally an Arab political faction, the Shiites came to differ increasingly in their doctrines from the Sunnis. (ibid. pp. 205–6.)

These events were still alive in the minds of villagers in the hinterland of Mashad in the 1970s and were constantly retold and embellished throughout the year as well as on the particular day of remembrance. On that day, the tenth of Moharram, villagers would gather in the mosque, many wearing black shirts of mourning and symbolically beat themselves with chains while chanting versions of the martyrdom.

Ennayat has traced the uses of the theme of martyrdom in Iran back beyond the events of the seventh century AD to concepts deeply rooted in Zoroastrianism, the dominant religion before Islam (Ennayat, 1972). In one sense, 'themes and formulae' developed in that era are re-created and re-presented through the passion plays and stories of Shiite Islam. We can find here, even more clearly perhaps than in other aspects of the Islamic tradition, that scope for poetic transformation and variation to which Finnegan and Phillips refer in relation to other oral traditions.

Those acquiring literacy in the 'maktab' in Cheshmeh tend to learn more details of these stories than others. Their literacy does not necessarily reduce the possibility for variation but may in fact enhance it, and the authority they have by dint of their learning may encourage them to play upon the themes and formulae for the benefit of others. They certainly seemed eager to play upon them for my benefit as a visiting scholar whom they wished to impress and they were often the leaders in conversations at the tea house when the subject of Islamic history, martyrdom etc. came up.

These men also became acquainted through the 'maktab' with the writings of learned Shiite doctors. They had been exposed to further elaborations on Islamic history and to interpretations of the rules of behaviour derived from that history. The commentary used by the young mullah in the 'maktab' in Cheshmeh, 'Tosi ol Mosa'el', is but one in a long tradition of such work and those attending 'maktabs' in other villages or with other mullahs may encounter different books and different interpretations. The writer of 'Tosi ol Mosa'el' happened to have access to and the right to use processes of publication in order to disseminate his particular interpretations more broadly than others. But his interpretation was only one amongst many circulating at any one time and, like the 'Hadith' of an earlier era, the selection, from this variety, of that which was written down and of that which was used for teaching purposes depends on a number of social and often political factors. As Finnegan suggests with regard to literary traditions in other cultures, we should not assume either a 'fixed' original, nor that this particular version then becomes 'fixed' because it is written down. Rather it can be seen as part of the 'storehouse of formulae and themes' on which users can play in a variety of ways.

The comparison of 'maktab' literacy with the various oral and literary traditions described by Finnegan is, in fact, particularly apt in the Iranian case. There is, in Iran, a rich oral tradition, including poetry, plays and memorised stories as well as religious interpretations, pronouncements and discussions. What is written down out of all of this and becomes available as literate text varies over time and space and in relation to specific conditions, such as access to publishing facilities and the judgement of 'experts'. Furthermore, the interpretation of what is written down continues to vary. The writing down of some of the vast corpus of what is said does not necessarily impair the scope for flexibility, and may in some ways enhance it. The extent to which a particular balance between these possibilities is developed depends upon the nature of the specific cultural and political traditions and not to any significant extent upon the nature of the media themselves. Students of the 'maktab' have learnt from written versions not simply to reproduce their specific content in fixed form but have also learnt those skills in playing upon formulae and themes that many have associated solely with an oral tradition.

'Maktab' literacy is derived from a historically mixed oral and literate tradition rather than being associated with a 'pure' type of either and it is this 'mix' that continues to be represented in the current circumstances. The 'mix' facilitates in different ways a variety of interpretation, not only across time and space in the grand terms conceived by Hodgson (1974, p. 85) but even within the limited environment of a small village. The mullah's school does not close people off from alternatives, as the concept of 'restricted' literacy that Goody applies to the Islamic tradition would lead us to expect.

The representation of Islamic schooling that I have offered has some support from another folk tradition in Iran, that of the 'Mullah Nasr-ed-Din' stories. Iranians love to tell 'Mullah' stories and they form a significant part of any leisured conversation. Mullah Nasr-ed-Din is represented as a sort of wise fool who shows up pretentiousness and hypocrisy in others and suffers himself when he exhibits such traits. As in all such traditions, the stories are adaptable to the relator's own circumstances and they can can tell us much about what the participants themselves took for granted in those circumstances. One such story suggests a way in which some Iranians, in some moods, might think about the mullah's type of education and about what goes on in the 'maktab'. It commences with what appears to be a standard description of rote learning and mindless memorisation, which it then puts into humorous perspective:

> If any boy [sic] in the village wanted to learn to read, it was the mullah's duty to teach. Sometimes a large class met in the small mud hut in the yard of the village mosque. Sometimes there was no class at all.
>
> Once Mullah Nasr-ed-Din was teaching a class of ten boys, all sitting cross-legged on the hard clay floor. Their one book was the Koran in Arabic. They sat there on a drowsy spring morning

reading the same words over and over. Each was reading a different selection from the Koran. Each was reading in his loudest voice to show how hard he was studying ... And so it went – ten selections from the Koran being memorised by ten boys with loud and monotonous voices.

The steady murmur was like a lullaby to Mullah Nasr-ed-Din. If a fly lighted on his nose or a raven cawed outside his window, he would rouse with a start. He would wonder if the boys were as sleepy as he was, and would think of ways of testing them. Sometimes he would ask questions about what they were studying. Sometimes he would ask the first question that popped into his head.

On this particular morning he was roused by the clink of the bells of cows passing in the street. Naturally, the first question that came into his mind was about cows, rather than about the Koran. (Kelsey, 1957, pp. 99–102.)

The mullah describes in slow and languorous detail two cows walking one behind the other in a narrow street, and how the horns of one pierce the rump of the one in front. He then asks the boys the question, 'Which cow can say "I have tail and horns at the same end of my body?"'. The story allows scope for lengthy elaboration of the replies, for repetition of the question and further description of the scene, until at last the mullah gives the answer. '"It is not the first cow or the second cow", grins Mullah Nasr-ed-Din: "You boys have forgotten that cows cannot talk"'. (ibid.)

The ironical description of the way in which the class is conducted and the representation of the mullah as aware that rote learning can be soporific and mindless should remind us that some at least of those who participate in the Islamic educational tradition can view it with humour and detachment and are aware of the difference between memorisation of facts and thinking about them intelligently. The stories can, of course, be read in many ways and those who might want to resist such an interpretation can do so easily by appealing to the folk knowledge of Mullah Nasr-ed-Din as something of a buffoon. Nevertheless, this story, and others like it, are widespread and popular and there can be few people who have not thereby been exposed to the broader possibilities they raise and, to some extent, legitimise.

Although the mullah in the 'maktab' in Cheshmeh was no Mullah Nasr-ed-Din, and purveyed a 'hard' view of the importance of Koranic learning, he was interested in debate and argument and keen to present himself and his pedagogy as rational and thoughtful. His students, too, were interested in asking questions about western life and thought and keen to identify what they saw as contradictions there. The literacy acquired at the 'maktab' interacted in complex ways with oral modes of communication, with folk traditions of story-telling (including, of course, that of the 'Mullah' stories themselves), and with peculiarly Iranian versions and interpretations of Islamic tradition. It was within this context that the learning of certain literacy practices by these Iranian villagers acquired meaning.

We can, then, approach the description of literacy practice in Iranian villages from a broader and more open perspective than that provided by either the 'autonomous' model of literacy or by common western stereotypes of Islamic learning. We can, with Parry, question the assumption that in religions of the Book sacred texts are immutable and that knowledge is transmitted in dogmatic, inflexible ways. Rather we can keep open the possibility of looking for the varieties of interpretation that some forms of literacy may facilitate and we can investigate how particular individuals and groups may adapt literacy to their own political and ideological purposes. Similarly, with Finnegan, we can recognise that what is transmitted may not necessarily be a fixed content but a 'storehouse of formulae and themes', which skilled practitioners may play upon in imaginative and creative ways, learning for instance to eschew memorisation and word-for-word repetition in literacy as much as in oral practice. We can identify a 'mix' of oral and literate modes and an interaction between the two such that what is taken as 'text' at any time should not be seen as 'fixed' or 'frozen' but rather as socially contingent and changeable, a product of specific political and ideological conditions. We can, then, look for malleability and flexibility in literacy practices as in other modes of communication, in Islamic contexts as in others. It is within this open framework of thought that I shall attempt to describe in more detail the 'maktab' literacy of Iranian villages.

'Maktab' Literates in Cheshmeh

In Cheshmeh, only a small proportion of each generation had attended the 'maktab', but these tended to be the ones who were the formative influence in the particular Islamic tradition that evolved there. They were the ones who put forward for the community interpretations of the kinds of texts and laws outlined above and who provided the framework within which discussion of them took place. As a first step towards analysing the nature of the particular form of 'maktab' literacy which they employed, and comparing it with other forms of literacy, I shall describe some of the ways in which the men of this group represented their ideas, their religion and their relationship to western developments.

In the hours and days when they were not working in the orchards, these men would sit in clusters at certain points in the village and discuss a range of topics. Inevitably my presence stimulated certain topics, particularly the relationship of western concepts of religion and history to those of Islam. What they found strange and difficult to comprehend about western Christians was that they should be so far 'ahead' of Iran in material and technical progress (putting a man on the moon being only the most dramatic of the technical achievements of which most villagers were aware), and yet be one step behind in comprehending the larger cycle of history, that apparent in the succession of the prophets. They were all well versed in the cycle of the prophets from Adam to Mohammed and knew some lives in considerable detail. They recognised Hazrat Esau (Jesus Christ) as a great prophet whom they respected and whose teaching was appropriate to its time, superseding that of previous prophets; but it was obvious to them that Hazrat Mohammed had similarly superseded Hazrat Esau and that his teaching was more appropriate for the current period. Recognising this, they saw a strange contradiction in western intellectual life, every bit as strange and difficult to explain as the apparent contradictions in Iranian life are for the westerner. This was not represented as a matter simply of blind faith handed down by their fathers but of what happened when they applied their minds fully to this particular question. If the cycle of prophets is meaningful, and the evidence of centuries suggests to them that it is, just as the history of British political institutions, monarchy etc. or of scientific discovery can be for an Englishman, then it is a matter of logic rather than of faith that the latest of the prophets supersedes his predecessors just as the latest discoveries of a scientist are embraced by the scientific community and outdated ideas are then rejected.

This raises for many villagers the problem of how so many people in the world, and obviously intelligent ones at that, for they are respectful of western learning, have missed this obvious point. This perception and the explanation they offer for it may, in fact, be understood in terms of the integration of science and morality in Islamic culture and its dissociation in the west. It is within this framework that, I would suggest also, we can understand the Iranian villagers' similar assessment of their own society's recent history. In particular, they were concerned to explain the lack of scientific progress in Iran and to understand the reason why Iran did not participate in the recent scientific and industrial revolutions having, as everyone knows, been a world leader at earlier stages of its history. There too they saw the explanation in moral terms.

The villagers were very conscious that important scientific developments had taken place in Islamic countries and they frequently cited the Koran itself as having anticipated the achievements of western science. Thus individuals would claim that the moon landings were originally described in the Koran and that Ali, the first Imam, had himself anticipated many of the findings of modern medicine, if one only knew how to read the texts in the appropriate way.

One mullah visiting Cheshmeh had a fund of such sayings. Although many of them were so forced and trivial that even devout villagers satirised him for them, they do illustrate the character of many local responses to western science. He cited Ali as advising 'don't urinate in water because urine is bad for animals' and he interpreted this as meaning that Ali had anticipated western scientific discovery, through microscopes, of the microbes which are present in water and are the cause of various animal diseases. Some Cheshmehis would justify the elaborate ritual washings prescribed by the Islamic texts in terms of modern hygiene. The rule of fasting, I was also informed, was based on the medical need to clear out one's stomach periodically. Likewise, the prescriptions about standing, kneeling and bending over in careful sequence during prayer were, it was argued, intended to keep the body fit and healthy.

Such conceptions are familiar to anyone who has worked in the Third World, especially in areas with religions of the Book. Parry, for instance, describes a similar phenomenon in Hindu India:

> In Benares I have often been told – and I have heard variants of the same story elsewhere – that Max Muller stole chunks of the Sam Veda from India, and it was by studying these that German scientists were able to develop the atom bomb. The *rishis*, or ancient sages, not only knew all about nuclear fission, but as (what we would call) mythology testifies, they also had supersonic aeroplanes and guided missiles. Of a piece with such claims is the commonly made assertion that every ritual detail prescribed by the texts has some justification or other in terms of modern science. (Parry, 1982, p. 10.)

Parry suggests that a first response to such claims might be to see them as a 'kind of defensive reaction to the encounter with cosmopolitan science and British imperialism' (ibid.) similar to the 'cargo cults' widespread in Melanesia. However, while recognising that there might be an element of this present, he thinks that there is more to it than this and argues that: 'The interpretation of religious texts as technical know-how is not the departure it might at first appear' (ibid.). He sees it, instead, as an integral part of the Hindu theory of knowledge: 'The essential point is that in traditional Indian thought there is no conceptual divide between "religious" and "scientific" knowledge. Without any sense of incongruity, the texts known as Puranas contain terrifying accounts of the fate of souls of sinners, sandwiched between sections on – say – mineralogy and medicine' (ibid. p. 11). India, as well as the west, has promoted scientific development, but it has done so through religious preoccupations rather than through a specific institutional distinction between science and religion as in the west: 'In the Hindu case there is neither a secular nor a scientific realm apart from religion. The shastras contain the last word on both science and salvation. Religion encompasses the whole and there is consequently no space left for a domain governed by its own laws and investigated by rules and procedures of its own' (ibid. p. 25) such as Christianity allowed in the west.

A similar explanation can be offered for the views on western science expressed by many Iranian villagers. Science and religion are not demarcated into separate compartments as in the Christian west. While westerners are not considered to have 'stolen' the secrets of science from sacred texts, as Parry suggests some Hindus believe, they are thought to have abused the knowledge they have acquired partly in fact as a result of the very separation from a moral context that many westerners see as a positive characteristic of their ideology. Moreover, it is recognised (accurately to some extent) that a significant part of that knowledge does derive from Islamic learning. The overriding context for such descriptions is a moral one. The misuse of·this knowledge is conceived of primarily in terms of westerners having abandoned religious rules and morality to concentrate on material achievements alone. The western countries, which now controlled such remarkable resources and power, were morally bankrupt: they did not know how to use these things rightly. Once Muslims had learnt the technical skills, they could then assert their moral superiority in order to use them properly and the dominance of the west would then cease. Iran had fallen behind in such knowledge because it had itself gone through a period of moral decline, apparent for instance in the decadence of the Qajars, the ruling dynasty before the present Pahlavi regime. Elements of this decadence were still to be seen in the gross westernisation of modern cities, in the behaviour of youth, and in the unseemly dress of women who abandoned the veil for mini-skirts. Men wanted their male children to attend the westernised schools of the city in order for them to take over for Islam the achievements of science and technology which were currently being abused by the west.

This could be interpreted as a typical example of any 'in group' or culture setting itself above those it encounters and assimilating what it wants of foreign achievement without having to take on the accompanying ideology or surrender local beliefs. Certainly Iran has a long history of such assimilation and has been notably successful in doing so, as in the adoption of Islam itself from the Arabs while maintaining clear distinctions between Iranian and Arab culture. But the villagers with whom I discussed such matters were not content to see the failures which they ascribed to the west in simple, ethnocentric terms. They were searching, as it were, for universal principles by which to explain such problems and they appealed to 'reason' as much as to faith in doing so. It was in these terms that they continually asked me to explain to them why it was that westerners, whom they recognised to be able, intelligent and highly successful in many ways, could be so blind in such crucial matters and it was in these terms that they explained their own society's temporary 'backwardness'.

The men who had attended the 'maktab' were particularly eager to argue about and discuss these issues. They held a regular round of dinner meetings at their houses to which one of the mullahs would be invited and at which they both recited from sacred texts and discussed commentaries and their application to current circumstances, such as those I have been considering. Many of their pronouncements of 'belief' stemmed from such meetings which were, in a sense, a continuation of the 'maktab' tradition in which they had been trained. They did not represent these beliefs as matters of faith only but as recognisably rational and reasonable, such that anyone not previously exposed to them would be convinced once they were explained. It was this framework which led them to be so perplexed about western intellectuals and the 'unreasonableness' of some of their thinking.

The mullah on one occasion publicly represented this claim to rationality by announcing to a crowd gathered around us in the tea house as we discussed these issues that he would be obliged to convert to Christianity if my arguments proved stronger than his. No such event was, of course, likely but the claim serves to demonstrate the ideological framework within which those in the mullah's school represented their learning. The ideology can, perhaps, be explained to some extent by the pressures of the contemporary situation, in which western learning and its claims to 'objectivity' were being powerfully extolled by the Shah's regime. Also, of course, the knowledge in the village that I had taught in the University of Mashad and was a 'roshan fekr', a 'thinker', was a factor in the specific situations that I am able to describe. But, as I suggested above, there was already an argumentative, interpretative tradition in Shiite Islam which some of those who attended 'maktabs' were likely to have been socialised into and which contributed to the particular response to western culture that was evolving in such villages.

The description of a particular incident in which I was involved may bring out the point about the ideological pressure on villagers to present beliefs and rules as reasonable. It also illustrates the variety of interpretation to be found, not only in Islam in general, as Hodgson suggests, but also within a single village. There were two public bath houses (hammams) in the village, one at the higher part and one built more recently by those who lived in the valley bottom, near the tea house in which I was staying. From 1970 onwards I had made regular use of the men's sections of these. One would undress discreetly in an outer room of a bath house, where a towel would be provided to cover one's sexual parts and then enter the main steam-filled chamber. In this chamber there was a line of separate shower cubicles and around the sides of the other walls were hot-water taps. One would sit by a tap, rub soap on oneself with a rough cloth and then douse oneself in hot water from a rubber bucket filled at the tap. Frequently friends would take it in turns to wash each other and then tip water over each other and the atmosphere was friendly and sociable. Over the years I often joined in these activities with friends, chatting pleasantly while we washed and doused one another. On the occasion I am presently concerned with, in autumn 1977, I had finished my wash in the bath house at the higher part of the village and was returning through the entrance from the bath-room to the changing-room, when the younger of the two mullah brothers appeared in the changing-room and created a dramatic scene. He ordered me to stop where I was, shouted at others in the room to provide a number of towels to lay on the floor in front of me on a line to the door, pulled everyone back, and then made me walk across the towels and into the corridor to the outer door. He bundled my clothes after me and told me to get out of the bath house and never to use it again. He continued to express considerable anger and shouted at the others, especially the man in charge, for letting me in.

Later, in the tea house, I complained to people I knew. A range of responses was evident. A good friend of mine, Joseph, who was shortly to marry the daughter of the mullah's brother, became extremely angry and rushed to the steps of the lower hammam, from which he shouted out that I should be allowed entry and that he would fight anyone who refused me, and it was only with difficulty that I restrained him. Another man commented critically on the mullah and suggested that I should wait until things had quietened down and then just use the bottom hammam, where I was better known. He also suggested, in keeping with his pragmatic outlook, that I should use it at quieter times so as not to upset the 'religious' people. The keeper of the lower bath house said that he did not mind me coming in himself, but he was frightened of the mullah and did not want to lose his job.

One of the 'religious' men, with whom I frequently had discussions and who was always friendly, if indulgent, of my theological wrongheadedness, tried to explain to me through metaphors the reason for the mullah's concern. He picked up some dust from the ground and let it slip through his fingers, pointing out how easily it ran away. Then he pointed to some mud which was being mixed ready to be stuck on the side of a house and said that it differed from the dry dust in that it would 'stick' ('chasp') to his hand and not run away easily. This, he said, was comparable to the water which had been on my body in the hammam. Being uncircumcised, my body was polluted ('najes'). In normal daily contact, when I was 'dry', my pollution was like the dust and simply ran off me without 'sticking' to anyone else. In the bath house, however, the water on my body made the pollution contagious – it would 'stick' to others who came into contact with it. A circumcised Muslim must therefore avoid washing in the same place as me. This was why the mullah had been so excited and had to carefully prepare a path of towels for my exit from the hammam.

The mullah himself came down to the tea house that evening and held a public discussion about the incident. He explained that if I were converted to Islam and got circumcised then I could use the bath house; he would be willing to go to a hospital in Mashad with me to have it done. He had heard of many Americans who had been converted, including famous academics who now used their Muslim names and were an example to others.

One function of this public address was to ensure that villagers who did not know what was going on, or did not care, would enforce the ban on my using the hammam. Indeed, one person whom I knew well said that he had not realised before, and so had not objected to my using the bath house, but now he understood the truth and accepted the mullah's word, unfortunate though it was for me. The mullah was clearly attempting to establish his authority on the villagers by both creating the incident and then making public comments on it in this way. He was the younger of the two mullahs who ran the 'maktab' and had always seemed to me to be in the shadow of his calmer and more respected brother. If he put down and even could convert a westerner then he would greatly increase his prestige in the village, and come out from under the shadow. He would also prove the power of his own arguments since I, the westerner, was a university teacher who would need convincing. His whole discussion was presented in terms of such rational argumentation and it was on this that he was staking his future prestige. His mention of 'najes', in fact, had already embarrassed a number of people who felt that it was discourteous to a guest and a friend to apply this term. When a young boy shouted out 'najes' during the discussions, an older man grabbed him and pushed him roughly aside to save my feelings. The mullah obviously felt obliged to put the issue into a more neutral and less socially charged context and so appealed to a rationalistic and academic framework for support. He explained to everyone that the rules about pollution were to be found in a religious book that he would produce to show me, and that they simply followed the logic of the beliefs they all held. As an academic, I could not fail to be persuaded: there was no personal comment in all of this and he was only trying to make things clear to everyone.

A little while later my friend Joseph married the elder mullah's daughter and he invited me to the feast afterwards in the house which the mullahs shared. The younger mullah made great play of the fact that he was happy to welcome me as a guest to his house and of his respect for western scholars. The hammam incident, he repeated, was based on the rules of Islam and was not to be interpreted as a personal gesture to me, whom he considered a friend. Later in the evening, when a number of us were gathered in one room, those left being mainly the men who had been educated at his 'maktab', he produced a copy of the book he had mentioned, called 'Tosi ol Mosa'el', and read out the relevant passages on pollution. The book was occasionally used in the 'maktab', mostly for the more advanced students, and was, in fact, a recent commentary by an Islamic scholar from Esphahan. It consisted mainly of a series of explanations of key concepts and rules and was, I was told, known to be used in the theological college at which the mullah had trained.

The use of such a text to claim authority for specific rules and interpretations reinforces what Parry said about the way in which literacy can both serve to justify the claim that there is only one interpretation and at the same time facilitate the range of interpretation that anthropologists find in practice. For each interpretation can claim to be more than just individual perception: the appeal to a written text claims an authority that insulates the interpretation from the apparent volatility of the oral mode of communication. Parry's point was that Goody was overstating the difference between written and oral traditions. Where Goody saw the oral tradition as malleable and volatile and the written as 'fixed', Parry suggests that in the Indian case there is considerable scope for 'fixing' the oral tradition, through remembrancers etc., while the written texts are malleable and open to a constant process of change. The situation that I am describing in Cheshmeh suggests that in some areas at least the Islamic literate tradition may be similar in that the texts are more malleable than either Muslims themselves or many outside commentators have led people to believe.

The fact that some villagers had acquired literacy in the 'maktab' did not, as Goody would seem to expect, lead to a 'fixing' and lack of adaptability in stories and commentaries. The ability of the young mullah to introduce a written commentary did not prevent alternative interpretations, as we have seen in the case of the hammam incident. The mullah himself certainly attempted to play on the authority of writing to attempt to privilege his own position, but this was a political process, not the consequence of the intrinsic qualities of writing. At the time that I am describing, the mullah had clearly not succeeded in convincing everyone. Indeed those who had read more or less than him were probably the most sceptical, if for different reasons, while within the circle of 'maktab' literates itself there was scope for imaginative play upon the meanings being offered and not just fixed reproduction of the word as handed down.

In the Mullah Nasr-ed-Din story cited above (pp. 142–4) the boys only learnt to read. In the 'maktab' in Cheshmeh there was a variety of literacy practices. While some simply learnt to recognise the words on the page as a sort of mnemonic for stimulating recitation of passages, many learnt to read in Arabic and Farsi and used their skills to read other texts than the Koran. Some developed skills in interpretation and argument and some learnt to elaborate on basic themes and to express their 'meaning in various forms'. A few learnt the rudiments of writing.

The ideological framework within which these practices occurred and in particular the scope for flexibility that I have been describing, was an important factor in the ability of Cheshmehis to adapt their 'maktab' literacy to the demands of marketing and commerce during the 1970s and so to develop a new 'commercial' literacy. In order to compare 'maktab' literacy with the new kinds of literacy that some Iranians were developing during the 1970s, we require a framework for describing the particular features and abilities associated with these different literacies. This framework cannot, for reasons I have tried to outline, rest on traditional assumptions about the 'technical' nature of literacy skills; these 'skills' are, in fact, social skills, not neutral, 'autonomous' ones and so the framework for generalisation and comparison must be a broader, more open-ended one than that offered by exponents of the 'autonomous' model of literacy.

A useful starting point for developing such a framework, which might be fruitfully adapted to the Iranian material, is provided by the Adult Literacy and Basic Skills Unit (ALBSU) in the UK. This unit is attempting to develop concepts for approaching the practical questions associated with literacy acquisition, training and assessment which complement in many ways what I term the 'ideological' model of literacy. As part of the advice given to teachers of literacy to adults, one of ALBSU's booklets suggests a 'list of literacy skills' (ALBSU, 1981, Ch. 2). The authors go out of their way to emphasise that such a list is only tentative, that the teacher and students may add their own, and that it can never be exhaustive. Since reading and writing are seen as essentially *activities*, undertaken for specific purposes, rather than simply as forms or 'mediums', then what is involved in 'literacy' will constantly change according to the needs and interests of those using it: 'No one ever gets to be "absolutely literate" – the idea is ridiculous' (ibid. p. 14).

Some of the skills described in this list can be usefully referred to in explicating what is involved in 'maktab' literacy in Iran. At the most basic level, this literacy provides knowledge of what the ALBSU 'list' calls 'understanding links between speech and print'. Students at the 'maktab' in Cheshmeh were made aware of the crucial point that sounds are represented by letters or combinations of letters and even those who got little beyond rote learning had also to learn some further complexities to be found in Arabic script. The Arabic alphabet, used in Farsi with minor variations, provides a number of different forms for the same letter, according to whether it appears at the beginning, middle or end of a word. A reader has to know and be able to recognise these different forms in order to discriminate words as units from strings of letters and to distinguish one word from another in the script before him. Furthermore, in some written conventions of Arabic script, which a 'maktab' student was likely to encounter, there is little or no use of punctuation so that knowledge of such differences has also to be used to determine where a sentence begins and ends. These are precise skills different, for instance, from those necessary for reading the Latin alphabet, where these functions are generally fulfilled by punctuation marks and the use of capitalisation. Moreover, just as Cole and Scribner observed that the specific skills acquired by those who were literate in Vai script were transferrable to other tasks, so the specific skills imparted by 'maktab' literacy were transferrable to new literacies, developed for new functions, as in the case of 'commercial' literacy discussed below (Chapter 6).

'Maktab' students also learnt other features of the 'link between speech and print'. They learnt, of course, the basic convention that Arabic script has to be read from right to left and from top to bottom of a page and they also learnt of more complex conventions regarding layout and presentation. Many of the texts used in the mullah's school displayed more complex layouts than the familiar, straight parallel lines of letters, words and sentences, evident on this page of print. The page in the religious texts and commentaries used in the 'maktab' is often broken up in various ways: blocks of words may be set at different angles, they may be placed in the margins or across corners of the page, and different kinds of print and lettering may be used for different purposes. In some cases, words in the margins may represent a commentary on the 'main' text that is constructed more familiarly across the middle of the page. Students thus learn that different conventions of written representation may indicate different levels or categories of meaning within the text: that 'meaning' is contained not only in the content of the language itself but also in the form, layout and conventions of its presentation.

This is one aspect of literacy knowledge that teachers in the adult literacy programme in the UK realise is seldom taught in English schools. Some students may pick up such knowledge implicitly, but many, not having been brought to realise that such a possibility exists, may go through life lacking the skill associated with it. In some cases, where such skills are necessary for specific functions, the lack of them may lead to real practical problems and to the individual being labelled 'illiterate', even though he or she may have a lot of other 'literacy skills'. By these criteria, then, 'maktab' students cannot be deemed 'illiterate', although they may well appear so in government and formal school tests designed to examine other, less 'hidden' skills. What students of the 'maktab' in Cheshmeh acquired as part of their 'maktab' literacy was not an obvious, or even a universal, aspect of literacy skills: it was a specific skill derived from the specific nature of the literacy materials they used and of the context of learning in which they encountered them.

It is in this sense that I am suggesting that the 'literacies' acquired in different contexts may be quite different, or conversely, may have similarities at levels that have not been recognised. Many of the characteristics traditionally associated with literacy may rest on superficial identifications of features relevant to the investigator's own literacy conventions but inappropriate for more universal statements. Conversely, many of the characteristics associated with different literacies may remain hidden and so have not been available as a basis for cross-cultural comparison (or, of course, for testing). For instance, some of the skills acquired in learning literacy in an English school context are hidden skills, not explicitly addressed by the teachers at all. According to ALBSU, many of the English children who arrive at school with a working knowledge of the alphabet have not done so because of the explicit teaching of the letters undertaken by conscientious parents, but because 'parents have done lots of other things which convey the message and have got their children so interested in reading that the process got started without any conscious effort' (ALBSU, 1981, p. 22). Many of the literacy skills learnt in the Iranian 'maktab' have been acquired in the same way, through implicit, often hidden, frameworks stimulated by specific commitment to and interest in the message contained in the texts they encounter. A number of students of the 'maktab' were genuinely inquiring about their religion, its history and its relevance to the current situation, and this stimulated their development of specific literacy skills associated with the religious texts used by their teachers. They were not taught explicitly about the relevance of format, layout and page design for 'meaning', but they became familiar with these concepts implicitly, just as children in the English context picked up from their parents a number of 'hidden' literacy skills even while their parents thought that they were teaching them different ones.

The ALBSU 'list' also refers to some of the hidden skills employed in using a text as a whole. It cites, for instance, 'using clues that help you to thumb a text for specific information'. One may elaborate this, in terms of the kinds of skills referred to earlier (Chapter 3) as part of the 'academic literacy' taught in English universities. Students there are taught to 'read' a text by skipping bits, searching forwards and backwards, using contents and index and focussing on what is required for specific purposes rather than simply reading from beginning to end. Teachers in universities have no little difficulty imparting these skills to students, which suggests that they are not a prominent part of earlier stages of English education. Students of the 'maktab', on the other hand, become relatively familiar with such forms of non-sequential reading. In the 'maktab', and in the reading sessions outside which some 'maktab' students attend, the purpose for which they have learnt reading itself entails also learning skills of selection and of 'thumbing' texts. Cheshmehis, meeting in each other's houses over dinner, for instance, to recite and discuss sacred texts, would choose suras of the Koran according to events and issues of immediate relevance. During my stay they would often choose suras on Mary and Christ, in order to confront me with them the next day and challenge the Christian view of them. Students with such purposes in mind learnt, then, to 'thumb' their way around the Koran and other texts and to use headings and contents pages as clues to finding specific passages. The suras of the Koran are numbered and most texts have a page listing their names and giving page references. As with skills in recognising layout and format, so these retrieval skills are learnt implicitly and because they serve a specific purpose, rather than explicitly, formally or for a general pedagogic rationale.

These particular skills associated with 'maktab' literacy were amongst those which were later transferred by some Cheshmehis to 'commercial' literacy and which served those purposes particularly well. In the change from one literacy to another, some of the skills previously acquired are appropriate and can be adapted to the new literacy, while others may atrophy and, without relevance or function, be forgotten. This reinforces the ALBSU advice to teachers of literacy to adults that they bear in mind not only the 'range of opportunities the printed word opens up', since this can be limitless, but more precisely 'its links with their [students'] own background knowledge and experiences' (ALBSU, 1981, p. 6). This approach requires the teacher to do more than simply offer a formal training in the 'medium': it recognises that the 'medium' is meaningless if divorced from the 'messages' of the specific literacy being imparted and their relation to specific purposes and more general cultural values (ibid. p. 13). A literacy teacher cannot construct a basic, technical model of literacy skill and assume that needs and interests can be added afterwards. Rather, it is the other way around: different needs and interests lead to new and different 'skills'. It is in this sense that the list of 'literacy skills' offered by ALBSU, and which I am adapting to my present purposes, is a list of 'social skills'. It is in this sense, too, that the skills acquired by students of the 'maktab' in Cheshmeh are properly called 'ideological'.

The ALBSU type skills which we have so far applied to the 'maktab' – 'understanding the specific links between speech and print'; the significance of format, layout and conventions of presentation for meaning; and the skill of 'non-sequential reading' – are all related directly to the purposes for which students came together in 'maktabs' and in reading sessions at village dinner parties. The 'skills' only acquired meaning for their exponents in these contexts – those of the Islamic tradition and of Iranian village values and 'ideology'.

This emphasis on the 'ideological' rather than the supposed 'technical' nature of literacy and its associated skills and abilities has recently been given strong support by an American educational linguist, S. B. Heath, whose work I examined above (pp. 121–5). Her analysis of the different literacy-related abilities and tendencies that were developed in three communities in south-east USA, provides both an elaboration and a 'fleshing out', as it were, of the list of social–literacy skills provided by ALBSU and provides helpful terms of reference for examining the ways in which students of the Iranian 'maktab' were socialised into the uses of literacy. In Iran, too, hidden pedagogic processes and 'ways of taking meaning from books' can tell us a great deal about how specific beliefs and values are acquired and reinforced and how the components of an ideology are built up. On the one hand, like Heath's Mainstream children, those in the 'maktab' were learning attention to books and were being conditioned to apply the information and attitudes learnt in that context to daily life and non-literacy experience. Ways of framing the world orally were being affected and to some extent shaped by the experience of books. On the other hand, the experience of 'maktab' students was like that of Roadville children, in that the content of the books they were exposed to concerned mostly 'true' events, largely incidents in the lives of holy men, described in a religious context in order to impart a moral message and similarly constrained by naturalistic conventions. It was in their learning of these conventions and how to employ them appropriately in social contexts that students learnt the hidden ideological assumptions of their culture, notably in these particular examples, assumptions regarding the connection between story-telling and morality. While the teacher's primary task in both cases was to bring his students to remember the stories and their messages, in fact he was also socialising them into specific, ideologically-based, 'literate mentalities' that carried over into oral contexts. Like the children in Roadville, young 'maktab' students learnt from their literacy training to think of stories as 'true' events and to look for moral truths in them and, conversely, they learnt to frame their moral sense in terms of such stories. Although conventions concerning how and when story-telling was appropriate were less rigid in Cheshmeh than it appears to have been in Roadville, nevertheless there were similar formal rules and expectations about their truth value and purpose. In both cases such rules and expectations were learnt through the particular ways in which literacy was 'taken' and in both cases they articulated with deeper aspects of the community's ideology.

Some of the specific social–literacy skills being learnt in the 'maktab' correspond to those described by Heath for Maintown children, others to those evident in Roadville or Trackton, while still others require different terms for their analysis and description than were appropriate for these small towns in America. 'Maktab' students, for instance, unlike any of Heath's subjects, learnt from their books, to express and develop their moral sense in terms of argumentation and dispute. The suras of the Koran and the commentaries taught in the 'maktab' explicitly raise and confront 'false' arguments in order to dismiss them and students learnt forms of expression and styles of dialogue from this that they carried over into oral discourse. Ways of thinking and talking that were derived from books, and from how students learnt both to approach books and to interpret and display the knowledge acquired from them, framed and coloured oral discourse in the village. The study of the acquisition of literacy is, then, directly relevant to understanding the uses of language and ideology in non-literate contexts in such a community. One of Heath's crucial questions was 'Just how does what is frequently termed "the literate tradition" envelop the child in knowledge about interrelationships between oral and written language?' (ibid. p. 50). How, she asks, does a reader make use of books for the representation and interpretation of everyday experience and knowledge?

In order to answer such questions she was obliged to examine not only 'hidden' literacy processes and 'skills' of the kind identified by ALBSU, but also more fundamental aspects of the community's language and ideology. Similarly an exposition of literacy in Cheshmeh has required further elaboration of the culture which gave it meaning and to which, in Heath's terms, it gave meaning. In relation to 'maktab' literacy this demanded some analysis of the particular form of the Islamic tradition to be found there and analysis of the ideas and arguments of those who learnt their literacy within this framework.

I now turn to an application of these concepts of literacy to what I term 'commercial' literacy, as it was manifest in Cheshmeh and other mountain villages in Khorosan Province during the 1970s. Using the framework developed here, with reference to the 'literacy skills' described by ALBSU, the 'hidden literacy' elaborated by Heath and the more general features of what I have termed an 'ideological' model of literacy, I shall now attempt to provide a description and analysis of this 'commercial' literacy and to consider how it developed out of, but differed from, the 'maktab' literacy that has been the subject of this chapter. The exposition of what 'literacy' means to those who practise this particular form of it will require specific and detailed description of the trading and economic processes of the village. This exposition and description will form the basis of the next chapter.

6

'COMMERCIAL' LITERACY

In order to investigate the nature of what I term 'commercial' literacy, I shall firstly describe more fully the structure and organisation of the kind of villages in which it occurs and outline their relationship to general developments in Iran during the 1970s.

Under the Shah's regime in Iran agriculture was downgraded. Investment was concentrated in urban, industrial programmes (cf. Halliday, 1979; Keddie, 1979) while rural areas declined to the extent that, by the end of his reign, the country was importing foodstuffs that it had traditionally exported (cf. Keddie, 1968, 1972 and 1979; Lambton, 1963 and 1969; McLachlan, 1968). The decline was not, however, uniform and mountain, fruit-growing villages like Cheshmeh successfully expanded their production during this period. Strangely enough this was a sector of the economy that was organised on the basis of individual small-holdings, a system generally considered less appropriate for adapting to modernisation with its large-scale demand than landlord and tenant systems which classically lend themselves to agricultural industrialisation. Lambton, for instance, has written: 'Where grain land is concerned it is probably true that the maximum productivity is not achieved where the land is split up into small holdings ... The natural conditions under which agriculture is carried out would seem on the whole to favour large landed proprietorship.' (1963, p. 28.) During the boom of the early and mid-1970s, following the oil price rises, it was small-holding, mountain fruit-croppers who were better placed to respond to the leap in urban demand for agricultural products than were the peasants of the grain-producing plains.

There are a number of factors which contribute to the ability of such villages to adapt to the new conditions. Lambton, for instance, points out that her generalisation does not apply to them: 'Where the main income is not grain but fruit ... it is doubtful whether productivity rises with the number of large landed estates.' (ibid.) When fruit-cropping is undertaken on a relatively small scale, and within such a structure of small-holdings, it is easily adaptable to increases in demand: production can be increased without major structural changes. Improvements require only small machinery such as spraying equipment, packaging materials etc. which individual owners can afford in a way they could not the expensive tractors and combines now essential to cash-cropping in the grain-producing plains. Moreover, fruit is not an immediate subsistence crop, as wheat can be: it entails the development of an exchange system, with some transport and organisation. The existence of such a system means that fruit-growing villages are institutionally more adaptable to cash-cropping and the demands of a modern economy than those which have traditionally produced mainly subsistence crops. A further factor was the residential flexibility of fruit-growing villagers: Cheshmehis, for instance, were able to migrate to urban centres for part of the year and still maintain their village holdings on a part-time, part-year basis.

In plains villages, on the other hand, the means of production had been concentrated in the hands of a few, distribution was less developed, residence more fixed and increases in production required more radical changes in plant and equipment. It was because of these structural and organisational differences that the response to the oil-money boom of the 1970s was different in the plains and the mountain villages.

The main thrust of my argument, however, is that a significant factor in enabling villages with the infrastructural advantages I have noted to actually cash in on the economic possibilities provided by the 1970s boom was the fact that a number of them had previously developed specific literacy practices and skills. This basis in 'maktab' literacy, as I have described it in Chapter 5, facilitated the development of a new 'commercial' literacy practice and associated skills. It was the presence of this practice and these skills, together with the advantages given by the organisation of small-holdings and the distribution system, that enabled the mountain economy to 'take off' in a way that did not happen in plains villages in the same area. The contrast between mountain and plains villages, then, helps to clarify what is meant by saying that literacy is an 'enabling' rather than a 'causal' factor. 'Maktab' literacy in Cheshmeh facilitated the development of 'commercial' literacy and 'commercial' literacy 'enabled' economic growth. The fact that literacy 'in itself' was not the *cause* of this growth is apparent from comparison of the structural features of the two kinds of village. The lack of these infrastructural features meant that economic growth in the plains villages was less developed and as a result 'maktab' literacy there did not develop into 'commercial' literacy. On the other hand, the presence of these features alone does not explain the economic growth of the mountain villages. In Cheshmeh such growth required also the mediating skills associated with 'commercial' literacy and they, in turn, rested on the prior development of 'maktab' literacy. While, then, I hope to employ knowledge of the different literacy practices in Iranian villages in order to illuminate the processes of change there, I do so within a framework of analysis that rejects mono-causal explanation and that recognises the interconnection of structural and ideological features in generating social change in the villages concerned.

I begin with a description of the social and economic structure of one mountain village and will then attempt to relate these features to the literacy practices I have been describing and to new practices that were developing during my stay there. In particular I shall attempt to identify the elements of 'maktab' literacy to be found within what I term 'commercial' literacy and to suggest· the extent to which knowledge of the former facilitated development of the latter. In the course of this analysis I shall introduce evidence from plains villages in the same area for purposes of comparison and to provide a basis for assessing how significant the particular literacy practices I am describing were in 'enabling' certain changes to take place.

Cheshmeh

Cheshmeh is a village in the Kuh-i-Binalud mountains west of Mashad, the capital city of Khorosan Province in North East Iran. It is situated in a deep valley about two hours drive from the city along a rough mountain track. The houses are built up the south-facing hillside, stacked on top of each other such that the flat roof of one is the courtyard of the one above. On the opposite side of the valley and for miles upstream and downstream are dense orchards, divided by dry-stone walls and irrigated by 'jubes' or water channels running along the hillside. Below the 'jube' is fertile land, above it is dry and barren.

The crop patterns, determined both by the seasons and by social decisions about what to grow and how to use it, provide the framework for the annual work cycles and for residence patterns.

Crop and Work Cycles

During the winter months heavy snow lies on the ground and no work can be done in the orchards. Apples are taken from the stores for sale in the city when conditions allow, the last being sold for the 'Noh Ruz' (New Year) holiday commencing on 21 March. By the end of this two-week holiday period the snows are melting and it is raining a great deal. Damage done to trees, water channels, walls and river banks by snow and floods is repaired at this time, paths are relaid and new trees planted, while work is also done on houses. During April, manure from the winter stables of animals now in the higher hills is carried to the orchards and spread on the earth, while donkeys carry paraffin-driven motors to the orchards to spray trees against worms. By May it becomes necessary to irrigate the orchards, each owner taking water from the 'jube' according to a cycle worked out by the water foreman or 'mir ab'. For those who have a number of orchards this can be a time-consuming task as each one requires irrigating on average every eight to twelve days. However, a good deal of the week is still spent by many men sitting around in groups at favoured spots or strolling through the orchards for relaxation as well as work.

In June some families move into houses in the orchards to be handier for fruit-picking, irrigating etc. and they stay there until autumn. By early July the first cherries are being picked and from then until autumn some fruit will always be ripening and the pace of work is relatively intense. After the cherries of June come the 'albalou' (sour cherries) of early July, then pears and peaches until late August when the summer apples ripen. The work involves picking the different fruits and then carrying, selecting, boxing and either storing them or transporting them immediately to town. Nevertheless, even at this period men can still spend two or three days a week or more sitting around talking, the intensity of each family's effort depending on the number and kind of orchards they own, whether they work for others as well as themselves or have workers employed in their orchards, and whether they have additional interests such as a saw mill, tea house, carpet factory, shop etc. At the height of the season of fruit-picking, August through September (and in cases of winter apples for storage, into October), this same pattern continues: brief periods of intense work followed, for the men at least, by more relaxed times, the pattern of work being decided by each owner within the constraints of his situation, of fruit-ripening and of irrigation cycles.

In September walnuts and winter apples are ready and the final storing and clearing up takes place. From mid-October until the following spring very little work is done in the village and some families move to the city. Those who stay in the village for the winter move their sheep and goats down from the high hills and put them in stables, often directly below the living quarters. Families sit around a 'corsee', a tray of charcoal placed in the middle of the room and covered by a large quilt spread across people's knees to the walls, to keep the heat in. Men continue their social life at the tea house and at each other's houses.

Residence Cycles

It is feasible for an orchard owner to live in Mashad during the slack winter season and to visit Cheshmeh only occasionally to keep an eye on his land. A number of these families have a house in their orchard rather than in the village itself and they live there only in the pleasant summer months as a kind of rural retreat. The extra intensive labour necessary for periods of a few days at a time as each fruit ripens can often be provided by a man's own family, including schoolchildren visiting on holidays or taken away from school, or by hired labour if he can afford it. Other families live permanently in the village and visit the city only occasionally, staying with relatives there. Those with interests other than orchards, such as shop owners or trade specialists like butchers or tailors, often fall into this category. Most residence patterns vary between these two extremes.

There is thus no clear-cut, geographical boundary demarcating the social unit that comprises (or the social units that comprise) Cheshmeh. To speak of Cheshmeh is to refer to different groups of people in different contexts. Indeed, some families who have only orchard houses outside the village may not consider themselves to be 'Cheshmehis' at all. However, their participation in land that is considered by villagers to be part of Cheshmeh necessitates their inclusion, particularly when we are referring to such aspects of village social structure as access to and control of the means of production and exchange. It is in this light that the census figures for the village of Cheshmeh, giving a population of 10,000, should be viewed. When I refer to Cheshmeh and Cheshmehis, then, I am identifying systems of social organisation rather than corporate groups of people.

Ownership of Land and Materials

Most Cheshmehis own at least a few orchards and there is practically no one who is simply a landless labourer. Some also own donkeys and mules necessary for the transport of fruit from orchards higher up the valley, where trucks cannot go. A few have their own trucks and lorries for transporting the fruit from the village to Mashad or even further afield. Stores, spraying machines and all of the equipment that goes with packing and handling fruit (boxes, rubber buckets, props for laden branches etc.) are also individually owned. In some cases this equipment is bought outright, in others it is made from primary products by the farmer himself: most orchards, for instance, contain a few poplar trees from which wood products are obtained.

Although land can be bought and sold, Cheshmehis do not like orchards to go to 'outsiders' and most land changes hands through inheritance. According to Islamic law (and Cheshmeh is 'orthodox' in this respect) a father will divide his goods amongst his children in the ratio two parts for each son to one part for each daughter. A man will give a child his or her share at their marriage though he may retain a portion for himself until he is too old to work it. It is thus difficult for anyone who cannot trace descent to a land-owning Cheshmehi to set up as a farmer in the village. As with all peasant small-holdings, the land does not in practice get divided up quite so neatly as the mathematical formula demands.

One problem that strict adherence to the formula would create would be the need to constantly shift the physical barriers that demarcate orchard plots each time land was distributed to larger or smaller numbers of inheritors. Since this demarcation is materially embodied in dry-stone walls or water channels directed vertically down the hillside from the 'jubes' above, then constant realignment would entail substantial material activity. To avoid this some brothers may organise their orchards as 'sherkat' (lit. 'company'), that is in combination, sharing the work, irrigation charges, transport and other costs and splitting the proceeds. A more common procedure recently has been for one or more brothers to go to Mashad, to pursue their education and get a job, leaving their portion to be worked by those who remain. They may return at weekends and during vacations to help in the orchards, both their own and those of their family, particularly for the periods of most intense work. They thereby keep a foothold in the village against city insecurity (cf. Parkin, 1975) at the same time as providing the flexible source of labour required by those who remain. The eventual distribution of the proceeds in these circumstances varies according to family and individual agreements.

When a woman marries she takes her portion with her, but it is usually under the control of her husband and becomes merged with the family land for purposes of subsequent inheritance. Some women, however, attempt to maintain greater control over their portion and to maintain its separate identity. An orchard may often serve as the bride's 'mahrieh', the dowry she brings to the marriage but which must be returned to her father's family if the marriage breaks down. Some divorced women and widows use this right in land to provide an independent base for themselves, rather than having to return to their natal family. This is rare, however, and they are subject to accusations of prostitution by men who conceive of women as wives, mothers or daughters, the residual category being 'whore'.

Labour

The labour that goes into production is organised and controlled rather differently than are the means of production themselves. The individual owner and his wife and children usually work their own orchards: at the height of the fruit season this may involve living in an orchard house and working from dawn to sunset picking fruit, putting it into panniers and carrying it to stores on donkeys, although, as I suggested above, this intense pattern is seldom sustained for more than a few days and men in particular are likely to retire frequently to the tea house. Their wives, apart from participating in all of the fruit-picking activities, are also obliged to provide meals and to organise the home which may involve transporting blankets etc. to the orchard house, keeping a samovar bubbling and looking after children and small babies. Children may help out in the orchards of their relatives and men may exchange labour at times, although it is more common for one to sell his labour to another for a set fee. Although practically everyone owns some orchards, so that no one is only a labourer, there are some who own so few orchards that they are obliged to work for others to make a living. Village stratification is drawn along these lines: the highest strata consist of large land owners who do no orchard labour of their own, while the lowest consist of some landless labourers from other areas who have been imported as permanent servants.

Communal Ownership of Water and Utilities

While the primary means of production, orchards, are individually owned, mainly through inheritance, and labour power is either controlled by the labourer himself or bought and sold, the other major component of the production process, water, is communally owned. Without the 'jubes' that run along the hillsides from many miles upstream, most of the valley could not be fertile. Cheshmehis say that these 'jubes' were built as much as one hundred years ago and that the main ones were a communal enterprise. In recent times individuals have made side valleys fertile by building their own 'jubes' there and then planting private orchards, but this mode of operation is less feasible as regards the large jubes which serve the main valley and which provide water for probably 80% of Cheshmehi orchards. There were various examples of the communal mode of operation during my stay, in relation to such public enterprises as the building of mosques, roads and a bath house, and these may serve as a helpful pointer to the way in which the main 'jubes' were built in the past. The construction of a 'hammam' or bath house in 1972 provides a particularly vivid example.

Those living at the bottom of the village decided that they wanted their own 'hammam', rather than climbing up to the one higher up. A few men organised a collection, going around the tea house and the homes culling cheques and promissory notes from individuals according to what they could afford, which on occasion was as much as 50,000 rials (£2,500). Each donation was carefully recorded and publicly announced and the list of donors was frequently displayed. With this money, outside specialists were hired for the construction work. When the building was complete it blocked the main path up the valley, so one Friday morning a crowd of men and boys proceeded to rebuild the path out over the stream. It was a complex piece of engineering, accomplished at a feverish pace amidst apparent chaos, although one or two respected figures appeared to be in control of the more technical aspects. One could certainly imagine the 'jubes' being built in this way, as the Cheshmehis claim, although there is little definite information about this. What these events do illustrate is that some areas of village life do operate in terms of pooled labour, even while others such as landholding and fruit distribution are more individualistic and, in the latter case, distinctly entrepreneurial.

The allocation of water from a 'jube' to the orchard below is also conducted on a communal basis, although in a more organised way and with specific office holders allocated and paid a fee. A 'mir ab' or water foreman is appointed annually to each 'jube' by a meeting of all those with orchards bordering a particular 'jube' and he is responsible for indicating the times at which water may be taken by each owner in turn. As I mentioned above, an orchard has to be irrigated about every eight to twelve days in the summer, though this varies from year to year according to the rainfall earlier that year. There are five main 'jubes', three on one hillside and two on the opposite one, and it is not always easy to find enough people to take on the five posts. The recompense is not large – a fee paid in proportion to the size of each orchard bordering the 'jube' – and the 'mir ab' frequently has to deal with disputes as owners take water at the wrong time or for too long. He also has to attend to his own orchards.

What is important about this system of organising water distribution is that it remains outside individual control. It ensures that those higher up the valley, for instance, cannot withhold water from those lower down. This would effectively give control over land and orchards since they are useless without irrigation. The system may allow individual cases of greed and deception to slip by, such as the payment of a bribe to the water foreman, but this same system prevents these cases being expanded into control of the supply as a whole. If a man were noticeably depriving those lower down the valley of water, then they would combine together to free the supply. The technology is simple enough, involving damming up one side of the 'jube' where it flows above one orchard and undamming it above another.

The fact that fifty or sixty people might have orchards along a single 'jube' ensures the political feasibility of this maintenance of communal interests. If the 'mir ab' were seen to be colluding in a significant reduction in supply to those lower down, then he would be sacked and possibly beaten up. Over the years fights have broken out over water, sometimes on a large scale and leading to deaths and serious injury. These fights, however, have remained fragmentary, their individual character representing no challenge to the system as a whole, and, where they have involved a group resisting one individual's depredations, they have actually served to reinforce the communal nature of the system. Moreover, numerous individuals have orchards at different points along a 'jube's' course so that blocking water to another individual's land below one's own might well mean blocking water also to one's other orchards lower down the valley: on these steep hillsides there is no way of diverting the water courses to bypass particular orchards. No one individual controls a large enough consolidated block of higher orchards to exert significant dominance over the water supply from a particular 'jube' and the land dependent on it. It is, then, difficult to envisage, and I saw no evidence of, a permanent faction controlling the water supply. The communal ownership of water, and its distribution through a system of jointly elected and controlled water foremen, represents a structural response to the requirements of individual small-holding in such a physical setting and serves to support and maintain that form of ownership and control.

Distribution and Exchange in Mountain Villages
The production of fruit entails the development of a system of exchange whereby subsistence goods and necessities can be obtained in return for the fruit. It therefore requires a more developed organisational structure, including liaison with transport facilities, than production for subsistence. Moreover, as we have seen, where production has been for some time on an individual, small-holding basis, it will have developed some communal organisation of irrigation and utilities.

In Cheshmeh both this organisation and the system of exchange were well developed. Many producers took fruit to dealers in Mashad themselves, or they had arrangements with a Tehran dealer. In the latter case, the boxes of fruit would be despatched from the village and recorded and the Tehran dealer totted up the amounts over the months with occasional checks by Cheshmehis travelling to the city, until the 'Noh Ruz' holiday when the producer went to collect his dues. These men handled trade in a 'hard-nosed' and sophisticated manner and were not disadvantaged in the way that various writers have observed was the case for the new peasant small-holders in the plains. In recent years, in fact, the scale and range of the operation have been considerably enlarged while production and ownership have been maintained in the hands of individuals.

The 'Tajer'
During the 1970s there was one important development that was altering the system of exchange, though without at that time radically changing the system of ownership and production. This was the development of the role of the village 'tajer' or entrepreneur. The 'tajer' bought fruit at an agreed rate from fellow villagers, who then took it to his stores as it was picked. There it was weighed and accounts were drawn up: the parties would negotiate whether the producer would be paid when his whole harvest or all of a particular fruit was in the store, or after the 'tajer' had himself been paid by city dealers. The 'tajer', whose stores in summer would be bulging with the produce of various villagers and, more recently, also with fruit bought from other villages too, would take bulk loads to town where he had arrangements with wholesalers to whom he sold at considerable profit. Ali Dadkha, for instance, bought peaches in Cheshmeh in 1977 at 20 rials per kilo and sold them in Mashad at 25 to 30 rials.

'Lebnon' apples (the result of grafts bought from government agencies) were bought at 100 rials (10 tomans) a mann (3 kilos) and sold at 150 to 200 rials. There was some control over prices, apart from free market forces, through government intervention in fixing prices at the canning factories which took a large proportion of the harvest. The 'tajers' dealt directly with these factories in the city and with middlemen there. They would often specialise in a single fruit. Hossein Ghorbani, for instance, practically held a monopoly on handling 'albalou', the sour black cherries that were made into jam and exported to Europe by the canning factories.

The 'tajers', with their expertise, their transport facilities and their bulk purchasing provided an organisation lacking in the new plains co-operatives (see below p. 169) and which enabled villagers to take full advantage of the upsurge in urban demand. Cherries, for instance, had to reach Tehran within twenty-four hours of being picked. For each producer, with his one or two trees, to organise this, to pay hire fees to truck owners, to make arrangements with city dealers and to keep track of the produce and the bills, as well as standing credit until they were paid, would have been extremely arduous and complex, especially as the producer was at the same time collecting other fruit and tending orchards. Winter apples, likewise, entailed difficulties in marketing that were unacceptable to many. They had to be kept in cool store-houses from the time of picking until the following spring and be taken out at times and in quantities that both responded to urban demand and ensured the best prices. Many living in Mashad in the winter preferred not to have to keep coming back to the village for this. The setting up of an intermediary wholesaling system in the village itself, through the role of the 'tajers', provided the organisation and flexibility necessary if these different orchard owners were to be able to respond to the growing urban demand for their produce and to take full advantage of it in terms of their preferred work and leisure patterns.

There were in 1977 about a dozen 'tajers' in Cheshmeh owning large, brick-built stores, trucks and big lorries and buying on a big scale. Their presence and their affluence were more obvious at this time than they had been in 1971, when I first visited the village. They were now building large additional stores in the main street, importing city builders, using iron girders, steel frames and fired, instead of mud, bricks. As a result of all of this they were acquiring a higher profile in the village. In the summer months particularly they were constantly loading and unloading their stores and their lorries, employing helpers, organising deals and making their presence felt in the few streets of the village.

If the village was able to cash in on the economic boom of the 1970s to some extent because of the efforts of the 'tajers', conversely the boom enabled the 'tajers' to 'take off' economically. They sported Mercedes cars (despite the rough mountain track), wore city suits and spent the winter in smart urban houses. Some of them were having similar homes built for them in the village itself, with electric points built in against the day when the wires reached Cheshmeh (which, at that time, was assumed to be quite soon). The rich in Iran have traditionally kept a rural retreat and newly affluent mountain villagers, aware of the disadvantages as well as the advantages of city life, did not simply migrate out of villages. In the summer months the cool, mountain village was far more comfortable than the dusty, busy city of Mashad in the hot plains below.

The way in which the 'tajer' system developed to the point where, with the urban boom, it reached these proportions in the village is perhaps exemplified by the continuing process whereby individuals in Cheshmeh were themselves trying to become entrepreneurs on a smaller scale. Mahmood Mashhadi, for instance, who owned a shop near his brother's tea house, decided one year to try to make extra money for his trip to Mecca by becoming a small-time 'tajer'. He arranged to buy up the harvests of other villagers and to store them where he usually kept his shop stores. He could then take the fruit to town in the truck he used to bring goods from town for the shop, thus making more efficient use of this resource too. A number of people dealt with him, partly because of under-capacity on the part of the big 'tajers' and partly because of ties he had established through his shop trading. From the proceeds of these activities he was already building a fired-brick house and planning the trip to Mecca, from which he would return as a figure of some note in the village. He might then branch out to become a larger scale 'tajer'. It was probably in this way that the present big 'tajers' had built up their position: some in 1971 had been no bigger than Mahmood was in 1977. Whatever the scale of their individual operations, it was the development and growth of this system of trading which enabled villages like Cheshmeh to cash in on the oil boom in Iran in the 1970s.

Plains Villages

The underpinning of the system of individual small-holding through a structure of communal institutions that provide such basic necessities as water, roads and utilities gave the fruit-croppers of the mountain villages an advantage that the new small-holders in the plains lacked. After years of absentee landlordism, the Shah's Land Reform gave portions of land in the plains to the peasants who had worked them. The new peasant owner, however, did not have the institutional infrastructure to organise on a scale that would make grain production efficient. McLachlan points out, in his survey of the Iranian Land Reform: 'the most serious difficulty was not the opposition of landlords but teaching the new co-operatives to carry out the role they had played as providers of credit, management and social welfare facilities since there were few experienced and trained staff available' (McLachlan, 1968, pp. 708–9). Moreover, the land that was handed to the peasants tended to be the least productive and fertile portions of an estate. Lambton writes: 'The land owned by large proprietors tends also to be that which is most productive. An analysis of the relation of large landholdings with average rainfall illustrates a correlation such that that owned by small peasant proprietors had least rainfall.' (Lambton, 1963, p. 271.) She adds, interestingly in relation to the comparison I am making, that: 'Owners of gardens and orchards, however, tend to be more fortunate than those who own grain land and are relatively more prosperous.' (ibid.)

In the plains the size of the new small-holding was often inefficient for a process of grain production that now demanded large-scale machinery and labour organisation. As Keddie remarks of the new peasant proprietors: 'if they get a plot of land based on the crop division it will in most cases be too small to provide subsistence and will rarely provide a surplus' (Keddie, 1968, p. 86). In the village of Hosseinabad, for instance, the Land Reform led to a situation where more farmers than before were cultivating areas of less than ten hectares: 'in 1962 the number had been 4 out of 88 farmers, by 1964 after the redistribution created by the Land Reform, there were 39 out of 88 cultivating less than 10 hectares' (Jones, 1967, p. 33).

The fruit-croppers of Cheshmeh and other mountain villages experienced no such difficulties. Fruit and gardens were not in fact subject to the Land Reform, but in any case the organisation of fruit-growing on a small-holding basis was more efficient than was grain production on this basis. The Cheshmehis had developed a system which balanced individual and communal organisation in a way that was well geared to the demands of the modern State. This system arose to some extent from the exigencies of fruit production and distribution itself.

Plains Co-operatives

The response to urban growth and increased demand was less successful in the plains villages. In those areas which had been handed over to the peasants in the Land Reform, the new owners were not able to replace the old expertise of the landlord, who had controlled transport and market outlets and an organisational structure for handling the produce, as McLachlan pointed out (cf. above). A United Nations survey reinforced this point in a comment that, by implication, stresses the advantages of the communal organisation I have been describing for mountain villages:

> The third immense problem is to find some rapid substitute for the organisational and physical services formerly provided by the landlords and their agents. It is not clear how effective the new co-operatives will be in this respect, in view of the fact that Iranian farmers have very little experience of egalitarian co-operation ... By December 1963 nearly 2,000 co-operative associations had been formed, but it is certain that many of these were co-operatives in name only, their sole function being to enable the tenant recipients of redistributed land formally to conform with the requirements of the law. (UN, 1966, pp. 24–5).

In these circumstances the man appointed by the co-operative was often none other than the former landlord, as the UN survey continues: 'in those villages where the land reform has left a stratified population with a few of the large landholders being the only obvious candidates for office, there are equally clear dangers – the possibility of an oligarchic system of exploitation of the poor by the rich' (ibid.).

Many large absentee landlords had, in fact, gladly taken payment for their lands at the Land Reform and invested in the new, urban industries. As Lambton says: 'The comparative economic wealth and security of commercial investment and of factories have tended to make many city-based landlords even less interested in their land and the purchase of their land by the government was welcomed by many since it transferred uncertain investment in land into investment in industry and commerce' (1963, p. 29). In addition to their other disadvantages, then, the plains villages were also starved of investment during this period. When the oil price increases of the 1970s made large amounts of money available in Iran, those who controlled that money were more interested in the profits being made in urban building speculation, car assembly plants and 'Coca Cola' factories than in that possible from agriculture.

Moreover, even where individuals did hold on to some rural property it was often not for purposes likely to lead to increased production and development. For urban Iranians it was a mark of prestige to have a rural estate in which to entertain guests as a retreat from urban smog and heat and as an investment against the financial insecurity of city life. As Lambton says: 'Many landlords invest in land because of its value in terms of social and political prestige not economic considerations alone as they were not concerned with production but ownership.' (ibid.)

Cheshmeh and other fruit-producing mountain villages, with their system of individual small-holding combined with communal utilities, lower investment requirements and developed exchange and marketing processes, were far better prepared to respond to the boom in urban demand when it came in the mid-1970s. The scale of this response in Cheshmeh can be seen in the quantities of cash coming into the village in the summer of 1976. Some individuals claimed to have made two or even three million rials (£14–20,000 at the then rate) from their produce, while some 'tajers' made this much from their orchards in addition to profits from dealing. A single lorry holds 160 crates of cherries at 300 tomans (£25) per crate (i.e. £4,000 per load) and in that summer twenty such lorries left the village, apart from smaller trucks etc. Even those with only one or two orchards were topping £1,000 in 1976.

'Commercial' Literacy and the 'Boom'

While the reasons for the success of villages such as Cheshmeh can be explained in terms of the institutional factors that I have cited, particularly in contrast with plains villages during the same period, I would like also to consider the extent to which a certain knowledge of, and acquaintance with, specific literacy practices was also significant. The factors I have already considered make it clear that there is no one determinant to which the changes described can be reduced and the arguments put forward throughout this book weigh against any attempt to ascribe causal significance to 'literacy'. However, what I hope it is now possible to do is to consider more precisely and with less grandiose ambition just what significance specific literacy practices might have.

I have already considered some aspects of the specific literacy practices associated with the Islamic school in such Iranian villages. I shall now examine, in a similar way, the literacy practices associated with trading and commercial enterprises there. I shall then suggest that some of the features of that 'maktab' literacy can be identified in what I term this new 'commercial' literacy and that the earlier practice might to some extent have facilitated the latter. In particular I shall argue that the 'tajers', who were the crucial group in enabling villages like Cheshmeh to cash in on the new economic circumstances, were able to achieve their successes partly on account of a basic knowledge of, and acquaintance with, forms of literacy acquired in the 'maktab'. My evidence is mostly circumstantial since the 'tajer' system was already flourishing when I arrived in the area. Although it is, in fact, possible to identify some examples of the process I am referring to in the contemporary ways in which individuals such as Mahmood Mashhadi were taking on a 'tajer' role, the main way in which I shall attempt to establish the point is through the identification of often hidden features of 'maktab' literacy within the practice of 'commercial' literacy. It can, I believe, be reasonably argued on this basis that 'maktab' literacy facilitated the emergence of 'commercial' literacy. Given the importance of this 'commercial' literacy in the system of distribution and exchange, it can then be said that these literacy practices were an 'enabling factor' in the remarkable commercial success of such villages at this time.

What, then, were the particular uses of literacy associated with the distribution and exchange processes in these villages? As regards writing, they involved specifically the signing of cheques, the writing out of bills and the labelling of boxes in ways that we have seen. There was a branch of the Bank Sadarat in the village and it was in constant use as Cheshmehis brought in wads of cheques, filled in the numerous forms and went over their often large and busy accounts. When the hammam was being built, the organisers carried a book with the names of donors, listing their contributions, and they accumulated wallets full of cheques which were then deposited in the bank. During the fruit season, individual 'tajers' similarly carried thick wadges of cheques around, often to the sum of several thousand pounds. A 'tajer' would frequently give a producer post-dated cheques in return for the produce unloaded in his stores, and the producer would use these against other deals and against shop credit, apart from simply banking them. Status would often be indicated by public exhibition of such large sums of money in the form of cheques or promissory notes.

In the shops, flour mills etc. men reckoned their accounts in school exercise books. The layout of these was often precise and conventional: a page might be allotted to each separate deal; columns would be neatly lined down the page for sections of the account, with indications for weights, money etc.; space would be designated for signatures. Similarly, as items were weighed into a store, the 'tajers' would record them in the appropriate section in their notebooks in such a way that the specific prices and quantities and the final totals and the way that they were arrived at were clear to both parties. They would then sign their agreement to the deal. The 'tajer' might indicate that he owed the producer a specific sum rather than handing over a cheque and the page would then serve the function of a medium of exchange within the village. When the account was finally settled a cheque would be passed over which the recipient could use to pay off accounts that had been run up on the strength of such pieces of paper and the parties would over-sign the page and cross through it. For the hire of my room in the village a page of my notebook was used, the weekly amount was noted at the top and then each week the date and the amount paid was entered with a signature from my landlord that he had received the sum due.

In all of these transactions, use was being made of the 'hidden' literacy skills that I identified above (p. 154) within 'maktab' literacy. These skills were being elaborated in new ways and particular new conventions were being adopted relevant to the expanded commercial enterprises.

In Chapter 5 I used some of the concepts developed by the ALBSU in the UK in order to describe some of the 'hidden' literacy skills acquired within 'maktab' literacy. The most significant of these were skills in recognising layout and format and retrieval skills, including 'thumbing a text'. I linked these skills to the specific ideology of 'maktab' literacy and described some of the cultural factors associated with particular skills, using work done by Heath in America as a further guide (see pp. 156–7 above). It is apparent that some of the skills described there can also be identified within 'commercial' literacy, although they were adapted and developed in specific ways. Through 'maktab' literacy, for instance, students had learnt to recognise that meaning was carried not only by the content of the words on the page but also by conventions concerning their position on the page. These ways of indicating meaning through the format and layout of religious texts had included the relation of groups of words on the page to other groups by such devices as columns, blocks of print placed at angles to the paper etc., different styles of print, headings, cross-references etc. The ways of classifying, ordering and retrieving information in 'commercial' literacy evidently involved some of these same features. Within 'commercial' literacy, for instance, the layout and presentation of lists, tables, columns etc. were the crucial indicators of meaning as in 'maktab' literacy and information was retrieved in similar ways through the separation of categories and the associated use of headings, page numbers etc.

'Commercial' literacy, however, was not 'textual' in the sense that the encounters of 'maktab' students with literacy through the Koran and sacred texts were and so the two literacies were also different in specific ways. In 'commercial' literacy the devices and skills were developed in particular ways. Dealers and producers alike, for instance, constructed their own classification systems, taking a more active role in this than students of 'maktab' literacy. The ALBSU skills of 'recording and communicating for self' and for others had not been particularly significant within 'maktab' literacy while in 'commercial' literacy they were crucial. Those involved in the sale and distribution of fruit in the village had to learn to develop for themselves specific conventions for recording versions of these transactions that could be agreed to by different parties and put to future use. They developed conventions for classifying and separating different transactions, for instance, through the use of notebooks that were divided up both by groups of pages and within a single page. This was done by the use of columns, headings etc. and by adaptations of the ways in which space had been used on the page in 'maktab' literacy.

Furthermore, the 'tajers' had to learn how to themselves give authority to writing and to the papers they were producing, whereas in 'maktab' literacy the authority had been passed down to students from outside as it were. The new representations, once produced in whatever form, were then legitimised and given quasi-legal status by means of new conventions and authority structures. The concept of a 'signature', for instance, as indicating agreement to a transaction rests upon an institutional framework that specifies, whether implicitly or explicitly, formal relations between commercial and legal processes. The concept was widely employed in the village in the 1970s and those who could not write their names simply impressed inky thumbprints on appropriate pieces of paper, indicating participation in and agreement to this institutional framework and its new status.

The setting up of a 'khane ansaf', or local court, gave some formal support to this process. The court was run by a local man who had gone to the 'maktab' about forty years ago, and had been in the same class as one of the mullahs and some of the 'tajers'. He had a small office full of bulging ledgers in the village as part of the government drive to establish central institutions in local idioms. He would handle problems and disputes through the mediation of piles of paperwork, using the ledgers and the panoply of bureaucratic processes to add to his sense of importance and to legitimise and mystify his role. Disputants would come to the office on specified days to present their arguments and he would have them recorded on sheets of exercise, or other readily available, paper. They would then be asked to sign or attach a fingerprint to the paper and he would stamp it to make it into a document with official standing. He could then proceed to give his verdict with the authority of a government agency.

Thus ordinary scraps of paper were legitimised and given status *in situ* rather than, as in many western-style bureaucratic processes, having their status confirmed beforehand by use of headings, formatting etc. An agricultural bank spokesman, for instance, travelling round the villages to determine loans to farmers, would both enhance his authority and officialise a transaction by transforming with stamps and signatures what was an ordinary scrap of paper into a document – something that gave entry to such official establishments in the city as banks and which could be exchanged for money there. The immediacy and flexibility of the process makes more apparent and conscious the social power of specific literacy practices. Similarly, the occasional appearance in Cheshmeh of a town gendarme was always enhanced by his use of paper and writing.

In these ways, then, new literacy associated skills were developed in the village and what I have termed 'commercial' literacy emerged. All of this experience of specific literacy practices contributed to a social and conceptual framework within which reading and writing acquired specific meaning. In this process the uses of literacy were integrated with the new commercial practices in such a way that those who knew and had expertise in specific literacies also had significant power within the expanding commercial processes within which it was playing such an important role.

Knowledge of the implicit rules and conventions that made up the hidden structure of 'commercial' literacy were crucial components of that expertise and therefore of that power. A form of this knowledge had been imparted to those who had been educated at the 'maktab', as we saw above. The present generation of 'tajers' had all been educated at the 'maktab', often in the same period and even in the same class as each other. The hidden literacy skills which they had acquired there thus contributed to their ability to establish positions in the new village power structure which rested on command of both the expanded distribution and exchange systems and of the new 'commercial' literacy. These 'skills' in isolation held no significance. But, in relation to their development by specific groups of people in a context where they facilitated commercial expansion and economic growth, they were a crucial component of the power structure.

'Maktab' literacy did not, however, only provide a few leading figures with skills and knowledge in literacy. It also provided a number of others in the village with the ability to recognise and to use the new 'commercial' literacy, albeit in a more passive way. 'Maktab' literacy thereby facilitated the wider use of 'commercial' literacy and ensured the broadening of the power base of those who had special expertise in it. The 'tajers' were thus able to establish power relations over larger numbers through common participation in literacy practices. Those who could not themselves write, for instance, had still learnt some reading skills that were adaptable to the new circumstances. When crates of fruit were sent to town, the names of the producer and of the urban dealer were written on the outside along with indications of the type and quantity of fruit. The truck driver had, then, to be able to identify and interpret this writing and to recognise the classification in order to distribute the goods appropriately.

The experience of hidden as well as overt literacy skills in the community as a whole also extended to those who had not been to the 'maktab'. On one occasion a woman with little overt literacy skill came to a 'tajer' offering her cherry harvest and apples in return for instant cash, which she needed for her son's wedding. The 'tajer' prepared a paper to this effect which he got her to 'sign' with a fingerprint and he gave her a cheque which she could cash at the bank, or use to purchase goods at village shops. It was their expertise in these processes that helped establish and maintain the power of the 'tajers' over less expert participants. The commercial activity of the village, then, and the control of it by the 'tajers', depended not only on there being a number of people able to read and write in overt ways, but also on the wider spread of hidden skills and knowledge.

Some of these, as we have seen above, are associated with knowledge of lists and tables and the recognition of format and layout acquired in the 'maktab' in relation to a different content. But other literacy skills were also being developed in other areas of daily life in this period. Some men were writing letters to relatives in other places, most frequently in the case of sons who had gone abroad to study. Official documents would be nailed to trees in the village, as with the bad carbon copies of a notice from the governor's office regarding military service. On visits to Mashad some villagers were beginning to look at newspapers, although they seldom brought them back home. On occasions, however, some did bring back propaganda leaflets or newsletters from government agencies, such as the Rastakhiz Party or the Rural Development groups. The skills required in finding their way around a rapidly expanding and westernising city were also, as Graff has shown in another context (Graff, 1979, p. 310), connected with literacy concepts and practice.

The development of such skills and knowledge and the construction of such literate forms is neither an individual matter nor is it necessarily the product of specific formal training: it is a development at the level of ideology, a social construction of reality embedded in specific collective practices in specific social situations. The social group which shared perceptions and uses of literacy in the village may not have all exhibited comparable levels or kinds of skills but they did share a common ideology and a common understanding of the 'meanings' of that literacy. Farmers and 'tajers' alike became used to the practice of handling cheques, notes, bills of sale etc. and of seeing particular transactions represented in material form on paper, against a shared background of 'maktab' learning on the one hand and commercial change and expansion on the other. In this sense those who imprinted their thumb on a page shared an experience of literacy practice with those who could write. This shared experience facilitated the control of positions of power by those with more developed expertise in that area. The 'tajers' were able to expand their power base precisely because a significant number of people had also acquired the literacy practice in which they had expertise. The common and ideological nature of this experience of literacy becomes apparent when we compare the literacy we have been discussing with that of young State school students.

A large number of boys and girls from Cheshmeh continued their studies in Mashad, many going on from high schools there to universities in Iran or abroad. During the summer months they tended to return to keep an eye on orchard interests, to visit families and to escape from the heat and dust of the city to the cool, fresh and shady bowers of the mountain village. The ways in which they used and perceived literacy, and were seen to use it by the villagers, differed considerably from that of the people whom I have been discussing.

These youths would sit in the orchards revising from text books and conversing during the summer months, establishing a group style through their dress and manner that clearly differentiated them from the 'ordinary' villagers. Abbas Tehrani, for instance, a youth of nineteen (in 1977) brought books and magazines and the occasional newspaper to read while he was selling fruit from his orchards or city goods at a temporary stall in a village square. Another boy brought books of Hafez and Sa'adi, classical Persian poets, scribbled over with his own translations. He would show off his knowledge of them in the tailor's shop, where youths often gathered, and the tailor would gasp at the difficulty of understanding his own language when it was written in this poetic style. Another youth carried a translation of a book on psychology by Jean-Paul Sartre which he was reading in anticipation of going to university to study psychology. His younger brother had an exercise book full of drawings in which he was copying out a map of the universe with the names of the planets, partly from interest and partly with an eye to high-school projects. One young boy, sophisticated in western manners and with a city job, read glossy magazines on the one hand ('Ta'alimat Haftegi') and *Lessons from the Book of Islam* on the other. Another man could explain to fellow villagers about the history of British imperialism and its decline on the strength of his general reading. These uses of literacy clearly took place within a different framework from that I have described above for either 'maktab' literacy or 'commercial' literacy. They involved a different set of social practices and a different ideology.

One explanation for these differences lies in the different employment structure that these city-oriented youths were involved in. They were anticipating salaried employment probably for a government agency; their work life would be structured by set hours, holidays and retirement pensions and their literacy practices related to this structure. Their parents, on the other hand, had developed their literacy in a religious context and then adapted it to an entrepreneurial economic context that was individually controlled within its stark dependence on the climate. Modern students acquired literacy within a context of secular literature and school text books and applied it to pre-existing bureaucratic institutions in which they were wage labourers. These differences determined the differences in the meaning of literacy to the various groups and the kinds of literacy practices and skills they developed. The shift to 'commercial' from 'maktab' literacy for the older generation had taken place within a shared context, with communal interests in and perceptions of literacy. The situation within which literacy was acquired and took on meaning for high-school students was quite alien from this environment and from both the 'maktab' and 'commercial' ideology.

For instance, although the young high-school students appeared to have the basic literacy skills necessary to conduct 'tajer' deals, they could not easily apply their literacy to them in practice. Socially, they had not cultivated the contacts necessary for 'tajer' deals and they did not command the kind of respect that these transactions were based on. Respect for their new learning was differentiated in the minds of the villagers from respect for the kinds of qualities that the 'tajer' system rested on, including the specific literacy practices associated with it. They did not make the mistake of many western observers and assume that literacy was a single thing, applicable once learnt to any context; the literacy which their children were learning was not easily transferred or transformed into the practices associated with 'commercial' literacy. The transformation of their own 'maktab' literacy to these commercial practices had been a specific process involving, as we have seen, the development of certain skills and concepts and the abandonment of others. Students visiting for short periods did not have the time to go through such a process and so remained outside the forms of village literacy I have been describing and the social practices associated with them.

The villagers were quite acutely aware of these differences and were fairly confident in ascribing relative value to the various literacies. They would select and identify different aspects of literacy, ascribe value to them and then put different users in their appropriate place on the scale according to each separate aspect. Thus some old men trained at the 'maktab' would point to the writing of a young student and say that their own careful script was superior. They would say that students at the State school played up and fooled about, and so learnt nothing; that there were so many subjects that they could not learn any one properly as at the 'maktab'; and that the teachers, who were all from town, showed no real interest in village students and were geared simply to getting an urban appointment as soon as possible, after working through their obligatory two years in the rural areas. On the other hand, the same old men would point to their children's ability to read from school text books and admit that they themselves could scarcely manage the third-grade ones; they would recognise their disadvantage when a student was reading a poem from a text book since they knew neither the vocabulary nor the rules of that particular discourse; they would point out an old hadji who had not done very well at the 'maktab' and who could scarcely write his name and they would talk about 'progress' and the bright future for the younger generation who were 'literate'. Most saw some of their children as going on with their education in the city, getting urban, white-collar desk jobs, free from the dirt and uncertainty of farming, and they denigrated their own work and skills in contrast.

Their children, however, were increasingly finding it difficult to live up to these expectations as too many qualified students were chasing too few 'respectable' jobs of the kind their families wanted for them. They often finished up in less comfortable circumstances than their village parents and depended on their rights to village land and profits for security.

The contradictions and ambiguities of these arguments and perceptions are familiar enough in any developing society. It is common for those who reproduce western stereotypes of urban sophistication and rural backwardness to at the same time resist the domination of alien western ideology. In the particular circumstances that I am describing, one way in which such people were able to hold both positions at once was through their sense that there were different kinds of literacy appropriate to different purposes and contexts. While not, perhaps, representing explicitly, as I have tried to do, the nature of the 'hidden' literacy skills entailed by the practice of 'commercial' literacy, villagers nevertheless had an implicit recognition that what they were doing required learning, was itself skilful and to be valued and that their children, for all their urban education and literacy, could not handle it, at least without specific training. The different literacies related to different socialisation processes, to different ideologies and to different employment situations.

It was these local literacies that were significant in enabling such villages to cash in on the urban boom of the 1970s. In examining reasons why Cheshmeh and similar mountain villages in Iran were able to capitalise on these new economic possibilities we have to look, then, not towards the increase there in modern-style education nor towards the general 'improvement' in the rural illiteracy figures claimed by the government, but instead to the development there of a specific set of literacy practices associated more closely with local ideology and developing out of such indigenous institutions as the 'maktab'. The fact that a significant number of people in Cheshmeh had developed specific literacy skills through the 'maktab' meant that, given other favourable factors, such as the balance of individual small-holding and communal institutions, villagers were in a better position to develop the specific literacy skills now required for commercial enterprise than were villagers in the plains. A few individuals were able to develop these skills further and set up as 'tajers', while enough 'ordinary' farmers were familiar with certain forms of script to enable the 'tajers' to deal with them on an organised and elaborate basis. This sophisticated entrepreneurial system facilitated distribution of an increased product to centres of expanding demand and hence was a crucial factor in the increased wealth of the village in this period.

In plains villages, on the other hand, when urban demand for wheat and other grain crops likewise increased, there was not the same institutional preparedness nor the same development of literacy practices. Under the traditional landlord system, commercial transactions with urban traders were carried on through the owner's agents and the peasant's contacts were limited to such transactions as borrowing to purchase grain for next year's crop and running up debts on food and household goods from town shops. When the landlords departed or withheld investment, new peasant owners were not able quickly to develop the infrastructure necessary to meet urban demand and indigenous agriculture flagged in competition with cheap imports.

Moreover, the experience of literacy in these villages was less developed than in the mountain areas. Villagers had been employed on a wage-labour basis and so had less control over their own time and less to devote to 'maktab' study. Those who had learnt to read and write in these circumstances had not done so in a context where it could be directly applied to commercial activity since the village system of production and exchange was outside their control. The learning of literacy bore quite a different relation to the economic infrastructure than it did in the fruit-growing villages and so, in practice, their literacy was of a different kind. The literacy skills associated with the particular commercial practices I have described were not just a set of techniques to be easily and quickly acquired but part of a complex ideology, a set of specific practices constructed within a specific infrastructure and able to be learnt and assimilated only in relation to that ideology and infrastructure: the acquisition of literacy is, in fact, a socialisation process rather than a technical process.

It is in these terms that the study of the significance of literacy in relation to economic development and change needs to be conducted. In the case of Cheshmeh and the fruit-growing mountain villages of Iran, this approach leads to the conclusion that it was the combination of specific literacy skills with an economic infrastructure facilitating entrepreneurial activity that enabled the villagers to successfully take advantage of Iran's growing wealth in a way that other groups, without those skills and infrastructure, could not.

Literacy in Practice

7

UNESCO AND RADICAL LITERACY CAMPAIGNS

Some aspects of Unesco literacy campaigns, and of the radical challenges to them issued in recent years, can be seen to involve aspects of the 'ideological' model although seldom worked through in the way that I suggest above is happening in some of the academic literature. I would like to examine some of these campaigns and the literature about them in order to bring to the surface the underlying theories that often remain implicit in them and to relate these theories to the more explicit concepts developed within what I term the 'ideological' model of literacy.

A statement made by Unesco in 1962 defines a literate person as one who: 'has acquired the essential knowledge and skills which enable him to engage in all those activities in which literacy is required for effective functioning in his group and community and whose attainments in reading, writing and arithmetic make it possible for him to continue to use these skills towards his own and the community's developments' (cited in Oxenham, 1980, p. 87).

The conception of 'functional' literacy underpinned development and literacy programmes across the world in subsequent years. It was open-ended enough to cater for all interests and its relativity subsumed the variety of political and ideological positions represented by a Unesco conference without making any particular one explicit and without appearing to require any reference to the material and political conditions in which those particular 'functions' operated. A decade later, at the 'Persepolis International Symposium on Literacy', some participants were able to be more forthright about their political beliefs. This was as a result partly of what many people there recognised as 'the overall failure of literacy campaigns undertaken in the course of the past decade' (Unesco, 1975, 3.1.5) and partly of the critical challenge to conventional thinking mounted by Freire and others in this period. These participants considered that the 'neutral' position of the earlier conference should be abandoned in favour of a more explicitly ideological approach to literacy. The report of the Symposium states:

> Several speakers noted, in the first place, that the notion of functionality had evolved considerably in the course of the period ... As desired by the United Nations Development Programme, this had, to begin with, been associated chiefly with the direct im-

provement of labour productivity. However, this notion subsequently broadened to encompass other dimensions, particularly insofar as it came to be seen that production-related objectives were inseparable from other objectives concerned with the transformation of economic and social structures. A number of participants agreed that the effectiveness of literacy training – as with education in general – depends upon the political and ideological functions it is expected to fulfil, both in the productive set-up and in the society as a whole. (ibid. 3.2.3.)

This shift in thinking had been influenced by the critique of Unesco literacy programmes made by a number of radical writers. Carol and Lars Berggren summarise these approaches in a pamphlet entitled *The Literacy Process: A Practice in Domestication or Liberation?'* (1975). Literacy, they argue, is not neutral nor simply a technology: it contains the moral philosophy of a particular society and its education system. Thus the concept of 'functional' literacy disguises the relationship of a particular literacy programme to the underlying political and ideological framework. The earlier Unesco input, for instance, was in fact tied to a particular developmental and economistic ethos. It subserved the interests of foreign investment and multinational companies on the premise that productivity and profits could be raised if 'literacy levels' were raised. From the point of view of many States, who badly needed such investment, literacy programmes represented an input factor whose success was to be assessed in terms of the economic return. This meant that ultimate determination of the programme lay with financial and commercial interests, with governments acting simply as mediators and as providers of the 'risk capital' in terms of the infrastructure of education and training. The subjects themselves were a form of 'plant' whose effectiveness could be maximised by the employment of new 'educational technology' in the form of 'literacy skills', thereby enabling greater surplus to be extracted from them.

The assumptions that lay behind these particular developments of literacy practice were, on the one hand, those of international capitalism and, on the other, those of the 'autonomous' model of literacy. Whatever interests capitalists might have had in Third World investment, their willingness to relate it to literacy programmes stemmed from what academics had been telling them literacy could do. Anderson's conception of a development threshold at a 40% literacy rate, for instance, affected perceptions of what investment in literacy might lead to, and it in turn was 'explained' by various theories, of the kind summarised in Section 1 as the 'autonomous' model of literacy, regarding the significance of literacy for logic, problem-solving abilities and other 'cognitive' skills.

Oxenham, for instance, explains the startling expansion of literacy campaigns in the second half of this century in terms of the 'yeast' effect which, he says, literacy is thought to operate. He cites, for instance, the assumptions that literacy was variously connected with 'a modernisation syndrome'; the development of 'empathy', 'flexibility', 'adaptability', and 'willingness to accept change'; the concept of 'modern man'; and 'proneness to adopt innovations' (1980, p. 15), all of which represent popular versions of the more esoteric researches discussed above regarding the 'cognitive' consequences of literacy. Oxenham suggests that these academic researches were simply rationalisations for decisions made on other grounds: 'The findings of social scientists served to justify and reinforce policies already launched' (ibid. p. 16).

Although this is often true, the work of academics of the kind discussed in earlier chapters has probably had other significance too. Research and investment interests are often more interrelated and multidirectional than Oxenham suggests. Researchers like Hildyard and Olson did, in a sense, allow their research to 'follow' from policies which had already been launched. They took as the starting point for their investigation into the 'cognitive' consequences of literacy the fact that 'vast amounts of effort and resources' were being devoted to education which they then set out to 'justify'. However, they claim that it can only be justified if it can clearly be shown that literacy produced some demonstrable development in 'intellectual competence' (1978, p. 4). In this sense they are also contributing to establishing an alternative language and terms of reference for investment decisions than that of 'pure' economics. The fact that literacy programmes need to be 'justified' in this particular way suggests that social scientists have established some claims to be arbiters of the ideology to which those who control investment are required to appeal.

Nevertheless what governments and companies want from literacy is primarily technological competence and improvement. The relationship between this and 'intellectual competence' remains problematic and, even if the academics fail to establish it, literacy programmes will still be justified on grounds of 'productivity'. If 'intellectual competence' includes, for instance, 'critical consciousness', then it might well be in conflict with 'productivity'. Much 'productivity' in Third World factories, for instance, depends on routine and repetitive tasks being performed by a docile and non-unionised workforce.

It has often been on this basis that potential investors have been convinced that there was some connection between literacy rates and productivity. As Oxenham says 'calculations were elaborated to contend that the advance of a society depended not merely on its capital, its natural resources, its technology but also on the education (and hence literacy) of its workers. Educated people tended to be more productive, if only because they could handle more sophisticated machinery' (1980, p. 15). This view, he goes on to say, 'was underpinned by the experience of industrial employers who found schooled and literate people not only easier to train but also apparently more able to hold on to what they learned. The copper-mining companies of Zambia, for instance, had the impression that an illiterate who had been trained by them lost much of his skill if he returned to his home village for long leave: whereas personnel with schooling and literacy seemed to suffer no such problems' (ibid. p. 16).

The link between literacy and ideology is clear here, even if Oxenham does not quite couch it in these terms. Those who had been trained according to the 'development' model of education and literacy have been deliberately prepared for certain kinds of work habits that employers prefer; inevitably, then, the more they are outside those social contexts which reinforce that ideology, the looser will be its grip on them. As a speaker at the Persepolis Symposium said: 'literacy training often takes the form of a sort of conditioning' (Unesco, 1975, 3.2.5).

As with much of the development and the academic literature, however, Oxenham disguises this ideological nature of literacy by appealing to its 'technical' character. He writes, for instance, of State and commercial interests in literacy that 'literacy and schooling were seen as technologies which, by their very use, were to transform the users. Moreover, they were regarded as technologies indispensable to rapid socio-economic development.' (Oxenham, 1980, p. 17.) Later he summarises his own view in similar terms: 'Literacy, in short, is a technology, a "technical method of achieving a practical purpose"' (ibid. p. 41).

The various claims made by academics, then, that literacy improves 'intellectual competence' and that it is a technical means to a productive end may be used to disguise the fact that some forms of literacy programme actually impair criticalness and that what is being imparted is not a technical skill but an ideology. This is certainly what Graff suggests occurred in nineteenth century Canada and what Freire and the Berggrens believe is wrong with many Unesco-oriented literacy campaigns. Freire saw literacy learning as an integral part of acquiring values or 'forming mentalities'. From his political position, then, it should involve, for instance, not 'problem-solving' but problematising the total social reality within which the 'problems' occur and within which the training itself is offered. Acquiring literacy, he believed, is an active process of consciousness and not just the learning of a fixed content, so he wanted that process to be geared to people's own interests and not simply to those of profit-making by commercial interests. Unesco programmes, being related to economic growth models and productivity, tended to be selective: they were not trying to make everyone literate but selected out those most likely to be productive, which tended to be those in a stable political structure and who already had some skills. Freire's method, on the other hand, was addressed to everyone and was more likely to be subversive since it aimed at 'conscientization', raising the consciousness of the person's own position in a wider society and in particular of their exploitation and its political and social causes. He stressed the importance of motivation and, as part of this, built up a literacy programme based on the production of texts by the students themselves.

The apparent failure of the conventional Unesco literacy project enabled this radical view to have considerable impact at the 1975 Unesco Symposium on Literacy. In the account of the debates there, we can trace the process whereby, firstly, the distinction between the two approaches was made clear and some of the arguments outlined above were introduced, before a compromise was worked out in which both were then accommodated beneath a 'broadened' definition of the concept of 'functional' literacy.'

> Certain participants suggested drawing a distinction between the two main categories of function: the first, economic in character, concerned with production and with working conditions; the rest cultural in character, encouraging the development from primary consciousness to critical consciousness (the process of 'conscientization') [sic] and the active participation of adults in their own development. A number of speakers emphasised that narrowly economic functions were liable to shore up the established order in a social system founded on injustice and inequality: indeed, literacy training may even take on a reactionary character as with education in general, moreover, it tends to assure the mechanical reproduction of the system of social relations taken as a whole ...
>
> One speaker condemned the present state of chaos engendered, in his view, by the type of educational system adopted, and the Development model imported, by a good many non-socialist Third World countries ... [which involved] increasing dependence upon the outside world. In these countries, this speaker went on, literacy training and all other forms of education, take the form of a 'poor man's luxury', and more closely resemble a sort of conditioning than education properly speaking. In these circumstances, literacy training in some ways serves to consolidate the existing division of labour between a privileged minority, invested with the exclusive responsibility for resolving problems, and the majority, which is reduced to merely implementing solutions that have been arrived at without it being consulted. (Unesco, 1975, 3.2.5.)

This speaker, however, was content to retain the concept of 'functional' literacy since for him it could mean something quite different from the

simply economistic part of the definition. He concludes: 'If literacy training is to become truly functional this dichotomy will have to be eliminated' (ibid.). As some earlier speakers had said: 'production-related objectives are inseparable from other objectives concerned with the transformation of economic and social structures' (ibid. 3.2.3). To define 'functional' literacy according to these two categories, one economic, 'the rest'
'cultural', is to separate the 'inseparable' and, indeed, to define most of
social life as a residual category of the economic. What the 'functions' of
literacy are taken to be will, then, vary according to the political and
ideological stand adopted. According to Freire and others the version of
literacy functions that had predominated in Unesco circles was the economic one. This bias and the persistence of the false dichotomy had been
disguised by the concept of 'functional' literacy which appeared as in the
opening quote on pp. 183–4 to be referring to something broader than
this. Nevertheless, the speaker just quoted is willing to employ the term,
simply giving it his own bias instead of the conventional one.

Many participants, however, appear to have recognised that their dislike for the economistic view of literacy entailed a radical rethink of the
very concepts by which literacy was defined. The report indicates, for
instance, that in one session:

> Most participants attempted to re-examine the concept of
> literacy training. Some even went so far as to consider that the
> term literacy training no longer accorded with the reality it now
> embraces, and that it would be desirable to agree on a term better
> suited to the new tendencies, one better able to restore the global
> significance of a process that is supposed to enable man to partic-
> ipate in the making of his own history: seen as a reading of the
> world and not simply a decoding of words. (ibid. 3.2.9.)

This move towards something like what I have termed the 'ideological'
model of literacy, which caters for the tendencies that I have outlined in
this book as well as for some radical Unesco campaigners, was however
deflected. The conference noted the shift in ideas but preserved the concept of 'functional' literacy, simply 'broadening' the definition to make it
acceptable to the radicals as well as to the conservatives.

What, then, are the implications of these debates and compromises for
actual literacy programmes? I will briefly consider some Unesco-oriented
programmes in Iran and Tanzania as examples of how the arguments
relate to practice. I shall attempt to make explicit some of the concepts
and theories that, I argue, underly not only these projects but much
Unesco work and so to relate them to the 'ideological' model of literacy.

The project in Tanzania was a 'work-oriented' literacy campaign reported on by M. Viscusi, an American 'author and journalist'. She based

her account 'on the broad principles of functional literacy', although the work is represented as a personal approach and not an official Unesco responsibility (Unesco, 1971, p. 1). The perspective adopted by many developmentalists with regard to literacy in the Third World is classically represented by the journalistic introduction which, the author admits, provided the frame for the whole study. As she flew in to Mwanza, where the project was centred, she reflected on its purpose: 'I went with a head full of theories acquired from reading about how work-oriented literacy *should* function, with a notebook full of questions to ask. But in those few moments as the plane prepared to land, I unconsciously formed one overriding question: how is it possible to link the slow-moving world of the farmers living in those squat thatched huts, the fishermen rowing those fragile craft, to that of the air-conditioned plane soaring overhead?' (ibid. p. 5).

At first glance one might indulge this simple stereotype as providing local 'colour' and the 'personal approach'. But, as with many such images, it is not just an aside but, as Lamb points out (1983, p. 12), serves to focus, imaginatively and conceptually, the writer's basic approach to the 'strange' culture and the literacy practice she had gone to study there. She continues:

> After several days in the literacy project area – visiting teacher-training sessions and literacy classes, talking to local education, rural development and agricultural officers, bombarding the project staff with queries – I grew more and more grateful for that first glimpse of farmers and fishermen almost lost in an untamed landscape. As I tried to fit each different activity I saw into an overall view of the literacy project, I asked myself how it related to these people. This persistent image came to symbolize for me the true view of work-oriented literacy: that it can reach out to groups of peoples engaged in particular activities in a particular setting, that it can provide education rooted in their daily work, education they can use to make tomorrow's farming or fishing more profitable than today's, that it closes just a bit the gulf between the world of the modern aircraft and that of the wooden hoe and the hand-fashioned net. (ibid. p. 5.)

There is not space here to explore, as I have done elsewhere (Street, 1975), the kinds of stereotypes exposed here: the use, for instance, of technological differences to indicate deeper differences; the romantic primitivism and associations of nature/culture evoked by describing members of other cultures as inhabiting 'an untamed landscape'; the stress on difference rather than similarity as in the comparison of aeroplanes with 'fragile craft' and 'wooden hoes' which is, of course, not a comparison of like with like in the two cultures although it is used as the central symbol of the general comparison between them. What, however, primarily concerns us here is the significance of these ethnocentric and misleading images for the view of literacy practice in the particular circumstances. The use of a spatial metaphor to indicate difference – a 'gulf' – for instance, leads to the concept of 'reaching out' to provide education which sets the whole project in a hierarchical and western framework. These images disguise from the developmentalists the true gap between their own ideals and what actually happens on the ground. As we shall see, the literacy that was provided for local farmers was not, in fact, 'rooted in their daily work': indeed, since the local farmers had no integral use for what they had been taught it soon began to 'atrophy' and the project staff had to construct an artificial 'literacy environment' to try to sustain it. The suggestion that 'tomorrow's fishing and farming' could be affected by literacy levels was also an illusion in a context where urban markets and pricing mechanisms were the determinants of profitability and, indeed, of what was produced in the first place. Also, the concept of 'improvement' regarding rates of work and allocation of labour, which the project organisers believed was linked with literacy, turns out on closer examination to have been crudely ethnocentric in its representation of time and work and its inability to recognise indigenous conceptions. This, then, is the kind of 'development model' that speakers at the Persepolis Symposium referred to, where 'the majority is reduced to merely implementing solutions that have been arrived at without it being consulted' (Unesco, 1975, 3.2.5).

The project being investigated was, in fact, a pilot scheme for a possible national programme. It was decided to choose an area 'where the right kind of investment in modernisation can be expected to pay high dividends' (Unesco, 1971, p. 13). The Mwanza lakes region was one of the 'country's best endowed agricultural areas' and it was chosen because the fundamental object of the programme was to teach 'good' agricultural practice. This involved, for instance, 'teaching' people to use cattle functionally and 'not just' for status. This approach seemingly ignores the fact that in many of the Unesco organisers' own countries much important economic production is for non-functional reasons: production involves a complex of motivations not simply the economistic ideal being foisted on the local farmers in this particular case.

The attitude of mind that the literacy programme hoped to instil was one of 'problem-solving'. Thus Viscusi points out that literacy enables farmers to take notes on the lectures regarding better cotton-growing practices: 'Only a literate farmer can take notes on what he sees and hears, refer later to his notes and other written instruction, expand his knowledge by reading pamphlets, brochures and books' (ibid. p. 14). This is indeed an important aspect of literacy and, as we shall see below (Chapter

8), framed within a more explicitly 'ideological' model of literacy it can lead to participants using various literacy skills and practices for self-selected ends. However, within the framework offered by Viscusi's interpretation of 'functional' literacy, it lays itself open to the criticisms levelled by Freire and others and by many at the 1975 Symposium. This framework, for instance, is constructed in terms of a hierarchy with the project organisers 'reaching out' to 'ignorant' farmers and failing to take account of the subjects' own culture and values. The organisers themselves, for instance, seem 'ignorant' of the fact that some of the 'problems' that they hope to teach the locals to overcome have, in fact, been created by the imposition of this external framework in the first place.

For instance, the organisers criticise the farmers for being foolish enough to 'sell milk from cows and eggs from chickens ... for cash' (ibid.) while at the same time suffering from malnutrition. What the analysis fails to indicate is that cash-cropping was introduced by the colonists as part of their structuring of the local economy and that the farmers had become tied to it through continuing pressures exercised by the western-oriented economic structure that emerged. Freire would take this as a classic case of the importance of a politically conscious literacy campaign that alerts learners to the causes of their 'problems' and of their own exploitation. A further example of the 'problem-solving' approach reveals its narrowness in failing to recognise that local peoples might have their own conceptualisations of the processes they engage in. Viscusi describes the approach as requiring the participant to learn 'certain intellectual as well as manual skills' (ibid.) as though they did not already have such skills:

> Sometimes the required change is very abstract, a matter of improving management or efficiency rather than substituting one activity for another. For example, in one Tanzanian village it was suggested to farmers that by devoting three weeks to building a well they could cut the time each village woman spent in getting water from two hours to fifteen minutes a day. At first the villagers replied a bit condescendingly that two hours was a very little time compared to three weeks of labour. But when they became skilled enough to grasp that two hours multiplied by *all* the women in the village and *all* the days in the year was an enormous block of time, they undertook the improvement with enthusiasm. (ibid.)

Clearly, both sides are being 'a bit condescending' since both are concerned with deeper aspects of their belief system and ideology and not just with a 'neutral' technical or mathematical skill. Given the local division of labour, three weeks of the men's time in one stretch was not an equivalent to small daily portions of the women's time. Their time fetching water often serves a combination of functions and allows other tasks to be accomplished concurrently, whereas the men's labour on a well would take up time they would normally spend on other productive activity. Once the well was built the women would have to 'make' other time for fulfilling the functions traditionally carried out during water collection. If these had been calculated into the total equation one might find that the well does not represent much of a 'saving'. Alternatively, the women might well feel that getting some of the work done by the men, out of their allocation of time as it were, was no bad thing and their 'enthusiasm' might be the outcome of this political awareness and choice, rather than a 'grasping' of the sums. The project staff were confusing what they saw as 'productive' time with more complex areas of 'cultural' time. The decision is ultimately a 'political' one, in the broadest sense of the term, involving a balancing of priorities in the allocation of economic and cultural time and as between different interest groups, in a way that all cultures, including the developmentalists' own, commonly deal in. Viscusi, however, presents it as though it were to do with 'skills' in mathematics and with supposedly 'neutral' concerns with 'improved' management and 'efficiency'. It is precisely the imposition of this western management model in Unesco literacy campaigns, as though it represented simply general intellectual competence and objective judgement, that Freire and others were complaining of, and that the 'ideological' model of literacy is designed to avoid. The Tanzanian project demonstrates clearly how the link between literacy and 'cognitive' skills, which as we saw above is made by many western researchers, is employed by developmentalists on the ground. The work of social scientists offers reinforcement to the cultural prejudices of those taking literacy 'out' to supposedly 'backward' peoples.

Some of the teachers whom the project was training to impart these new concepts were themselves inclined to resist. They were given, for instance, text books which, Viscusi says, made 'great demands on them' (ibid. p. 26). 'The first page of the cotton primer reads simply: "Pamba ni mali. Pamba bulets pesa" (Cotton is wealth. Cotton brings money).' Viscusi points out, somewhat disingenuously, that teaching such things involves changes in thinking for teachers and students alike:

> The teacher's job is not only to get the learners to read these words. Using suggestions given in the teacher's manual, he or she must also draw the class into discussing the *concepts* represented by the words. What is wealth? What is money? What can you do with money? How can you get the most money for your cotton? Why is ridging (or any other improvement) recommended? For many teachers mastering this approach requires a complete reorientation of thinking about what it is to teach. (ibid. p. 26.)

The 'reorientation', of course, runs deeper than how to teach and includes most of what would normally be defined as ideology. The teachers appear to have understood this better than the project staff and they, like the students, were not always willing to concede that their own ideology was as inferior as was being claimed: hence the resistance found both here and in many parts of the world to the literacy programmes purveyed beneath the Unesco banner of 'functional literacy'.

The conflict of interests was further exacerbated in the Tanzanian case by a problem typical of many such campaigns: the differences between established school teachers and the 'volunteers' drafted in specifically for the campaign. Viscusi is very alert to these differences: 'Even in non-elitist rural Tanzania, primary school teachers undeniably constitute a privileged group. They practise an honoured profession, they are assured of a steady income ... Although they are respectful of authority ... they are sure of themselves, they know they have been trained for a task of vital importance in national development.' (ibid. p. 27.)

These teachers are increasingly called upon to bear the burden of the literacy campaigns, given the sheer scale of them, but they are not given extra money for conducting 'work-oriented classes for adults' after school hours. They also resent the unprofessional, inexperienced volunteers who were brought in to get the project off the ground but who clearly could not represent a permanent basis for a nationwide programme.

> Unlike primary school teachers, most volunteer teachers are able-bodied and articulate young men unable to find permanent employment. Their education is not sufficient to ensure them an income much higher or steadier than that of any illiterate farmer or fisherman. Volunteer teachers have first-hand experience of the degrading effects of illiteracy and underdevelopment, and they seemed to be more personally indignant about social conditions in rural areas and less satisfied by current efforts to improve them than primary school teachers. One volunteer teacher, for example, asked whether drop outs could be taken to court to compel them to attend literacy classes (he was told that persuasion and good teaching were the only weapon against class attrition).
>
> Volunteers are eager to teach; they sincerely want to help their illiterate neighbours, and the honorarium offered them is a welcome addition to their income. But they know an honorarium is not a salary: it cannot erase the stigma of being unemployed. (ibid. p. 27.)

Similarly in Iran, the 'Literacy Corps' teachers drafted in by the Shah were considered by villagers as 'second best' and a village felt that it had been insulted if it did not get a 'proper' teacher. In Tanzania one solution to the low morale and conflicts was the production of a newsletter for teachers of literacy. This represented, in a sense, a recognition that the teaching of literacy in the particular way envisaged by the project staff was a matter of shifting ideology and that if this were to happen then the teachers had to be re-conditioned as much as their students.

Like the teachers, the students soon fell back into their old ways if the new ideology was not constantly reinforced. The organisers discovered that, as Viscusi puts it, 'mental and manual skills atrophy without use' (ibid. p. 33). This, of course, contradicts the hopeful account with which she began where it was claimed that literacy would 'provide education rooted in their daily work'. Clearly, the literacy being imparted is not integral to that work otherwise it would not 'atrophy'. The Berggrens would suggest that the real motivation behind such campaigns was the attempt by the State to get foreign investment by proving that it had passed the development threshold. Multinational companies, for instance, see a correlation between literacy rates and their ability to sell consumer durables and this is what encourages their investment. There is, indeed, a hint of this in Viscusi's reference to the fact that deep-freeze facilities were being considered for the area of the literacy project. She notes that 'no large-scale programmes aimed at economic development will get far if the people they are designed to help are too under-educated to take advantage of them' (ibid. p. 14). This 'taking advantage' has classically involved their being sucked into a cash economy where they become an enlarged market for western consumer goods and, as a speaker at the Persepolis Symposium noted, includes 'increasing dependence on the outside world' (see p. 187).

Thus, when a literacy campaign founders on its stated aim of being 'rooted in daily work', it is necessary for an alternative set of institutions to be built to justify and maintain literacy levels, in order that the fundamental aim will still be met. In the Tanzanian case this took the form of the construction of what was called 'a literacy environment'. This environment, however, does not consist of the 'work-oriented' activity on which the project was initially based, since the locals have already resisted this, but instead it is a classroom and library-oriented construction that is, in fact, even more alien to the local culture. It consists of reading groups meeting in local schools and libraries to share experiences, swop books etc. It is, writes Viscusi: 'an environment that not only encourages and helps all new literates (including school drop outs) to maintain and develop whatever they have learned, but also inspires class members to attend class regularly and make fast progress and – perhaps most important – continues to draw illiterates into literacy classes by surrounding them with more and more evidence that literacy really does have a function in rural life' (ibid. p. 35).

This approach implicitly recognises that literacy is a matter of culture and ideology and that people will only adopt it if they are sympathetic to, and see the relevance of, the particular culture and ideology that shapes it. The Tanzanian farmers appear to have indicated that they were not happy with the economistic ideology of the 'work-oriented' project so the organisers retreated to that other category of 'functional' literacy, the 'cultural', and attempted to use this to shore up their project. 'Culture', however, is not just a residual category of the economic, nor is it a single thing to be imparted across the globe. The kind of culture associated with the 'literacy environment' being purveyed in rural Tanzania appears to be no more relevant or appealing to the locals than the economic literacy. The outcome, however, is a matter of political judgement and the shift towards a 'literacy environment' does represent some admission of this, even if the particular judgement does not appear very sound. Freire and other radical writers would argue that it is possible to conceive of literacies which are appropriate to people's particular circumstances and which would appeal to them. Following on his work the leaders of the 'Literacy Crusade' in Nicaragua, for instance, claim to have made a political judgement that is meeting with success. Whether this is true or not remains to be assessed; the point, for the moment, is that they have at least pitched their claims at this level, while the organisers of the Unesco-oriented campaign in Tanzania continued to present their activities behind the veneer of 'functional' literacy, as though it were not a political issue, even when their retreat to the concept of a 'literacy environment' makes it quite clear that it was.

Before I examine the implications of such radical campaigns as that in Nicaragua for my general argument, I will attempt to elaborate further some of the problems associated with the particular kind of literacy campaigns that evolved out of the Unesco concept of 'functional' literacy. We have already considered some aspects of literacy in Iran from the village end, as it were, and I would now like to use this as a baseline from which to view the large-scale campaigns and Unesco-influenced institutions set up under the Shah's regime to 'improve' literacy levels in the country as a whole.

The underlying principles on which these campaigns were conducted are exemplified by the reports and evaluations of a major 'work-oriented' literacy campaign that was conducted in the towns of Dezful and Esphahan, under the auspices of Unesco, between 1967 and 1973. The project was 'initially conceived primarily as an experiment in the application of a certain economic theory: that the supply of human capital was an operative, if not the operative, constraint on output in two selected geographical areas' (Unesco, 1973, Vol. I, p. 167). For the organisers and teachers this meant a 'work-oriented pedagogical base' and they found themselves 'defining and elaborating an efficient technology for the production of human capital' rather than 'causing a significant increase in the stock of human capital' (ibid.). The effects of the project were carefully monitored and researchers were drafted in to study the 'educational, social and economic impact, if any, of the work-oriented literacy in different areas in comparison with other forms of literacy teaching and with reference to the defined targets of socio-economic development projects' (ibid. Vol. III, Part I, p. 1). This involved assessing, for instance, the 'degree of literacy required for higher productivity' and the 'effectiveness of work-oriented literacy' according to measured changes that occurred as a result of literacy. Psychologists, for instance, reported on the 'behavioural changes related to the adoption of practices, use of literacy skills and attitudinal changes observed in former participants in the work-oriented literacy courses' (ibid. Part III, p. 35). These courses had, like those in Tanzania, been focussed around specific work skills such as, in this case, automotive maintenance, embroidery and civics.

The team brought in to evaluate the project found that, as in other cases, the aims of the organisers did not match those of the participants. The 'international experts', they write, saw the courses 'as a professional training with literacy integrated into them' while the Iranians saw it as a 'literacy acquisition method' (ibid. Part IV, p. 145). Many of the Iranians had been conditioned by their achievement-oriented and very westernised education system to see literacy in terms of the 'autonomous' model, as a set of skills which would get them a job. Some Unesco experts were already taking a broader view of literacy than this, as we have seen, and the two views came into conflict. The evaluators maintain that the result was a 'weak compromise which undermined the research' and also complain at the 'lack of research experience by the specialists and inadequate organisation of the structure responsible for the experimental project' (ibid.).

One outcome was to recommend that the government pay more attention to the main educational institutions of the country rather than expect too much of one-off campaigns. The report cites an international mission which proposed that the Iranian government 'give high priority to the development of primary education in the next national plan' (ibid. Vol. I, p. 69). One of the reasons cited for this provides an illuminating example of the 'economistic' bias of Unesco 'functional' literacy approaches. The report argues:

> Education at secondary and higher levels is likely to be socially discriminatory for many years to come. In fact, many of the proposals contained in this Report would increase the social exclusiveness of general secondary higher education in order to try

to secure greater economic efficiency in resource utilisation. It is more than normally necessary therefore to take steps to ensure that primary education is available to all. (ibid.)

The reason for the emphasis on primary education is made clear in a work by one American planner who had recently assessed the Iranian bureaucracy in terms of manpower needs:

> The main contribution of primary education to development may be its function in mobilizing a small number with natural talents useful for nation-building. This is a more important reason for the expansion of primary education than the creation of a literate work force. Functional literacy is also a less important justification for primary school expansion than increasing the number of eligibles from whom selection can be made for entry into secondary schools and universities. Thus first level education is primarily important as a selection mechanism for mobilising the natural talent in the population so that it can be upgraded with acquired skills. (Baldwin, 1967, p. 148.)

Although Baldwin explicitly rejects 'functional literacy', he is in fact putting forward a model of educational development that would fit perfectly well with many of the interpretations of 'functional literacy' that we have seen and certainly with the concept of 'work-oriented literacy' that arose out of it and is expounded in the Tanzanian and Esphahan studies.

It was in the light of these conceptualisations of education, and in response to the international pressures that accompanied them, that the Ministry of Education in Iran devoted a lot of effort and resources to setting up schools in rural areas during the years of the Shah's general expansionary programmes. One Iranian educational administrator, who has clearly assimilated these notions, makes it clear that these schools represent an ideological challenge to rural life and values: 'The psychological attitudes of the Iranian villagers create a great obstacle to [rural] reconstruction', and it is thus necessary for 'educated' Iranians to instigate a programme which 'will so change the outlook of the average villager, that he will desire reconstruction on certain lines, know how to bring it about and feel confident that he can achieve it through his own efforts' (Gharib, 1966, p. 88). This puts the teacher into quite a different relationship with students than in the traditional system where, as we have seen, he shared their ideology and way of life. As Arasteh notes: 'Whereas in the past the teachers continued the traditional patterns, in these days they have become the agents of change' (Arasteh, 1962, p. 86). This creates fundamental problems for all such uses of education for 'development'. The teacher is not integrated with the community but is an outsider: he does not try to teach the village children to integrate but to become outsiders. While education, and in particular literacy, are regarded as 'technical' processes this problem gets little attention since it is assumed that anyone professionally trained to impart 'skills' can do so to anyone 'intellectually' capable of acquiring them. Once, however, it is recognised that teaching literacy involves putting over a specific ideology, particularly one alien to the students concerned, then the 'problem' of the teacher beomes crucial and developmentalists are obliged to take some account of local values and ideology. This is what was beginning to happen in Iran during the 1960s and 1970s. Richard Antoun, who studied village life in both Jordan and Iran during this period, puts the point from an anthropological perspective. The villagers, he points out, are bound by multiplex relationships which involve the payment of dues and obligations so they can make demands on each other in a pattern which is known and can be predicted. The teacher, on the other hand, is frequently outside this system: 'he is in the village but not of it' (Antoun, 1965, p. 9).

Many teachers in Iranian village schools owed their allegiance to the central institution of education and saw their future as upward progress within it. They often lived in towns and commuted to the village to teach, treating the village school as a temporary step in their own careers and often looking down on the villagers as 'backward' and, in many cases, as scarcely worth the trouble. The Ministry obliged them to spend a few years in rural areas before they were allowed to move to urban schools, although the period was often negotiable and youths would spend long periods at the local Ministry of Education office attempting to get themselves a 'better' appointment. Even when they had got a city post, many youths would often take a job teaching part-time in a village in order to supplement what they considered to be an inadequate salary. University students, getting no grant from the government, would go to college in the morning and teach all afternoon, trying to read for degrees while teaching as many as thirty hours a week and supporting a family at the same time. Their journey to the village was, in these circumstances, a burden and they tended to have little sympathy for village schoolchildren. Eventually they would get a degree and an urban job and they would be replaced by another part-time teacher until he too was able to 'get away'.

In a country where the Shah and the western-educated elite were acutely conscious of the need to impress foreign agencies and companies that they were successfully 'modernising', the slow progress of the Ministry schools was perceived as a crucial problem. With their commuting teachers, salary costs and difficulties in getting enough trained teachers to cater for the large, unwesternised rural areas of Iran, they were not going to achieve the necessary 'breakthrough' on their own. In 1963, as one of the points of the 'White Revolution' which set out a programme of modernisation for all areas of Iranian life, the Shah instituted an 'Education Corps', the 'Sepah-ye Danesh', to speed up the work. It was composed of young people drafted in as part of their military service and remained under the auspices of the army. It was, indeed, referred to as an 'Army of Knowledge'. Young recruits from the high-schools were given training for four months, of which one-third was military, were then made sergeants and given an army salary and sent to a village to teach for fourteen months. Set text books were prescribed for them to use designed to bring children up to the second grade of primary school. The Corpsman or woman was also charged with the task of adult education and of teaching the villagers sanitation and first aid and of taking a leading role in the 'improvement' of village life. One of the 'Objectives of the Army of Knowledge' was that 'From now on the duty of the village teacher shall not be limited to the education of rural children, rather they shall be charged with the leadership of the village' (Ronduen and Dideban, 1970, p. 18). Similarly an order from the Ministry stated: 'That the heads and elders of villages should be encouraged to follow the useful social, public health and developmental instructions of the Education Corps conscripts which will be effective in the improvement of living conditions, the progress of society and in the development of the village' (ibid. p. 19).

Many youths drafted in for this task had become urbanised and to some extent westernised and, like State school teachers, saw their careers as moving up through national educational institutions to white-collar jobs. They saw their fourteen months in the village as a retrogressive step and an interruption. They were afraid that they would forget the English they had learnt and be out of touch with urban centres, where modern goals and life styles were being set and where fellow youths were expressing their modernity. An encouragement offered by the government was that after their service they could become fully-recognised teachers by merely taking a course lasting four months, although they were still obliged to spend further years teaching in rural areas before graduating to an urban school.

The problems that arose from sending these youths to not only teach but also 'lead' villagers were well understood by many involved in the system on the ground. An employee in the Ministry of Education in Khorosan Province, for instance, points out that 'these Corpsmen lack many essential things: they are young and inexperienced and they come mostly from cities and know little about the problems of rural people. They lack the ability to adapt themselves to, and identify themselves with, the community in which they work' (Hashemi, 1966, p. 109). A colleague of his added that the four-month training course for those drafted in was inadequate; that youths were often sent away from their own areas to places where manners and dialects were different; that it was often not possible to find 'suitable accommodation'; and that 'in some cases lack of understanding and appreciation of the programme of the Corpsmen results in lack of enthusiasm for the job which they have undertaken' (Gharib, 1966, p. 50).

Some recruits, however, did have a genuine vision that they could do something to help and they did work well with the villagers, gaining their respect and fulfilling some of their goals both inside the school and outside. But such success and such a self-vision often went to the head of a boy or girl of just twenty-one whose whole life had been within an insulated school system with little responsibility. The new status and power became an 'ego trip' that disrupted village life and further alienated the locals from central values.

Where Corpsmen and women did achieve 'success' these remained individual and personal achievements. The organisation itself did not evolve an overall strategy which would have enabled it to relate consistently and harmoniously with the villager; indeed, its very principles set it at variance with the principles underlying village life. Many villagers saw the Corps, even more blatantly than the schools, as an arm of central government power keeping control of village affairs, upsetting traditional goals and beliefs, and introducing outsiders whose first loyalty was to a system of beliefs external to the village and in conflict with what the villagers considered best for themselves. In Iran there has been a long history of attempts by centralising powers and invaders to impose their rule on local peoples and the Shah's efforts could be seen as part of this pattern. Indeed, the locals have, historically, often come off best in the end; they have learnt strategies for coping with alien rule and alien beliefs and local culture has reasserted itself after a period of invasion. The proponents of the present Islamic regime in Iran would certainly present the current situation in these terms. From a broader perspective we might recognise that the sheer affront to village life and values represented by the examples cited above was likely to produce an extreme reaction of the kind now being experienced. Reading over the literature of that period it seems remarkable how crude and ethnocentric the thinking behind the literacy campaigns and education programmes were, and yet they were founded, to some extent at least, on the theories and developments worked out by Unesco 'experts'. Although the Iranian example represents perhaps an extreme version of what radical writers have complained of in Unesco-oriented literacy theory and practice, it does highlight what that can lead to.

As in Tanzania, many Iranian villagers showed considerable resistance to the programmes being foisted upon them and this forced the 'experts' to search for a compromise – a means of getting their educational ideas accepted by adapting it more to the wishes and needs of villagers. One local administrator in Khorosan Province, for instance, put forward proposals for rural teacher training that were precisely in this spirit (Gharib, 1966). He believed that the government had put too much emphasis on the Sepah-ye Danesh, which was only a temporary solution to the 'problem' of rural education. Ultimately such education would have to be developed along the lines of having local men and women, trained in local teacher training centres, return to their own villages to impart some knowledge of the outside world while teaching rural children to better understand and use their own environment. The principle of urban men and women trained in urban colleges teaching in the villages must ultimately be abandoned. The fact that such compromises were being proposed, whatever their internal problems, indicates the extent to which the indifference of the villagers to the schemes of central government was a powerful political weapon, which could force that government to rethink its programmes. It also, of course, forced into the open debate about what the real, as opposed to the stated, aims of such programmes were. This is apparent if we examine the work of a Unesco expert, P. Ronduen, who was writing about Iran at that time. He advised teachers in his report on rural education there that they 'must appreciate the value of the rural heritage and the fine qualities and possibilities of rural people. They must use the rich educational possibilities of the environment for teaching the various subjects and for teaching civic relationships' (Ronduen, 1970, p. 117). He wanted village schools to integrate with the community and to use the whole environment and situation. He writes: 'It can be said that the very best education for a child during his/her formative impressionable years is to become thoroughly steeped in the atmosphere of his own environment' (ibid.). One is tempted to suggest that this is what she/he was before the outside teacher arrived. Taken to its logical conclusion such proposals contradict the basic purposes of the outsider in the village, although their presentation in this way does force the 'expert' to reconsider what those purposes are. In the Iranian case, as in many others, it was to get a sufficient proportion of villagers to 'participate' in the modern economy to fulfil its manpower and skill needs and to exercise central control over outlying areas.

Seen at this level, the relationship between government agents and villagers is a political one and there is scope for negotiation across the obvious lines of conflict. Indeed, many village youths did take to the new philosophy, or at least to its material inducements, and left the villages to pursue urban education and careers. From the government's point of view the 'problem' was that not enough of them were doing so to service the expanding modern economy, which therefore remained dependent on expensive foreign expertise. In order to get rid of the foreign 'expert' and to become self-supporting, it was considered necessary to, as it were, turn a proportion of the indigenous population themselves into western-type experts and this, as Baldwin pointed out, involved enlarging the pool from which 'natural talent' could be selected for 'upgrading with acquired skills' (1967, p. 148). The negotiation between government agencies and villagers hinged on these interests, although they were not always represented in these terms. The Shah saw the process in terms of metaphors of war. The recruits of the Education Corps were 'soldiers fighting in the first line of the front' and he believed: 'Today the world is observant of our history in this war. Obviously in this war I, who have ordered the formation of the Army of Knowledge, shall lead you everywhere as the flag carrier of this national holy war' (*Kayhan International*, 30. 12. 71). Some Unesco experts and local educators, on the other hand, were trying to soften the authoritarian nature of the literacy programmes and to pay more attention to local culture and interests. The conflict between these two extremes in Iran brings out at a somewhat stark level the arguments and debates taking place in Unesco circles and amongst international developers generally during this period.

Freire, for instance, attempted to emphasise the participatory and co-operative nature of literacy programmes rather than their conception as 'warfare', although he did want to make explicit the extent to which ideological struggles were integral to them. In fact his willingness to make explicit the political and ideological nature of literacy practice places him nearer to what I have termed the 'ideological' model of literacy than are many Unesco-oriented approaches, whether of the 'warfare' or 'local atmosphere' type. Freire is concerned with how people codify their own experience and with how their consciousness of that experience can be raised. His approach to teaching methodology is framed by this political concern with 'conscientization'. He proposes, for instance, the selection of key words and syllables from the experience of the people concerned which the teacher can then focus on to help them generate other, relevant words and so build up their own word picture. They would thus be learning to write and read what concerned them centrally in their own lives and would be motivated in a way that those receiving external 'education' would not (1972).

However, some of Freire's ideas have themselves been challenged in recent years and he has been accused of failing to appreciate the implicit hierarchy in his supposedly egalitarian and co-operative system. While his ideal was 'classless', it actually involved, according to Walker, making use of a 'petty bourgeois' class which had the skills to do the job (in Mackie, 1980, p. 134). Walker points out that the solution to this dilemma adopted by Amilcar Cabral was to admit that 'peasants can't take on their own liberation' and so that petty bourgeois teachers had to be employed in the first instance (ibid. p. 135). Cabral went on to suggest, however, that they should commit 'class suicide' once the revolution had been accomplished (ibid.). Walker disagrees, arguing that the concept of class is a material one and not simply a moral choice as the proposal for 'class suicide' implies. Freire's position, on which so many radical programmes have been built as an alternative to the Unesco kind cited above, involves a similar appeal to a 'mystical' rather than a material analysis: in Freire's case this is a sort of 'existential Christianity' rather than 'sound' Marxist analysis. The class position of the teacher cannot be so simply disregarded, or bracketed, claims Walker, since the methodology of teaching cannot be divorced from its political aims (ibid. pp. 136–7). The recognition of this contradiction in Freire's work requires, then, a refinement of the theory and of Freire's model of pedagogy which appears to be built on ideals rather than on practical experience. Again, as with some of the ideas put forward at the Persepolis Symposium on Literacy, some radical writers appear to be moving towards an 'ideological' model of literacy.

Freire, of course, did have a great deal of personal experience and his work has been used in a number of practical programmes. He influenced, for instance, the recent Nicaraguan Literacy Crusade, although the Nicaraguans have gone out of their way to claim some independence and to suggest that they have found ways out of the kind of dilemma highlighted by Walker. The material on Nicaragua provides an interesting comparison with that cited above from Iran and Tanzania. It should enable us to see how far the left of the political spectrum has rejected the model of literacy represented by those experiences and, in moving towards a more 'ideological' model of literacy, has managed to face up to or resolve the difficulties and contradictions outlined above.

There is certainly an explicit recognition of political objectives in the Nicaraguan campaign. Henri Weber in *Nicaragua: the Sandinist Revolution* summarises the campaign in these terms: 'Most impressive of all, however, was the political balance sheet of the "cruzada". The bourgeois parties made no mistake when they constantly denounced the "over-politicization" of the campaign. For the youth mobilized to serve the Sandinist revolution, and in doing so they internalized the values of the revolution. The rural proletariat now closely identifies with the new regime.' (1981, p. 85.)

The means of achieving this 'politicization' were similar to those proposed by Freire, with deliberate changes to cater for local circumstances. Black and Bevan (1980) describe the difference between the materials which Freire provided for teachers to use as the basis of 'dialogue' with students and those used in Nicaragua. There a single text book was provided for the whole country, consisting of twenty-three lessons focussed on specific photographs and key phrases. These were geared to an explicit political strategy – 'unification':

Freire's materials had focussed on the local reality of specific communities for use in regionally independent campaigns. In a country where there is a sharp distinction between the experiences and cultural values of a peasant in the remote mountains of Matagalpa and a factory worker in Eastern Managua, it was difficult for the Nicaraguans to select visual themes for dialogue which would strike a chord at national level but in choosing images which reflect the dominant elements of the revolution, they have managed to avoid the use of limited regional subjects. (1980, p. 64.)

The 'dialogue' is begun by reference to the photograph which is then related to a phrase, out of which other phrases and key words and syllables are developed as in Freire's method, except that he used a single word as the focus. The text book begins with 'Sandino, guide of the revolution' and progresses through such injunctions as 'To spend little, to save money and to produce a lot is to make the revolution', to the twenty-third phrase: 'The Sandinist revolution is creating close fraternal bonds with all peoples' (ibid. Appendix II). Black and Bevan point out: 'The key sentence of each lesson, in synthesizing the political message of the photograph, is tremendously important from a teaching point of view. If the illiterate learner recognises the letters and words and associates them clearly with the discussion themes the words will cease to be a meaningless arrangement of shapes and take on instead a direct association with concepts the learner feels strongly committed to' (ibid. p. 65). This is a clear representation of the ideological nature of literacy learning. There is no pretence that the process is a 'neutral' one or that, having learnt to 'decode' letters, readers can then make their own political choices, as in much of the academic and development literature we have been considering. The very pedagogy and the form as well as the content of literacy training are admitted as ideological. Some individuals may not like the particular political bias of the Nicaraguan revolutionaries but at least they are made explicitly aware of that bias. Their dislike for it is similar to that felt by people of a different political persuasion when they observe the political bias in Unesco-oriented literacy programmes and establishment teaching methods. As Graff (1979), for instance, has shown regarding nineteenth century Canada, or Mace and others regarding contemporary education in the UK, literacy training always involves some such political and ideological structure and content. The fact that these are not equally distasteful to many observers stems from the fact that, firstly, the political bias is often hidden and, secondly, that they are, in any case, in sympathy with it. When students in Tanzania are given text books with such phrases as 'Cotton is wealth. Cotton brings money' they are being subjected to ideological training in the same way as are the peasants of Nicaragua, although from a different political perspective.

The decision as to which approach is 'better' is then a political one. Similarly the resolution of the problems and contradictions within the campaigns themselves can only be reached by political choices and decisions. In the Nicaraguan case, for instance, the problems faced by the literacy campaigners are essentially those faced in other areas of the revolution. The crucial contradiction is that between a stated commitment to helping people to 'create their own history' and the evident imposition of specific central theory and practice on the regions. This takes the form in Nicaragua, as elsewhere, of a classic urban–rural tension. A quick survey after the revolution revealed 'profound regional imbalances':

> In the capital city of Managua and other heavily populated areas of the Pacific coast belt, where all industry, the agricultural export crops and the state bureaucracy are concentrated, urban illiteracy falls as low as 26.5%. Around Managua the Crusade has almost as many volunteer teachers at its disposal as there are illiterates to be taught. On the Atlantic coast, however, with its low population density and little economic development, rural illiteracy can reach 85% (100% in the case of women in some villages) and there is of course a corresponding shortage of locally available teaching volunteers. The problem of the Atlantic coast is increased because there are non-Spanish speaking settlements. (Black and Bevan, 1980, p. 50.)

The Literacy Crusade, then, consisted mostly of young people from the urbanised and 'developed' areas of Nicaragua who went out into the countryside bearing the specific forms of political literacy formulated in their areas. Similar tensions, then, could be expected, and were in fact experienced, as occur in other literacy campaigns of a different political colour but evolved out of the same structural features. As in Iran and Tanzania, we find local resistance. One Cuban volunteer who had responded to a call for help by the Nicaraguan authorities complained, for instance, of difficulties similar to those encountered by the Shah's Corpsmen: 'The problem is to make sure that they come to classes. I have 21 children, for example, but seven or eight of them don't turn up because they are working in the fields with their parents. As for the adults, it's really only the women who come regularly: none of the men attend classes very often' (ibid. p. 45).

This Cuban youth also hints at another familiar problem, one which was highlighted in different ways in both the Iranian and Tanzanian campaigns – the relationship between volunteer forces and the established teachers: 'It's frustrating not to be able to talk more to Nicaraguan teachers, which is almost impossible, partly because of the bad communications – and of course we share the same timetables' (ibid. p. 47). Judging from experience elsewhere it is likely that if they had met more often they might have found that there was much they did not share.

However, the increased interaction between rural and urban areas of Nicaragua as a result of the Literacy Crusade did not always lead to tensions. One of the positive aspects of the campaign, according to many commentators and participants, was that the middle-class children of urban parents came back from the villages with a genuine respect for the people they had worked with, a deeper understanding of how the peasants had been exploited by urban capitalism and a commitment to avoiding the old stereotypes of peasant life. Moreover, many of them began to convince their parents too: many urban-based parents went to considerable trouble to keep in touch with their teenage children out on the Crusade and this involved visiting outlying villages, for the first time for many of them, and establishing personal relationships with the peasants. Many of these ties have continued after the period of the Crusade, rather in the way that urban dwellers in Britain, who had been evacuated to villages during the last war, have maintained ties with the community they stayed with ever since. Many of the parents are also being infected with their children's new-found radicalism as a result of their experiences in the Literacy Crusade, which has further contributed to its political impact. These differences from the results of campaigns in Iran, Tanzania and elsewhere stem, to some extent, from the motivation behind the Nicaraguan campaign in the first place.

The overt strategic drive behind the Literacy Crusade was to keep up the momentum of the Revolution in the period after the victory. The material benefits promised by the overthrow of the dictatorship could not be realised immediately – although some benefits have come through very quickly, such as increased rice production as a result of participatory mechanisms, popular pricing systems and Land Reform geared to production (Marchetti, 1983) – and the Literacy Crusade was seen as a way of providing concrete action and involvement. Most families had lost a loved one in the war and the Crusade in a sense provided a positive demonstration of what they had died for. A comparison with the attempted Literacy Campaign in the neighbouring State of Honduras suggests that the revolutionary motivation is, in fact, crucial to the success of such campaigns (Bevan, 1983). The Honduran Campaign 'was launched by a rigid and authoritarian military dictatorship. Neither land reform nor primary school expansion are seriously on the agenda. Social and political relations remain unchanged. The failure of the campaign has as much to do with this as with its chaotic organisation and lack of planning' (ibid. p. 20). The Nicaraguan campaign, then, has achieved some measure of success for the same reasons as the Honduran one failed. As Freire says of the Nicaraguan campaign 'literacy only has meaning in a society undergoing revolutionary change' (quoted in Bevan, ibid.). Whether this fervour can be maintained remains to be seen. At present the Nicaraguans have not had to resort to artificial 'literacy environments' in order to prevent the new literacy skills from atrophying. This is perhaps because, for the moment, the revolution is continuing. Peasants can, for instance, use their new-found literacy to read or take the minutes of a committee meeting that will decide on matters of immediate and crucial importance to their lives. They thus ensure that the committee is not controlled by one person and reap the direct fruits of their literacy in participatory politics. Likewise they are using numeracy to avoid being swindled in trading deals and in order to 'run local industry and take part in the "participatory" rural economy' (ibid.).

While most commentators agree about these 'successes' in the country generally, whatever their prognostications for the future, there is more uncertainty regarding the effects of the campaign on the Atlantic Coast, an area different culturally and cut off geographically from the main centres of the revolution. The bad communications and the remoteness of many of the regions beyond the western industrial belt mean that in many cases, according to Black and Bevan: 'The population is unfamiliar with – and perhaps unready for – many of the political assumptions behind the Crusade (many remote communities only heard of the revolution weeks after it had triumphed) and there are at least four minority languages, some with numerous dialects' (Black and Bevan, 1980, p. 47). Although, as we shall see, the revolutionaries are committed to showing more sensitivity to these people than was demonstrated by many developers in the Iranian and other similar contexts, they nevertheless have their own version of the economistic model and their own priorities: 'Economic integration is', according to them, 'dependent on cultural integration, the development of a sense of national identity among the people of the Atlantic coast' (ibid. p. 59). Some aspects of the campaign are, then, similar to those evident in political regimes of quite a different political persuasion. This extends to the language in which the issue of literacy training is couched. As with the Shah's 'Army of Knowledge', the Nicaraguan attempts to take central beliefs and practices to outlying areas are conducted in military terms: 'The metaphors of the crusade are military: it is the "cultural insurrection" or the "second war of liberation". In each region where literacy is eradicated, the teachers will raise a banner declaring the place "liberated territory". The literacy brigades will be arranged in "battle fronts" identical to those used by the FSLN during the insurrection and similarly divided into brigades, columns and squadrons' (ibid. p. 54).

This is hardly surprising after the evident success of such language and organisation in defeating the Samoza dictatorship, but it makes explicit the tension between those bringing the ideology and literacy and those intended to receive it. It also brings out the contradiction in revolutionary ideology between wanting people to 'make their own history' and the imposition of specific ways in which they must do so. This contradiction exists also in the apparently more liberal Unesco projects, as is obvious from the Iranian material, although it is not always so explicit as in the Iranian case. Understanding literacy as a form of ideology at least enables us to recognise these problems at the level at which they might be resolved. The adoption of the 'autonomous' model of literacy can and has led to the mistaken assumption that they can be resolved at a 'neutral' level – that they have simply to be left to the 'experts'. As we saw in relation to proposals for 'community-oriented' literacy in Iran, this simply leads to new contradictions so long as the political nettle is not grasped. It is, in fact, the prevalence of this 'neutral' approach too often beneath the concept of 'functional literacy' that can be held to account for the continuing 'failure' of many Unesco programmes, as many participants at the Persepolis Symposium indeed recognised. While the adoption of the 'ideological' model of literacy will not necessarily provide immediate or simple answers, it will at least establish the analysis and discussion at the appropriate level and within a framework that, being by its nature political, is already geared to decision-making in relation to the society as a whole.

In Nicaragua it was this recognition of the ideological nature of literacy training that led, I would argue, to explicit efforts to be sensitive to local cultures in a way that does not happen either when teachers believe they are simply imparting a 'neutral' technical skill or when the ideology is explicitly elitist and scornful of village life as in Iran. Although in Nicaragua too a 'war' has been engaged in, tactics are to be varied to suit local interests and the troops are not simply ordered in to control and oppress the villagers as in the Shah's campaigns. Black and Bevan explain this sensitivity in terms that might be instructive for other literacy activists of the left. In the outlying areas, they write:

> A slower rhythm has been established for the campaign dictated by the combination of technical obstacles (different languages etc.) and political sensitivities. The inhabitants of the area, whatever their linguistic background, are not necessarily receptive to the ideology of the revolution. This ideology may be unrelated to the reality of an area which was marginal to the development of the revolutionary struggle: it may also be in direct conflict with a complex system of values formed by tribalism, racial factors, a resentment of 'Pacific Coast' influence and evangelical Christianity. (ibid. p. 60.)

The response to this different ideology represents a combination of political idealism and anthropological detail unusual in such campaigns. A local radio station set up to explain the aims of the revolution to these outlying areas also addressed itself, for instance, to briefing the teachers on 'local living conditions': "'It's important to brief people on the smallest details", said a radio worker "even on things like diet, which will cause problems of adaptation ... to tell the teachers that peasants in the area eat fried yucca three times a day, not beans and rice like the rest of the country'" (ibid. p. 60). It was also decided 'to teach ethnic minority groups to read and write first in their own language in a "transitional" period, before moving on to learning the "official" national language of Spanish' (ibid.). The situation gives rise to many of the problems experienced in other minority language programmes, with the added complication that in the case of one group, the descendants of slaves imported by the British in the eighteenth and nineteenth centuries, the 'mother tongue' is, in fact, English. As Freeland points out:

> MISURASATA [a new association of indigenous peoples] can argue cogently that a Revolutionary government should respect their ancient traditions of resistance to colonization, and allow them to follow their interrupted processes of development. But this argument does not apply, of course, to the English-speakers, whose languages and customs are the result of the very imperialism against which the Sandinistas fought and triumphed. Against legitimate claims that, whatever their roots, this *is* their mother tongue and culture, and that to attack it is to attack their identity, must be set the equally legitimate need to confront and modify alien values. Hence the language politics of the Atlantic Coast Crusade reflect in microcosm some of the larger complexities of a pluralist programme of reconstruction such as the new government has set itself. (Freeland, 1981a.)

Freeland adds an optimistic note on the basis of her experience of the way in which such problems are currently being approached in Nicaragua: 'As in other areas, these are being tackled with flair, imagination, and much tact.' (ibid.)

It is worth dwelling on this experience in some detail in order to demonstrate how a sophisticated 'technical' knowledge on the part of literacy campaigners can be combined with clear ideological commitment rather than confused with supposed 'neutrality', as in many of the cases we have been considering. Freeland writes, for instance, that the 'language politics of the Atlantic Coast Crusade' have involved the campaign organisers in close consultation with MISURASATA and the Churches on both the content and the methodology of mother-tongue programmes. One immediate problem raised was that the teaching materials had been designed for Spanish-speaking communities which had experienced the revolution in some form. 'It was argued by the Atlantic Coast teams that, in communities which had not directly shared this experience, the phrases might seem more like empty slogans, and arouse resistance or hostility' (ibid.). In the end the phrases in the Spanish *cartillas* were translated into local languages but 'links between the local and national frames of reference were established through different pictures in some instances, through oral discussion, and finally through the important process of creating new words and phrases from old' (ibid.). In the case of the English language speakers, however, the ambiguity of English orthography makes it difficult to apply Freire's technique of breaking words into syllables in order to build up new words.

As Freeland points out: 'English, of course, is neither written phonemically, nor so easily broken down into syllables [as Spanish], for creative recombination. So, at the vital stage of making new words from old, the awkwardnesses of English orthography are liable to set up barriers, when *heat* not only rhymes with *meat* (or is it *meet?*), but also with *feet*.' (ibid.) She shows how the campaigners dealt with the problem within the terms of their ideological commitment to the learner's own participation: 'The idea is to start from words offered, at a certain stage of the lesson, by the learner: where these present orthographic problems (meat/meet, for instance), the teacher will need to show learners that there are variants, but without working them too emphatically. They will then refer back to them for practice and production later in the course. Also from the start, words are combined into simple sentences, so that function words are learned by sight as part of statements. Matching exercises are used here, to help foreground key words and patterns, and allow unobtrusive practice in recognising irregular but common forms' (ibid.). Writing in 1981 Freeland recounts the initial success of this strategy: 'only eight months after the launching of the national crusade, the Atlantic Coast's literacy campaign for ethnic minorities is well on its way, a remarkable feat considering all the complications ... not to mention the purely logistic ones of establishing the original surveys and preparing the necessary support organisation of accommodation and transport in such difficult areas' (ibid.).

There were, however, problems: the campaign ran 'against a background of regional unrest which must have sorely strained the atmosphere of trust necessary to its success. During this time, several attempts were made to manipulate cultural differences to counter-revolutionary ends' (1981b, p. 7) and MISURASATA was accused by some of having separatist tendencies. One of its leaders did, in fact, turn out to be a Samoza informer who has since escaped to Honduras and broadcasts anti-Sandinist propaganda from there, but it would be a mistake to infer from this individual's activities that the movement as a whole is 'counter-revolutionary'. Its interests are not so much separatist as trans-national, a point of considerable general significance in considering the ways in which local and central groups compete over such issues as literacy and language programmes. In December 1981 the Nicaraguan government entertained a delegation from the International Work Group For Indigenous Affairs (IWGIA), inquiring into how the interests of the indigenous peoples could be recognised within the overall framework of the new nation state. The delegation is reported to have left positive that the issue of local versus national language and literacy practices was at least being recognised by the Sandinistas and that, given the outside pressures, it was being handled sensitively (IWGIA, 1982, pp. 5–38). Freeland is equally optimistic: 'It is not yet clear precisely how these events [on the Atlantic coast] interacted with the Literacy Crusade ... [but] official reports on the Crusade in Spanish lead one to expect a clear-sighted document that will draw out the implications of this complex experience for future policy. Verbal reports suggest a level of success which, though modest beside that of the Crusade in Spanish, is considerable in view of the problems confronted' (Freeland, 1981b, p. 7). The pace of learning was slower and the cost of the campaigns in this area was much higher than elsewhere, but:

> against all this must be weighed far subtler social effects of the mutual teaching and learning involved in such a venture. The role of local leaders cannot be minimised ... The dialogue between government and communities is a tangible gain, which will be of immeasurable importance during the delicate transition to Spanish-medium teaching which it is now planned to make, through the follow-up programmes designed to complete the basic education of the newly literate. A difficult, but essential task will be to accompany this change with the development of convincing channels through which the minorities can express their identity, if they are to resist the seductive propaganda of separatism ... So far one can only speculate, and it is clear that the diversity of this region will be only gradually harmonised. But the record so far of imagination and patient attention to detail promises an interesting future (1981b, p. 8).

She concludes the *WUS News* article with a positive affirmation of a principle of no little relevance to other such campaigns: 'The signs are hopeful that interchange, rather than importation of forms, will mark this latest attempt to overcome the isolation and consequent suspicion and withdrawal of this area of Nicaragua' (1981a).

There are clear lessons here not only for 'Establishment' practitioners but also for more radical teachers of literacy in other parts of the world, including the UK and the USA. Left-oriented teachers, for instance, often find themselves in daily contact with literacy learners through adult literacy campaigns and other non-formal learning situations. The Nicaraguan example might remind them that rejection of 'Establishment' bias in literacy training does not necessarily require or justify immediate imposition of 'revolutionary' ideology on their subjects. Many working-class people and so-called 'illiterates' may not be 'receptive' to such ideology and, indeed, as in Nicaragua it may be unrelated to some aspects of their lives and in conflict with deeply-held values. The recognition that literacy is ideological, and therefore involves imparting a point of view as well as simply teaching a technical skill, does not mean that that point of view has to be imposed in authoritarian or insensitive ways. The local language, culture and thinking has to be taken into account and not simply written off. A 'slower rhythm' might have to be established than some enthusiasts would wish. Teachers and organisers on the left, and indeed those liberals who have come to recognise the limitations of the 'autonomous' model of literacy, might, then, learn from the Nicaraguan experience not only the importance of adopting the 'ideological' model of literacy but also the importance of applying it with sensitivity to different cultures and class groups. It is with this crucial aspect of literacy in practice that the final chapter will be concerned.

8

ADULT LITERACY CAMPAIGNS IN THE UK AND THE USA

In the late 1970s in the UK and the USA government money and institutions began to be directed towards what was defined as 'the problem of illiteracy'. 'Unacceptable' levels of illiteracy were identified by various criteria and programmes were developed to overcome them. I would now like to examine these definitions and activities in the broader context developed in Sections 1 and 2. I would hope thereby to provide a framework for approaching the more familiar features of our own literacy practices in a detached and critical frame of mind, independent of both official definitions and equally independent of, though taking into account, the participants' own perceptions. This, as we have seen, raises a number of issues that can only be briefly sketched in here. They include; the hegemonic uses of literacy both within the educational system and in communication media generally; the relations of production, distribution and control of literate forms and their implications for the assessed consequences of literacy; the relationship of pedagogic practice and tradition within the education system to that being developed in adult education programmes and in radical groups; the concept of literacy as 'technology' and 'skills' as opposed to that of literacy as social practice and activity; the significance of student production of their own texts as opposed to passive consumption of them.

The sudden perception of 'illiteracy' as a 'problem' in the 1970s in the UK and the USA has a specific history, not necessarily directly related to any changes in the real situation. Levine (1980) suggests that in the UK it was related to the power of specific pressure groups whose strategies involved the unsubstantiable claim that two million adults in England were 'functionally illiterate'. This figure was a powerful focus for a campaign to raise consciousness about and inject funds into an area that had previously been subsumed under 'schooling' both in terms of the concepts applied and the finance availabe. In the USA the discovery of 'illiteracy' and the use of numbers to shock opinion was equally dramatic. Some estimates suggested that as many as sixty million 'suffer significant disadvantages because of their limited education' (Hunter and Harman, 1979, p. 103). The authors of a major American inquiry into the issue pointed out, further, that 'studies of functional competency suggest that one in five American adults has difficulty with *many* tasks required in daily living

213

and that more than one-third have trouble with some of those tasks' (ibid.). They suggest that, as in the UK, these findings were explicitly brought home to the public in the mid-1970s: 'the Americans have recently been confronted and confounded by dramatic headlines about the level of illiteracy among the adult population. The *New York Times* of 24 April 1977, declared: "Illiteracy of Adults Called U.S. Disease".' (ibid. p. 1.) One effect of the publicity was that resources were allocated to researchers investigating the 'problem' and Hunter and Harman's book is one of the more prominent outcomes of the very process they were studying. Levine, in a comparable study commissioned by the SSRC in the UK, describes how the focus of research altered as the researchers themselves altered the nature of the 'problem'. Researchers at first followed a 'policy' orientation concerning themselves with questions of 'aggregate provision' and 'aggregate need' (1980, p. 3) in relation to the desire to mobilise support. This stage was followed by 'action research': those responsible for the overall organisation of the new provision wanted to find out what was actually going on in the 'one to one' teaching sessions that were the main mode of adult literacy training. More recently, in contrast with earlier researchers who saw 'illiteracy' as an individual problem, writers have posed it as a 'social problem' and looked for causes in the institutional values and practices of school and other 'establishment' institutions.

Hunter and Harman, for instance, in the USA, concluded that the 'problem' of illiteracy could not be separated from the larger structural problems of the society in which it occurs: 'Just as the problems faced by people everywhere are interrelated, so too must be the efforts to solve them. This study looks at adult education as an integral part of the larger social and economic system.' (1979, p. 3.) They expect resistance to this approach and line up their arguments to rebut it:

> It is our conviction that a mere rearrangement of educational furniture is too simplistic an approach to the resolution of the social and economic issues of which illiteracy is only a symptom ... We believe that the interconnectedness between policy decisions and assumptions in the field of education and in other areas that affect the total life of a people call for new alliances and an integration of insights from different disciplines and from diverse segments of the population. (ibid. p. 4.)

This leads them to reject attempts by the government in the USA to emphasise the relationship of literacy to job prospects, in keeping with the economistic model of literacy and the perspective that puts the 'blame' for illiteracy and unemployment alike on the individual. They point out for instance how the Adult Basic Education Program in the USA was based on the claim 'that *anyone* who becomes literate is automatically better off economically, is better able to find employment, and becomes a better citizen'. This, indeed, was enshrined in law: 'Literacy, it was claimed, would help those with low-level literacy skills "to eliminate their inability to get or retain employment", would make them "less likely to become dependent on others" and would increase "their ability to benefit from occupational training" (Title II of Public Law 91 – 230, Amendment to the Adult Education Act, Section 303c).' (ibid. p. 15.) In keeping with Graff's findings in nineteenth century Canada and his rejection of the 'literacy myth', they argue that 'poverty and the power structures of society are more responsible for low levels of literacy than the reverse'. Much of their research findings are devoted to exposing this 'myth'. For most persons who lack literacy skills, illiteracy, they point out, is 'simply one factor interacting with many others – class, race, and sex discrimination, welfare dependency, unemployment, poor housing and a general sense of powerlessness. The acquisition of reading and writing skills would eliminate conventional illiteracy among many but would have no appreciable effect on the other factors that perpetuate the poverty of their lives.' (ibid. p. 9.)

In the UK, too, however, the government has recently attempted to invoke the literacy 'myth'. The ALBSU, which as we shall see below has been responsible for some important innovations in thinking and practice in the UK, was asked by the Minister responsible for it to change its remit to include responsibility for 'communication and coping skills without which people are impeded from applying or being considered for employment' (ALBSU, 1982a). After some resistance from the Unit, however, the government has softened the line to make it responsible 'for those related basic communication and coping skills without which progress in and towards education, training or employment is impeded'. (ibid.) The Unit had argued that 'to concentrate on the motivation of a job may be very misleading at a time when over three million are without work'. They stressed that: 'It is important to recognise ... that the quality of life and the quality of our society as a whole does not depend only on employment and that mastery of basic skills is just as important in many other aspects of an individual's life.' (ibid.) Being a government-funded institution they record their victory modestly: 'That central government has recognised this view at a time when so much concentration is placed on work, is important for everyone involved in the development of basic education.' (ibid.)

Research and experience in both the UK and the USA, then, is suggesting that, whatever governments may say, the only long-term way of dealing with the defined 'problem' of literacy levels is to change the institutions themselves. Some radical literacy teachers, however, despairing of achieving such a goal, have opted in the short term for changing the 'victims'. In England, Mace for instance, whose book *Working with Words* has been seminal in putting literacy on the political agenda, at least on that of the left, directed tutors to the students' 'loss of self esteem' as a result of bad schooling experience and proposed that literacy programmes should be directed to the explicit political aim of 'comprehensive resocialisation'. *Tribune* reviewed her book under the headline 'Literacy as a Political Issue' and selected out the pedagogical aim of 'helping the student to regain his [sic] self confidence in a learning relationship established on the basis of trust and mutual respect' (22.6.79). This involved doing more than simply inculcating skills in 'consuming print' but was a whole education so that the student would 'no longer see his illiteracy in terms of a personal failure, marking him as an incompetent devoid of moral virtue, but in terms of an educational system which had failed him in the past' (ibid.).

Levine questions Mace's approach and asks whether the people who came to literacy programmes actually saw themselves in the terms she posed. He wonders whether many of them in fact underestimated their 'problem' or simply did not experience any difficulty until some crisis occurred for them. The kind of situation he has in mind is exemplified by the experience of an individual I encountered at a literacy centre in Brighton. He was a mechanic who had been used to handing out 'MOT' (Ministry of Transport Car Test) forms to customers on the basis of his ability to 'read' layout of forms and the few conventional terms they employed. One day a customer returned telling him that the form had been wrongly completed and he discovered that the Ministry had changed the format. At that point he decided that he needed more general literacy skills to enable him to adapt to such changes: those he had successfully exercised for many years no longer seemed to be adequate. Levine would argue, rightly I believe, that individuals such as this had not perceived themselves as 'deprived' and did not lack 'self-esteem', so that Mace's approach would not adequately cater for their particular experience and demands. Research in the USA suggests that the same conclusions are true there. Hunter and Harman, for instance, say that 'literacy is seldom a first priority among those who are themselves unlettered. When given an opportunity to define their own needs, they are likely to stress first their economic problems, followed by such personal concerns as family living, child care, health, and nutrition.' (1979, p. 8.)

Hunter and Harman in the USA and Levine in the UK highlight, then, a crucial problem in Mace's approach. A project for altering an individual's consciousness, which is all that Mace in the end offers us as a form of political action with regard to literacy practice, will remain marginal if it fails to challenge the central establishments themselves.

Activists have to ask, in this as in other areas of struggle, is it right to opt out of the establishment institutions and to work instead at 'comprehensive resocialisation' in alternative sites of struggle? Or does this deflect energies from the major task of changing those institutions themselves? In order to act on this larger front, I would argue, we need a more general theory of literacy practice: a theory which combines understanding of just how establishment institutions are really 'depriving' working people (without falling into the 'cultural deprivation' trap) with understanding of why they themselves do not necessarily perceive it in that way.

From this perspective current researches do pose a challenge to Mace and to the main direction of thinking on the left with regard to literacy. We would do well to listen when Levine, for instance, tells us that many people's experience of establishment institutions and practices does not necessarily entail loss of 'self esteem' or feelings of inadequacy. Middle-class radical intellectuals might sense that they would feel such loss if they were in those circumstances but this, as the anthropologists would say, is 'if I were a horse' kind of thinking. Such a framework blithely ignores 'folk models' or relegates them to the level of 'false consciousness' and thus prevents us from coming to grips with just why that experience leads the participants to that particular conception of it. Levine's findings remind us that solutions to political problems cannot be extracted from such 'if I were a horse' kinds of approach.

A theory of literacy practice that adequately explains the situation that large numbers of adults currently find themselves in cannot be satisfactory if it rests on the simple belief that 'they' have been directly deceived and that there is nothing in their situation that might reasonably lead them to the conceptions they evidently hold about it. Rather I would propose that we should examine that situation as an anthropologist would examine a culture or sub-culture, making explicit the judgements we would make from our own cultural and structural situations in order to discover how and why the structures to be identified there generate particular conceptions and perceptions amongst the actors themselves. Such a project requires a theory of literacy practice that is not embedded in the dominant establishment uses of and assumptions about literacy in this culture.

In order to disembed ourselves from this dominant ideology we firstly have to make it explicit. This, I would suggest, is what is offered by the 'ideological' model of literacy that I have been developing above.

At present there is very little interaction between this academic work and the actual practice of different literacies in the UK. On the one hand, those involved in the day to day practice of teaching adult literacy, particularly in the adult literacy campaigns to which I referred above, have had little time, or often inclination, to devote to an apparently jargon-ridden, ivory-tower set of theories of the kind I have been discussing. As one literacy worker put it to me: 'I just use my intuitions.' On the other hand, those producing the theories and ideas cited above have indeed operated at a remove, institutionally, conceptually and in terms of their empirical interests, even, from the workers 'in the field'. The substantive data on literacy practice to which they do refer ranges from medieval England to contemporary Africa and Asia, as we have seen, but it pays little attention to what is happening right now in the UK. Questions regarding the political and ideological nature of literacy practices, which they have posed in relation to other times and places, have scarcely been confronted by them or by others with regard to the UK. Research here, as Levine points out, has been either 'policy oriented' or conceived in terms of the 'social problem' approach. The academic literature that is used in literacy teaching tends to be from experimental and developmental psychology, and to be concerned with such individual 'problems' as reading skills, spelling, dyslexia etc. As Stubbs points out: 'most theories of literacy have been related to instructional techniques' (1980, p. 7). The 'ideological' model of literacy, then, has for a number of reasons scarcely penetrated studies of literacy practice in the UK. What we find here in terms of political and ideological debate are such arguments as that between Mace and Levine regarding the extent to which 'illiterates' see themselves as deprived, whether individuals or institutions are 'to blame' and, most recently, the relationship of literacy to job prospects. These are all important questions, but it is difficult to see how any of them can be resolved without recourse to a larger theoretical framework which would put them into perspective.

One area, however, where some attempt has been made to apply aspects of the 'ideological' model of literacy, albeit implicitly, to the practice of literacy teaching in the UK has been within the Adult Literacy and Basic Skills Unit. In doing so, this work provides some answers to the challenge posed by Levine. Instead of approaching adult illiterates as 'lacking in self esteem' and 'in need of comprehensive resocialisation', as Mace would have it, the Unit offers adults specific skills for specific purposes, respecting their own perceptions of what they need and putting a lot of its theoretical effort into providing a political and ideological framework in which that choice is possible and meaningful. Resource centres and even temporary caravans in city centres, for instance, provide a resource to which passers-by can come to discover what is available and to relate it to their own perceived needs. Some 'clients' may attend only once and never return, others may discover something they are looking for and then sign up for more substantial courses. The courses, however, remain more of a resource and more student-oriented than anything they are likely to have encountered at school. This framework is represented also in the ALBSU's primer for teachers in adult literacy programmes. Although entitled 'Working Together: A Functional Approach to Literacy' it in fact goes beyond the limitations of 'functional' theories of literacy and succeeds in conveying some of the ideas that I have described in terms of the 'ideological' model. The pamphlet begins by stressing that literacy is *doing*: it is only meaningful in practice. They have found it necessary to stress this fact as a result of realising the differences between the needs of adults regarding literacy and the kind of literacy normally imparted to children in schools. They write:

> Most tutors, teachers and organisers [in adult literacy] are dissatisfied with the use of school children's books because: 1. In the adult world we DO things with reading and writing. You cannot DO much with children's books except sit and read them. 2. Ploughing through children's reading books tends actually to be slower because it takes longer to get to the words and phrases an adult might urgently need to learn to read and write. (1981, p. 5.)

They propose, then, that teachers begin by 'helping their students to define their needs and interests'. This is not to suggest abandoning 'previous teaching strategies, concerned with teaching the relationship between sounds and letters or spelling skills' but 'the object is to put these skills into a more relevant setting' (ibid.). A lot of time has, then, to be devoted to establishing what particular literacy practice individuals are interested in or 'need', and this inevitably involves some analysis of their social position and of the social context within which that practice has relevance. In this sense, then, adult literacy tutors are employing something more akin to the 'ideological' model of literacy than to the 'autonomous' model which, they suggest, is still being employed in schools.

One reason why schools maintain this position is that the academic literature which they draw upon is still conceived largely within the framework described above as the 'autonomous' model. At its most general, this literature is concerned with questions regarding 'cognitive skills', such as in the attempt by Olson, Hildyard, Greenfield, Goody etc. to establish some link between the acquisition of literacy and the 'improvement' of mental processes. In educational policy circles this is used to 'justify' the large expenditure on schooling, as Hildyard and Olson indicate (1978). More specifically, within development psychology considerable knowledge has been developed regarding the nature of specific reading and writing 'problems', such as dyslexia and 'bad spelling'. These approaches, by the very way in which they are framed, tend to represent literacy as a 'skill' and a 'technical problem' to be solved, rather than as social practice. They inevitably put the emphasis on the individual and on whether he or she 'succeeds' or has 'difficulties'. The school teachers trained in this literature, whether explicitly through teacher training colleges and university education departments, or implicitly through the pedagogical strategies and theories they employ, have little opportunity or space in which to explore alternative models. It is in the knowledge that most teachers have been trained in this way of thinking, and that the schoolchildren's books and school methods of teaching that derive from it are particularly inappropriate for adults, that the ALBSU authors have been led to pose alternatives which I would identify with the 'ideological' model of literacy.

According to ALBSU, then, it is only *after* the social context and 'needs' of the individual adult student have been analysed that the tutor is able to work out which specific literacy practice it is appropriate to discuss with him or her, 'selecting from specific tasks those reading and writing skills that could be used in relation to a student's ability' (ALBSU, 1981, p. 5). This leads to an awareness of the 'actual skills' involved in performing such tasks and a consideration of how the teacher can 'make the student aware that those skills are needed' (ibid.).

Although the term 'skills' is employed here, it appears to have a broader connotation than in the 'autonomous' model. The authors point out, for instance, that 'the skills are only relevant when a context has been created for them' (ibid. p. 23) and that any such list must always be 'incomplete' (ibid.). 'New' and different skills will continually be developed in new and different contexts and the tutor is advised to continually add these to the list. They also point out how many of these skills are 'hidden' social skills rather than explicit technical or 'cognitive' processes. Parents and teachers alike may often not recognise this and instead expect to see literacy skills openly displayed, as for example with the superficial memory exercise of repeating the letters of the alphabet. The authors argue that it is 'nonsense' to believe that the acquisition of this knowledge means that the reader is 'well on the way'. Whereas 'a lot of parents with very young children *think* that they taught their children to read by this method long before they went to school' in fact 'what actually happens is that parents have done lots of other things which convey the "message", and have got their children so interested in reading that the process got started without any conscious effort'. Their misconception about what has actually happened is part of a general confusion of the 'medium' with the 'message': 'The children understood that the squiggles on the page were signalling a message: stories, poems, information and so on. Then they found the world full of such messages, all of which were patiently explained to them. (The lucky ones, that is.) In short they learned the purpose of print.' (ibid. p. 22.) This knowledge is social knowledge and its significance and content vary across cultures and over time and space. It is knowledge of the social practice of literacy and is not to be confused with knowledge of what ALBSU call 'the medium', which is what those writing within the 'autonomous' model of literacy tend to stress. It is this social and functional aspect of the learning of literacy that ALBSU want tutors of adults to grasp and emphasise: 'We should be showing them [adults] the range of opportunities the printed word opens up, and its links with their own background knowledge and life experiences.' (ibid.) It is in this spirit that they offer a list of literacy 'skills' (see Appendix pp. 229–31), a list that is more akin to what I have termed 'literacy practices' than to the technical, supposedly neutral, 'skills' described by exponents of the 'autonomous' model.

The value of the list is that it directs us towards aspects of literacy practice that tend to be ignored both in traditional teaching situations and in much of the research in the field. The question of what literacy actually is in specific contexts is made problematic for both the teacher and the researcher and both are forced to move away from a rigid conception of a fixed set of technical skills to be imparted across the board. For the researcher, for instance, the nature of the format and layout of written material, to which the list draws attention, raises questions which provide a concrete basis for cross-cultural comparison that might be more interesting than those raised by comparison of more explicit literacy skills, such as 'spelling' etc. With regard to my own anthropological field work in Iran, for instance, it suggests a way of comparing the traditional Koranic literacy taught in the mountain village I studied with the recent development there of commercial uses of literacy. In the 'maktab' or Koranic school students had, in their reading of sacred texts, learnt about various conventions regarding layout and format that, I argue, served them in good stead when the need arose to expand commercial literacy practices. In learning to interpret and use these conventions students acquired 'hidden' literacy skills and knowledge, of the kind highlighted by the ALBSU list. Some of them were able to transfer these skills and knowledge to the different literacy practices associated with the commercial expansion of the village and thus to establish positions of influence and power in the new circumstances following the oil boom of the 1970s. This is a knowledge that those literate in other contexts have not necessarily developed to such an extent and which varies according to culture, circumstances and the individual's role. ALBSU tutors suggest that it is a knowledge that is not explicitly taught in English schools, where the emphasis tends to be at the level of relating sounds to letters, and of learning 'literal' meaning of the 'words on the page'.

The ALBSU list also draws attention, under the same general heading as format and layout, to the ability to use 'clues that help you thumb a page for specific information' (ibid. p. 25). Again this is the kind of knowledge that, I suggest, is imparted through the 'maktab' literacy of Iranian villages and which, in some form, passes on to and facilitates practice of 'commercial' literacy there. In the UK, on the other hand, university lecturers tend to have great difficulty in teaching such skills and knowledge to students who have not been grounded in them in schools. Explicit attention has to be drawn in 'study skills' courses to ways of 'thumbing' a book which involve, for instance, use of contents and index pages and headings in order to move around within a text and between texts rather than simply reading consecutively from the first page to the last.

Adults who come to literacy programmes in the UK often tend to be asking for training in these kinds of skill and knowledge. In their daily lives they are often called upon to 'skim' a text, whether it be a leaflet, a newspaper or the instructions included with some technical object. A classic area where the ALBSU approach has highlighted a discrepancy in traditional school teaching of literacy is that of 'form filling'. A specific leaflet has been produced by the Unit for teachers in response to the frequent requests for assistance from adults and it clearly indicates that the skills involved are not the traditional ones of relating letters to sounds, or of spelling, but hidden ones that are seldom addressed in school (ALBSU, 1982b). The leaflet, for instance, makes explicit such skills and knowledge as 'understanding the concept of the "box" relevant to given information' and points out that 'the separate compartments could be difficult to orientate and therefore be confusing'. It indicates the importance of 'variations of print and spacing' and of 'focussing on key words and numbers'. Nor are these isolated as 'technical skills' to be learnt in a vacuum: the leaflet explicitly draws attention to the social skills that may be involved in, for instance, handling a P45 form (previous employer's statement of employee's tax and national insurance contributions). It tells teachers: 'A relaxed atmosphere and informal chat will help clear any misgivings about the P45. For many people it is a mysterious fact of life. Think, for example, how do you feel about it? We might know it as a P45 and that we must give it to our new employer or to the unemployment benefit office, but what it does and why our new employer should be told exactly how much we earned in our last job remains a mystery. Using the information given at the front of the pack ... you should be able to clear away some of the mystique through discussion.' (ibid.)

Such knowledge and skills and the way in which they are imparted vary, then, both between and within cultures and are often a latent rather than explicit aspect of literacy practice. Awareness of these and other 'skills' highlighted in the ALBSU list is clearly significant both for the researcher investigating literacy practices in different contexts and for teachers addressing students who have specific, culture-related needs and interests.

The application of these principles in the UK has led to the practice of groups producing their own literate materials rather than simply consuming what the teacher provides. 'Write First Time' groups, for instance, put out a regular newsletter (under that title) composed by adult literacy students who come together as editorial teams in different parts of the country for each issue. They design the format and choose the material on a collective basis. Much of it consists of poems and essays by students describing their own experience of different levels of literacy, or their own social background: the kind of material that they feel seldom gets represented in the school text book. Organisations like 'Queen's Park Books' and 'The Writers and Readers Publishing Co-operative' are developing these practices into an important branch of social history in which literacy and oral tradition 'mix' in ways that are relevant to producers and consumers alike.

In the USA a similar ideological shift in approaches to literacy teaching has been taking place. The same 'discovery' of 'illiteracy' led to the same initial responses as in the UK. There too, however, recent theoretical work has been more in the direction of the 'ideological' model, as we saw above in relation to S. B. Heath's work and to that of Hunter and Harman. This is also being carried over into practical programmes. One such example is described in *The Linguistic Reporter* (Oct. 1981), a newsletter published by the Center for Applied Linguistics in Washington. Jane Staton sets out a programme for using literacy in the classroom as a form of interactive dialogue. 'For the past year', she writes, 'The Center for Applied Linguistics has been involved in research on the classroom use of "dialogue journals" – daily written communication between students and teachers' (Staton, 1981, p. 1). (These findings have now been published more fully, Staton et al. 1982.) The philosophy behind this is not unlike that proposed by some of the English authors we have been considering: 'The purpose is always to communicate and understand, never to be evaluated. These dialogues combine the receptive (comprehension) skills of reading with the productive (communication) skills of writing, and they take advantage of the functional, interactive, self-generated features present naturally in first-language acquisition.' (ibid.) The assumptions demonstrate the developing link in the USA between important aspects of the 'ideological' model and its application to practical work. They include the following:

'Literacy' in our view means communicative competence in *using* written language – that is, mastery of the personal and social functions of reading and writing, as well as mastery of both forms. Communicative competence involves both comprehending written information and actively expressing one's experiences and intentions in writing to accomplish personally meaningful goals. Literacy is acquired most effectively when attached to one's own life experience, social context and life goals. Materials and curricula are less important for acquiring literacy than is a significant, interactive dynamic relationship with a teacher. The same principles should guide literacy acquisition that guide oral first-language acquisition: language use is natural and necessary to get things done, and it is our most important mode of social interaction. It is self-generated in that it is used voluntarily when the person using it sees the need, and its use is controlled and made meaningful by its real-life context. (ibid.)

In the English context, one outcome of this broadening of what is included under 'literacy skills' is that adult literacy programmes can concentrate on specific skills for specific purposes. They need not be drawn into imparting, as integral to literacy, conventions that are in fact only those of a particular culture or sub-culture. The classic case is that of 'academic' literacy practices which are often treated in schools as if they are 'universal' and vital. Olson and others would, as we have seen, associate these conventions with 'logic', 'rationality', 'objectivity' and 'intelligence'. If this were really the case then clearly we would want everyone to have equal access to this particular kind of literacy. If however, as I have argued, these grandiose claims for 'academic' literacy are merely those of a small elite attempting to maintain positions of power and influence by attributing universality and neutrality to their own cultural conventions, then we could do without them and suffer no great loss. This is, in fact, the case: 'logic', 'objectivity' etc. are equally possible in other literacy conventions, other forms of discourse and other media of communication than those practised by the specific academic sub-culture that much literacy in schools is modelled on. ALBSU, CAL (Center for Applied Linguistics), Write First Time etc. can, then, legitimately concentrate on teaching specific skills and knowledge for specific purposes without depriving their students of skills that are crucial to their full development, self-expression and participation in society.

This point was crucial in the 'cultural deprivation' arguments of the 1970s, although it was not often made with specific reference to literacy. The dilemma for progressive workers at that time was how to reject the claim that certain cultures or sub-cultures, such as working-class families, were 'deprived' at the level of 'logic', 'abstraction' and basic intellectual skills, while recognising and struggling to change the fact that they were 'deprived' in terms of access to power and wealth which in this culture are linked to certain linguistic and literacy performances. Bernstein, for instance, saw this latter kind of 'deprivation' as linked with differences in language 'codes' amongst different classes and social groups but then appeared to give credibility to the idea that this was also linked to the former kind of 'deprivation'. What makes these claims significant for our present interest is the similarity between Bernstein's claims for certain 'codes' and those put forward in the 'autonomous' model of literacy for the consequences of reading and writing. Thus his description of the 'elaborated' code, which working-class children were supposed to lack, is not just of relative, culture-specific skills and styles but includes the 'deeper' abilities such as 'abstraction' and 'logic', which some researchers have attempted to link with literacy. However much he claims that he is not making value judgements, then, his actual description of the consequences of employing different codes, just as that of exponents of the 'autonomous' model of literacy regarding different modes of communication, does include qualities, the lack of which is bound to lead to judgements of inferiority and would, indeed, call a person's very humanity into question.

All who use language do in fact engage in abstraction and, as anthropologists have demonstrated, 'logic' is to be found in all cultures, accounts of its absence in specific groups being due simply to misunderstanding on the part of travellers and observers from alien cultures. Similarly, Labov has shown, in relation to black working-class sub-cultures in New York, that the lack of 'logic' attributed by middle-class teachers and testing processes to many black youths there is often no more than mistaken interpretation of the rules and conventions of an alien language use and dialect – youths labelled 'subnormal' and 'illogical' turned out to be perfectly logical and intelligent once the tester had learnt to understand these cultural rules and conventions.

There is no need, then, to associate the evident deprivations suffered by many working-class and ethnic groups with deprivation of the deeper kind. The fact that many do not read or write 'standard' or 'academic' English, or that they speak 'non-standard' English, does not mean that they lack 'logic' or the ability to abstract. We should not, then, be concerned if 'academic' literacy is not part of the core curriculum – lack of it will not do any harm to students' intellects.

However, this still leaves us with the political problem (and it is a political rather than an 'academic' one) that 'academic' literacy happens to be a source of wealth and power in the particular culture we inhabit. If we ignore it – leave it to 'academic' classes as it were – then we can hardly complain if they continue to exercise hegemony through it. There are, I believe, two major answers to this dilemma. Firstly, we need to build institutions which enable people to acquire what they say they want and not what teachers, radical or otherwise, think they want. Levine, as we have seen, can provide useful information of what people say they want and more research of this kind is clearly essential to this project. The development of the kinds of 'hidden' literacy skills listed by ALBSU, and which people say they come to adult literacy classes for, will itself make a contribution to their ability to exercise power in the system as present constituted. The person who can fill in forms, for instance, has the power to extract funds from institutions, run garages and make use of bureaucratic process for their own particular purposes and organisations. This response is currently being advocated with positive results by many progressive elements within adult literacy courses, whether set up under MSC (Manpower Services Commission) programmes, funded by LEAs (Local Education Authorities) or WEAs (Workers' Educational Associations) or instigated by the 'pump-priming' work of ALBSU.

This approach has, of course, dangers of the kind previously identified in radical critiques of 'consumer' education in general. It could be argued, for instance, that people may have been indoctrinated into asking for the 'wrong' things. As I have suggested, I am suspicious of this argument and believe that people are generally more aware of their interests than middle-class researchers and 'providers' give them credit for. However, there is some point to the argument that crude response to 'consumer' demand simply reproduces the social framework and is not what 'radical activists' are about. Radical critiques of Bernstein's approach did point out that the political programme which followed from it simply offered a prospect of access to power structures as they currently existed rather than any way of changing them. The notion of 'giving' working-class adults or schoolchildren (and the problems there presumably require further elaboration) whatever literacy skills they wanted might similarly be seen as creating the illusion that this would change their fundamental disadvantage as a group when all it does is to give individuals greater facility within the system. I would hope, however, that we do not have to relive all of the earlier struggles and debates about education in general when considering literacy strategies. One of the functions of this book is to attempt to clear away some of the 'dead wood' and at least to bring discussion of literacy up to date with the work in related fields, if not to attempt to move it further ahead. This involves, for instance, recognising that, with literacy as with education strategies generally, there are in fact positive aspects of the 'provide what people want' approach (which are embodied to some extent in the ALBSU approach) and they should not be so readily discarded by those who see themselves as active or progressive. The 'ideological' approach to literacy is, I would argue, more complex than some of the earlier 'compensatory' or 'consumerist' theories of education. It involves, for instance, constructing a framework within which 'demand' takes on a different meaning than it does in establishment institutions. The 'choice' of literacy skills and knowledge being proposed in the ALBSU list, or being offered through such institutions as one-to-one teaching, caravans in city centre sites or 'Write First Time' sessions, is clearly of a different kind and range from that available in schools. One immediate and practical answer to the dilemma posed above is therefore to challenge hegemonic uses of elite literacy practices at base – within schools and other establishment institutions themselves – by introducing there the ALBSU and other 'progressive' approaches I have described.

Levine resisted this approach, in the context of his criticisms of Mace. He writes: 'if prisons, schools, and other similar formal organisations commanding considerable resources find comprehensive resocialisation a problematic and often impossible task, is it not over-ambitious to attempt it via very limited contact with students, limited finance and predominantly part-time and volunteer personnel?' (1980, p. 6).

This, however, misses the point. As a number of writers have pointed out both in the UK and the USA, it was precisely because of the kind of socialisation offered in formal establishments that the problems to which Mace alludes occurred. She does not expect those establishments to offer any help since they are the cause of the problem. The institutional framework and its establishment ideology, in her view, failed to give working people the confidence and learning experience that would raise their political consciousness as she would like. The adult literacy programmes were therefore a way of compensating not for the 'cultural deprivation' of class and family background, as educationalists following Bernstein would seem to suggest was needed, but for the failings of establishment education. It might be over-ambitious, as we have seen, for political activists to use the adult literacy programmes in this way, but not for the reasons proposed by Levine. As one strand of a larger project this proposal becomes meaningful and practical within the schools themselves.

Nevertheless, it is clear that, however effective in themselves, these approaches would remain marginal if they were not accompanied by more radical structural changes in the host society. The second answer to the dilemma posed above, then, is both more difficult and more crucial in the long term since it involves changes at the level of ideology within the institutions themselves. A step in this direction would be achieved by the dissemination of the 'ideological' model of literacy more widely amongst those responsible for the organisation of these establishments as well as amongst those engaged in day to day literacy teaching in them. The project would, however, have to be accompanied by the creation of direct links and influence between these practitioners and those I have described as engaged in the production of theory. Whether such a radical reshaping of the classic distinction between theory and practice could be achieved in the specific arena of literacy practice when it has failed at more general levels remains to be seen.

Appendix

(Extract from *An Approach to Functional Literacy*, Adult Literacy Resource Agency, 1981, pp. 24–8.)

Literacy Skills
Here is a suggested list of the literacy skills used when undertaking any of the [ordinary everyday] tasks [that teachers are helping their students to manage]. We give these suggested headings in alphabetic order, bearing in mind that, in any particular task the order in which they are used will vary. Not all the skills will be used in every case.

You may find it helpful to make this list into a set of cards.

Context:	Words vary in meaning. Expression alters meaning. Sequence builds expectations of words to come.
Find the main ideas in the text:	Get the facts: what is fact? what is opinion? Evaluate information in the light of your background knowledge: do you need another text?
Follow instructions:	Awareness of contents, order, and layout of text. Awareness of information required. Using clues that help you thumb a text for specific information. Skip 'padding'. Infer steps and details which are unclear or unstated. Re-sequence steps for your own purpose.
Reactions to text:	What is your immediate reaction to the text? Can you relate it to your feelings, and previous experiences in this area? Has it altered your outlook on the subject? What other information do you now want? Do you want to take further action?
Recording and communicating for others:	Awareness of needs of recipient. Awareness of layout and format required. Awareness of style and importance of clarity. Handwriting requirements. Spelling.

Recording and communicating for self:	Noting information for next steps in use. Appropriate storage of information according to future requirement.
Selecting the task:	What is your reason for selecting the task? What do you want from it? What are you going to do with it?
Source of texts:	Awareness of places, organisations and people as reference points for locating texts.
Spelling:	Awareness of ways of solving a spelling problem. Try out several variations. Does it look or feel right? Try the possible ways of spelling given sounds in context. Draw on knowledge of prefixes, suffixes and syllables. Use of the dictionary and other sources of information.
Understand links between speech and print: Words made up of sounds. Sounds represented by letters. Expression alters meaning.	Left to right. Top to bottom. Sequences made up of words.
Word recognition:	Context. Dictionary. Phonic. Structural– roots, prefixes, suffixes.

The next stage is to marry the skills to the task; the framework below is intended to help you to do this in a workable sequence.

Essential preliminary questions regarding the skill of the good reader	Developing these skills with students.
1 What is the task? What is the purpose for wanting to undertake the task?	What is a student's specific purpose? What practical need must be dealt with immediately? What general scheme can emerge from helping with that need?
2 Where is the relevant information to be found? Is there more than one text?	How can you help a student to be aware of this process of finding a text? Can he/she share in the search in some meaningful way?

3 Is the text suitable for the task? How is the suitability decided? What information is required? What problems, issues and discussion points need to be sorted?

How can your student help decide on such suitability? How far are these issues, and the consequent discussion, led by your student?

4 What reading skills does the good reader use for this task?

How can your student be made aware of these skills? What follow-up usage can your student make:
  of the actual passage,
  of a simplified passage,
  of his own dictated response,
  of the key vocabulary.

Essential preliminary questions regarding the skills of the good reader.

Developing these skills with students.

5 What writing skills does the good writer use for this task?

How can your student be made aware of the written requirements? What follow-up usage can your student make of the various writing skills the task requires?

BIBLIOGRAPHY

ALBSU. 1980a. *An Introduction to Literacy Teaching.*
 1980b. *Newsletter*, No. 3
 1981. *Working Together: An Approach to Functional Literacy*
 1982a. *Newsletter*, No. 10
 1982b. *Making the Most of Tax Forms*
 1982c. *Annual Report 1980/1*
Al Musavy, Hajji Seyed Abul Ghasem n.d. *Tosi al Mosa'el..* Mu'sasseh Enteshavat Qu'im
Anderson, C. A. 1966. 'Literacy and Schooling on the Development Threshold: Some Historical Cases' in Anderson, C. A. and Bowman, M. (eds.) *Education and Economic Development.* Frank Cass, London
Antoun, R. 1965. 'Conservation and Change in the Village Community: A Jordanian Case Study'. *Human Organisation.* 24 (Spring)
Antoun, R. and Harik, I. (eds.). 1972. *Rural Politics and Social Change in the Middle East.* Indiana University Press
Arasteh, R. 1962. *Education and Social Awakening in Iran.* Leiden
Avery, P. 1965. *Modern Iran.* Ernest Benn Ltd
Bakhshi, K. 1978. 'Literacy Organisations and Social Change in Iran'. Unpublished Ph. D. Univ. of Missouri, Columbia
Baldwin, G. 1967. *Planning and Development in Iran.* John Hopkins, Baltimore
Barbovitch, P. 1980. 'Assumptions about Literacy as a Determinant of Social Change in Pre-Revolutionary Russia.' Unpublished MS
Basso, K. 1974. 'The Ethnography of Writing' in Bauman, R. and Sherzer, J. (eds.). *Explorations in the Ethnography of Speaking.* Cambridge University Press
Bataille, L. (ed.). 1976. *A Turning Point for Literacy.* Unesco
Berggren, C. and L. 1975. *The Literacy Process: A Practice in Domestication or Liberation?.* Writers and Readers Publishers Co-operative
Bernstein, B. 1971. *Classes, Codes and Control.* Vol. 1. Routledge and Kegan Paul
Bevan, J. 1983. 'Each One, Teach One.' *New Internationalist* (April)
Black, G. and Bevan, J. 1980. *The Loss of Fear: Education in Nicaragua Before and After the Revolution.* World University Service
Bloch, M. (ed.). 1975. *Language and Oratory in Traditional Societies.* Academic Press
Bloomfield, L. 1964. 'Literate and Illiterate Speech' in Hymes, D. (ed.). *Language in Culture and Society.* Harper, New York
Bruner, J. et al.1966. *Studies in Cognitive Growth.* Wiley, New York
Bullock, A. 1975. *Report of the Committee of Enquiry Appointed by the Secretary of State for Education and Science: A Language for Life.* HMSO

Caheny, M. 1980. 'Literacy as an Enabling Factor: P. Freire'. Unpublished MS

Callaway, H. 1978. 'The Implications of Literacy in Social and Economic Change: N. Nigeria'. Unpublished MS

Charnley, A. H. and Jones, H. A. 1979. *The Concept of Success in Adult Literacy.* Adult Literacy Unit

1980. *Perceptions of Adult Literacy Provision in 1979.*HMSO/Adult Literacy Unit

Chomsky, N. 1957. *Syntactic Structures.* Mouton, 's-Gravenhage

1968. *Language and Mind.* Harcourt, New York

1976. *Reflections on Language.* Temple Smith and Fontana

Cippola, C. 1969. *Literacy and Development in the West.* Penguin

Clammer, J. 1976. *Literacy and Social Change: A Case Study of Fiji.* Brill, Leiden

1980. 'Towards an Ethnography of Literacy: The Effects of Mass Literacy on Language Use and Social Organisation' in *Language Forum* Vol. 4, No. 3

Clanchy, M. 1979. *From Memory to Written Record 1066–1307.* E. Arnold

Cole, M. and Scribner, S. 1974.*Culture and Thought.* Wiley, New York

1977. 'Unpackaging Literacy' Unpublished MS

1978. 'Vai Literacy Project: Working Paper 2' Unpublished Ms

1981. *The Psychology of Literacy.* Harvard University Press

Cole, M. et al. 1971. *The Cultural Context of Learning and Thinking.* Methuen

Cressy, D. 1982. *Literacy and the Social Order: Reading and Writing in Tudor and Stuart England.* Cambridge University Press

Crystal, D. 1976. *Child Language, Learning and Linguistics.* E. Arnold

Curle, A. 1964. *World Campaign for Universal Literacy.* Unesco Occasional Paper

Dale, R. et al. (eds.). 1976. *Schooling and Capitalism.* Open University

Derrida, J. 1978. *Writing and Difference.* Translated with an introduction by Alan Bass. Routledge and Kegan Paul

Ennayat, H. 1972. Public Lecture given at Middle East Centre, Oxford

Evans, M. 1980. 'The Cognitive Consequences of Literacy and Bernstein's Cultural Deprivation Theories'. Unpublished MS

Evans-Pritchard, E. E. 1937. *Witchcraft, Oracles and Magic Amongst the Azande.* Clarendon Press

1970. 'Lévy-Bruhl's Theory of Primitive Mentality', *Journal of the Anthropological Society of Oxford* Vol. 1, No. 1

Ferguson, C. A. 1971. 'Contrasting Patterns of Literacy Acquisition in a Multi-Lingual Nation' in Whitely, W. (ed.). *Language Use and Social Change*

Fernandez, J. 1980. 'Edification by Puzzlement: Logic, Memorization and Literacy among the Fang' in Karp, I. and Bird, C. (eds.). *Explorations in African Systems of Thought.* Indiana University Press

Finnegan, R. 1973. 'Literacy versus Non-Literacy: The Great Divide' in Finnegan, R. and Horton, R. (eds.). *Modes of Thought.* Faber

1979. 'Attitudes to Speech and Language among the Limba of Sierra Leone' in *Odu* ns, 2

1981. 'Orality and Literacy: Some Problems of Definition and Research'. Unpublished MS

1982. 'Oral Literature and Writing in the South Pacific', *Pacific Quarterly* (Moana), Vol. 7.2

Fisher, W. B. (ed.). 1968. *The Cambridge History of Iran*. Vol. 1. Cambridge University Press

Fought, J. 1973. 'On the Adequacy of Recent Phonological Themes and Practices', *Annual Review of Anthropology* (ed. B. Siegel), Vol. 2

Freeland, J. 1981a. 'The Literacy Campaign on the Atlantic Coast of Nicaragua'. *World University Service News*, Nos. 1. and 2

    1981b. 'Cultural Diversity and the Literacy Crusade on the Atlantic Coast'. Unpublished MS

Freire, P. 1972. *The Pedagogy of the Oppressed*. Penguin

    1976. *Education: The Practice of Freedom*. Writers and Readers Publishers Co-operative

    1978. *Pedagogy in Process: The Letters to Guinea-Bissau*. Seabury Press, New York

Furet, F. and Ozouf, J. 1982. *Reading and Writing: Literacy in France from Calvin to Jules Ferry*. Cambridge University Press

Gellner, E. 1973. *Cause and Meaning in the Social Sciences*. Routledge and Kegan Paul

Gharib, G. S. 1966. 'Training Teachers for Rural Elementary Schools in Iran'. Thesis for MA, American University of Beirut, Lebanon

Golden, H. 1965. 'Literacy and Social Change in Underdeveloped Countries', *Rural Sociology* 20

Goldhill, R. 1979. 'Literacy Amongst Men and Women in 19th Century East European Jewish Communities'. Unpublished MS

Goody, J. (ed.). 1968. *Literacy in Traditional Societies*. Cambridge University Press

Goody, J. 1977. *The Domestication of the Savage Mind*. Cambridge University Press

Goody, J. and Cole, M. 1977. 'Writing and Formal Operations: A Case Study among the Vai', *Africa* 47.3

Graff, H. J. 1979. *The Literacy Myth: Literacy and Social Structure in the 19th Century City*. Academic Press

    1982. *Literacy and Social Development in the West: A Reader*. Cambridge University Press

Greenfield, P. 1972. 'Oral or Written Language: The Consequences for Cognitive Development in Africa, U.S. and England' in *Language and Speech*, No. 15

Halliday, F. 1979. *Iran: Dictatorship and Development*. Harmondsworth, Penguin

Hargreaves, D. 1980. *Adult Literacy and Broadcasting: The BBC's Experience*. Frances Pinter/BBC

Hashemi, M. 1966. 'Adult Education in Rural Iran: Problems and Prospects'. Unpublished Thesis for MA, American University of Beirut, Lebanon

Heath, S. B. 1980. 'The Function and Uses of Literacy', *Journal of Communication*, No. 30

    1982. 'What No Bedtime Story Means: Narrative Skills at Home and School', *Language in Society*. Vol. 11

    1983. *Ways with Words*. Cambridge University Press

Heather, P. 1982. *Young People's Reading: A Study of The Leisure Reading of 13–15 year olds*. Centre for Research on User Studies, University of Sheffield

Heslop, A. 1980. 'Some Redefinitions of Literacy in The Adult Literacy Programme in England'. Unpublished MS

Hildyard, A. and Olson, D. 1978. 'Literacy and the Specialisation of Language'. Unpublished MS, Ontario Institute for Studies in Education

Hodgson, M. 1974. *The Venture of Islam*. 3 vols. Chicago University Press

Horton, R. 1967. 'African Traditional Thought and Western Science', *Africa*, 37, Nos. 1 and 2

Hoyles, M. 1977. *The Politics of Literacy*. Writers and Readers Publishers Co-operative

Hunter, C. and Harman, D. 1979. *Adult Literacy in the United States: A Report to the Ford Foundation*. McGraw-Hill

Hymes, D. (ed.). 1964. *Language in Culture and Society*. Harper, New York

Hymes, D. and Fought, J. 1975. *American Structuralism*. Mouton, New York

IWGIA. 1982. 'Nicaragua: IWGIA Participates in Seminar on Racial Discrimination, Managua', *IWGIA Newsletter*, No. 30 (April)

Jeffries, C. 1967. *Illiteracy: A World Problem*. Pall Mall Press

Johansson, E. 1977. *The History of Literacy in Sweden*. Educational Reports, No. 12. University of Umeå, Sweden

John, M. 1979. 'Libraries in Oral-Traditional Societies', *International Library Review*, No. 11

Jones, H. A. and Charnley, A. H. 1979. *Adult Literacy 1978/9*. National Institute of Adult Education

Jones, R. M. 1967. 'The Short-Run Economic Impact of Land Reform on Feudal Village Irrigated Agriculture in Iran'. Unpublished Ph. D, University of Maryland

Karp, I. and Bird, C. S. (eds.) 1980. *Explorations in African Systems of Thought*. Indiana University Press

Keddie, Nell. (ed.). 1973. *Tinker, Tailor ... The Myth of Cultural Deprivation*. Penguin

Keddie, Nickie. 1968. 'The Iranian Village Before and After Land Reform', *Journal of Contemporary History*, Vol. 3, No. 3

   1972. 'Capitalism, Stratification and Social Control in Iranian Agriculture, Before and After the Land Reform' in Antoun and Harik (eds.)

   1979. 'Oil, Economic Policy and Social Conflict' in *Race and Class*, Vol. XXI, No. 1

Kelsey, A. 1957. *Once the Mullah ....* Brockhampton Press

Kneale, W. and M. 1962. *Development of Logic*. Oxford University Press

Kuhn, T. S. 1962. *The Structure of Scientific Revolutions*. University of Chicago Press

Labov, W. 1973. 'The Logic of Non-Standard English' in Keddie, Nell (ed.) 1973

Lamb, D. 1983 'A Critique of Theories Underlying Adult Literacy Campaigns'. Unpublished MS

Lambton, A. 1963. *Landlord and Peasant in Persia*. Oxford University Press

   1969. *The Persian Land Reform*. Clarendon Press, Oxford

Lawton, D. 1968. *Social Class, Language and Education*. Routledge and Kegan Paul

Leach, E. 1954. *Political Systems of Highland Burma*. London School of Economics Monographs No. 44. Athlone Press

1976. *Culture and Communication*. Cambridge University Press

Leech, G., Deuchar, M. et al. 1984. *English Grammar for Today*. Macmillan

Léon, Lourdes de 1982. 'Semantic Classifiers'. Unpublished MS

Lerner, D. 1958. *The Passing of Traditional Society: Modernizing the Middle East*. Glencoe Free Press

Levine, K. 1980. *Becoming Literate: Final Report on a Research Project 'Adult Illiteracy and the Socialization of Adult Illiterates'*. SSRC

Lévi-Strauss, C. 1966. *The Savage Mind*. Weidenfeld and Nicolson

  1968. *Structural Anthropology*. Penguin

Lévy-Bruhl, L. 1926. *How Natives Think*. Translated by L. A. Clare, London

Lewis, M. 1953. *The Importance of Illiteracy*. Harrap

Lienhardt, R. G. 1980. 'Self: Public and Private: Some African Representations', *Journal of the Anthropological Society of Oxford*, Vol. XI, No. 2

Linell, P. 1982. *The Written Bias in Linguistics*. University of Linköping, Department of Communication Studies

Lockridge, K. A. 1974. *Literacy in Colonial New England*. Norton, New York

Luria, A. R. 1976. *Cognitive Development*. Harvard University Press

Lyons, J. 1977. *Semantics*. Cambridge University Press

  1981a. *Language, Meaning and Social Context*. Fontana

  1981b. 'Language and Speech', *Philosophical Transactions of the Royal Society*. B 295 (London)

  1981c. *Language and Linguistics*. Cambridge University Press

  1982. Personal Correspondence

Mace, J. 1979. *Working with Words*. Writers and Readers Publishers Co-operative/ Chameleon

Macfarlane, T. 1976. *Teaching Adults to Read*. Adult Literacy Resource Agency

Mackie, R. (ed.). 1980. *Literacy and Revolution: The Pedagogy of Paulo Freire*. Pluto Press

McLachlan, K. 1968. 'The Persian Land Reform', in Fisher (ed.)

McLuhan, M. 1964. *Understanding Media*. Sphere Books

Marchetti, P. 1983. 'Agrarian Reform, Popular Participation and Food Security', Paper presented to Conference on *Nicaragua After the Revolution: Problems and Prospects* at the Institute of Development Studies, University of Sussex

Martell, G. 1976. 'The Politics of Reading and Writing', in Dale, R. et al. (eds.)

Olson, D. 1977. 'From Utterance to Text: The Bias of Language in Speech and Writing', *Harvard Educational Review*, No. 47

Ong, W. 1977. *Interfaces of the Word*. Cornell University Press

  1982a. *Orality and Literacy*.Methuen

  1982b. 'Literacy and Orality in Our Times', *Pacific Quarterly* (Moana), Vol. 7.2

Osborn, J. 1967. 'Teaching a Teaching Language', Paper to the Society for Research in Child Development. New York

Oxenham, J. 1980. *Literacy: Writing, Reading and Social Organisation*. Routledge and Kegan Paul

Parkin, D. 1975. *Town and Country in Central and Eastern Africa*. Oxford University Press

Parry, J. 1982. 'Popular Attitudes Towards Hindu Religious Texts'. Unpublished MS

Polanyi, M. 1965. *Personal Knowledge*. Routledge and Kegan Paul

Popper, K. 1979. *Objective Knowledge*. Clarendon Press

Pulgrum, E. 1951. 'Phoneme and Grapheme: A Parallel', *Word*, 7
    1965. 'Graphic and Phonic Systems: Figurae and Signs', *Word*, 21

Rediske, M. and Schneider, R. 1982. 'The Indians of Nicaragua: Between Coloni-
    alism and Revolution', *IWGIA Newsletter*, No. 30 (April)

Rizvi, S. A. 1980. *Iran: Royalty, Religion and Revolution*. Ma'rifat Publishing
    House, Canberra, Australia

Romaine, S. 1982. Personal Communication

Rommetveit, R. 1980. 'On "Meanings" of Acts and What is Meant and Made
    Known by What is Said in a Pluralistic Social World' in Brenner, J. (ed.), *The
    Structure of Action*. Basil Blackwell
    1982. 'Conversational Analysis and Pragmatics'. Lecture Series to ESF Summer
    School in Linguistics, University of Sussex

Rommetveit, R. and Blaker, R. M. 1979. *Studies of Language, Thought and Verbal
    Communication*. Academic Press

Ronduen, P. and Dideban, Z. 1970. *Administration and Supervision for Better
    Rural Schools and Communities in Iran*. Unesco Mission, Ministry of Educa-
    tion, Tehran

Rosen, H. 1972. *Language and Class: A Critique of Bernstein*. Falling Wall Press,
    Bristol

Ryan, J. et al. 1975. *The Saveh Experience*. International Institute for Adult
    Literacy Methods, Tehran.

Scollen, R. and S. 1979. *Linguistic Convergence: An Ethnography of Speaking at
    Fort Chipewyan, Alberta*. Academic Press, New York

Scribner, R. W. 1983. *For the Sake of Simple Folk: Popular Propaganda for the
    German Reformation*. Cambridge University Press

Smith, B. 1960. *European Vision and the South Pacific*. Oxford University Press

Smith, M. 1978. 'Vai Literacy Project: Working Paper 1'. Unpublished MS

Staton, J. 1981. 'Literacy as an Interactive Process', *The Linguistics Reporter*, Vol.
    24, No. 2

Stierer, B. 1981. *Reading, Testing and Schooling: A Collection of Evidence*. Insti-
    tute of Education, London

Street, B. V. 1975a. *The Savage in Literature*. Routledge and Kegan Paul
    1975b. 'The Mullah, The Shahnameh and The Madrasseh: Some Aspects of
    Literacy in Iran', *Asian Affairs*, 62
    1982. 'Literacy and Ideology', in *Red Letters*, Vol. 12
    1983. 'Literacy Campaigns in U.K.', *Literature, Teaching Politics*, Vol. 2. (Uni-
    versity of Sussex)

Stubbs, M. 1980. *Language and Literacy*. Routledge and Kegan Paul

Torrey, J. 1973. 'Illiteracy in the Ghetto' in Keddie, Nell (ed.)

Turton, D. 1975. 'The Relationship Between Oratory and the Exercise of Influ-
    ence Among the Mursi' in Bloch, M. (ed.)

UN 1966. *Progress in Land Reform*. UN Department of Economic and Social
    Affairs, New York

UNESCO 1957. *World Illiteracy at Mid-Century*
    1970. *Literacy 1967–9: Progress Throughout The World*

1971. *Literacy for Working: Functional Literacy in Tanzania* (by M. Viscusi)

1972. *Literacy 1969–71*

1973. *Esphahan Work-Oriented Literacy Project*

1975. *Final Report for International Symposium for Literacy, Persepolis.* Iran

Vygotsky, L. 1962. *Thought and Language.* MIT Press

Weber, H. 1981. *Nicaragua: The Sandinist Revolution.* Translated by P. Cammiler. Verso Editions and New Left Books

Whitely, W. (ed.). 1971. *Language Use and Social Change.* Oxford University Press

Williams, J. A. 1972. *Islam.* Washington Square Press

Williams, R. 1961. *The Long Revolution.* Chatto

1974. *Television: Technology and Cultural Form.* Fontana

1976. *Communications.* Chatto

Wilson, B. (ed.). 1974. *Rationality.* B. Blackwell, Oxford

Wood, E. and N. 1978. *Class, Ideology and Ancient Political Theory.* B. Blackwell, Oxford

WRITE FIRST TIME 1975. *Let Loose: Writings by Adult Literacy Students*

Regular publications

Adult Literacy and Basic Skills Unit. Bi-monthly Newsletter

Unesco Year Books.

University of Reading Literacy Documentation Service. Monthly Bulletins

Write First Time. Quarterly Newsletter

INDEX

'abstraction', cognitive skill 23, 24, 26, 27, 31, 34, 35, 36, 38, 79, 80, 225
  definition of 30
'academic' literacy 75–7, 80, 224, 225
Adult Basic Education Program 214–15
ALBSU (Adult Literacy and Basic Skills Unit) 90, 152, 154–6, 157, 172–3, 215, 218–20, 221–3, 224, 226, 227
  see also literacy skills
'alphabetic' literacy 50, 51, 53, 61, 62, 63, 93, 154, 220
  Arabic 134, 153
  Semitic 51
  writing system 83–4
Anderson, C. A. 2, 13, 184
anthropology, and study of literacy 5–6, 7, 9–10, 24, 25, 26, 27, 32, 35, 40, 44, 45, 77, 79, 80, 87, 98, 102, 130, 135, 221, 225
Antoun, R. 198
Arasteh, R. 197
'autonomous' model 1, 4, 7, 9, 13, 69, 81, 89, 100, 101, 130, 137, 144, 152, 184, 196, 208, 212, 219, 220, 221, 225
  definition 3, 6
  'strong' version 19–65
Avery, P. 53

Baldwin, G. 197, 202
Berggren, C. and L. 13, 184, 186, 194
Bernstein, B. 3, 21, 22, 24, 27, 74, 75, 124, 225, 226, 227
Bevan, J. 206, 207
  see also Black, G.
Bird, C. S. *see* Karp, I.
Black, G. 203–4, 205–6, 207, 208–9
Bloch, M. 30, 35, 41, 48, 57
Bloomfield, L. 7, 66, 93
Bruner, J. 103

Cabral, A. 202–3
CAL (Center for Applied Linguistics) 224
'cargo cults' 6, 146
Charnley, A. H. *see* Jones, H. A.
Chomsky, N. 68
Clammer, J. 6, 42, 61
Clanchy, M. 10, 43, 46–7, 81, 82, 88, 97, 98, 106, 110–21, 122, 123

codes
  'elaborate' 2, 3, 24, 27, 74, 225
  'restricted' 3, 22, 24, 74
cognitive skills 2, 21, 24, 26, 33, 34, 46, 103–4, 184, 192, 219, 220
  consequences 2, 9, 24, 35, 46, 102–3, 109, 185
  deprivation 26, 33–4, 224–5, 227
  'flexibility' 22–3, 27, 34, 185
  see also 'abstraction'; 'logic'; 'objectivity'; 'rationality'
Cole, M. 9, 10, 92, 93, 102–4, 153
'commercial' literacy 11, 12, 114, 129, 130–1, 152, 153, 155, 157, 158–80, 221, 222
communication 86
  literate modes 4, 49, 151, 157
  'mix' of oral and literate modes 4, 5, 10, 42, 45, 46–7, 61, 95, 102, 110–21, 130, 133, 137–8, 141–2, 143–4, 223
  oral modes 5, 36, 44, 45, 46–8, 49, 50, 61, 62, 63, 81, 82, 94, 151, 157
'conscientization' 187, 202
context-dependent
  concept 30, 34, 35, 70, 71, 74–5, 77, 109
  speech 21, 30, 42, 81, 94
  thought 21
  writing 38, 81
context-free
  thought 2
  writing 38
cross-cultural comparison 1, 3, 8, 12, 20, 26, 56, 73, 78, 93, 123, 125, 154, 221
Crystal, D. 4, 7, 67
'cursive' script 113–14

'dabestan' (State school) 12, 129, 130, 131, 176–7, 178, 197–203
Dale, R. 19
Derrida, J. 101
Deuchar, M. 7, 66, 91–2
Dibedan, Z. *see* Ronduen, P.
Domesday Book 112, 113

'enabling factor', literacy as 96, 119, 159, 160, 171–2
Ennayat, H. 141

ethnolinguistics, and study of literacy 7, 68
Evans-Pritchard, E. E. 3, 24–5, 29

Finnegan, R. 45–6, 77, 95–6, 97, 137–9,
    140, 141, 144
Firth, J. R. 68
Fought, J. 68–9
Freeland, J. 209–10, 211
Freire, P. 14, 183, 186–7, 188, 191, 192,
    195, 202, 203–4, 207, 210
Friedman, M. 34
'functional' literacy 213, 219, 221, 229–31
    see also Unesco

Garuda Purana *see* Puranas
Gellner, E. 59
Gharib, G. S. 197, 199–200, 201
Goody, J. 9, 41, 42, 77, 97, 99, 119, 135–6,
    137, 138, 142, 151
    and 'autonomous' model 4–5, 6, 10, 43,
        44–65, 98, 102, 219
    theory of literacy 51, 65, 108, 109, 117,
        118
Graff, H. J. 8, 10–11, 19, 42, 43, 104–10,
    176, 186, 204, 215
graphemes 36
'great divide' theory 3, 5, 24, 28, 29, 30,
    38, 42, 47, 49, 62, 94, 95, 103–4
Greenfield, P. 20–4, 27, 28, 29, 30–6, 38, 39,
    41, 74, 83, 90, 103
    and 'autonomous' model 3, 43, 219

'Hadith' 136, 139, 140, 141
Halliday, F. 158
Harman, D. *see* Hunter, C.
Hashemi, M. 199
Heath, S. B. 121–5, 156–7, 173, 223
Hildyard, A. 4, 70, 74, 75, 83, 90, 93, 104,
    117, 185
    and 'autonomous' model 3, 19, 20, 24,
        28, 29, 35, 38, 39, 40, 41, 42, 43, 81,
        219
Hodgson, M. 134–5, 142, 148
homographs 91
homophones 91
Horton, R. 25, 77
Hunter, C. 15–16, 213–14, 216, 223
Hymes, D. 69

'ideological' model 1, 6, 7, 9, 11, 12,
    95–125, 130, 157, 183, 188, 191, 192,
    202, 203, 208, 212, 217, 218, 219, 220,
    223, 227
    definition 2–3, 8
'illiteracy' 14–16, 105–7, 109, 110, 120,
    153–4, 179, 193, 194, 212, 213–18, 223
Islamic schools *see* 'maktabs'

Islamic Tradition, and literacy 134–44
    history 140–1

James, H. 85
Jones, H. A. 15
Jones, R. 169
'jubes' (water channels) 160, 162–3, 164–6

Karp, I. 77
Keddie, Nickie 158, 169
Kelsey, A. 143
Kneale, W. and M. 93
Koran 104, 132–57, 173
    see also 'maktabs'; 'maktab' literacy
Koranic schools *see* 'maktabs'
Kpelle education 21, 35
Kuhn, T. S. 60

Labov, W. 4, 26, 27, 28, 30, 31, 38, 225
Lamb, D. 189
Lambton, A. 158, 169, 170
language 39, 67, 85, 86, 87, 225
    functions 20
    'language-specific' 68–9
    language-systems 72–3, 80–1, 85, 90–1
    oral and written 20–1, 39, 42, 66–9,
        74–5, 82, 87–8, 89, 91, 93, 94, 101,
        125
Leach, E. 25
Leech, G. 67, 75, 92
Léon, Lourdes de 69
Lerner, D. 13
Lévi-Strauss, C. 3, 25, 36, 37, 48, 49, 62,
    101
Levine, K. 15, 213, 214, 216, 217, 218,
    226, 227
Lévy-Bruhl, L. 29, 50, 53
Lienhardt, R. G. 7, 79–80, 81
    and 'essayists' 94
Linell, P. 7, 67
linguistics, and study of literacy 3, 6, 24,
    26, 27, 31, 35, 66–94
literacy, acquisition 1, 19, 186, 219
    in nineteenth century Canada 104–10
    in Iran 138, 141, 143–4, 196
literacy, consequences 2, 5, 38, 39, 40, 41,
    44, 57, 58–9, 95, 104, 108, 114, 215
literacy, malleability 100, 101, 136
literacy, uses 114, 123, 172–8
literacy campaigns 1, 2, 104, 114, 121, 133,
    216
    in Honduras 206–7
    in Iran 11, 13, 188, 197–203, 205, 206,
        207, 208
    in Nicaragua 14, 195, 203–12
    in Tanzania 13, 188–95, 200, 204–5, 206

in the UK 14–15, 42, 46, 90, 152, 153, 204, 213–31
Unesco 183–212
in the USA 14–15, 213–31
literacy 'myth' 10, 104, 110, 215
literacy programmes *see* literacy campaigns
literacy skills 152, 154–7, 172, 175, 176, 179, 180, 184, 196, 216, 219, 220–1
ALBSU list 154, 155, 156, 157, 172–3, 221–2, 229–31
see also cognitive skills
'literate' 5, 9, 10, 24, 30, 41, 42, 48, 49, 53, 58, 62, 63, 66, 81–2, 111–20, 135–6, 156, 190
definition 51
versus 'illiteracy' 105–7
versus 'non-literate' 5, 30, 48, 53, 58, 62, 103, 116–17, 120
see also communication, literate modes
'logic', cognitive skill 4, 5, 6, 24, 27, 31, 35, 38, 44, 47, 50, 53, 60, 63, 64, 77, 88, 117, 184, 224, 225
and Islam 145–6, 147–8
and language 20, 26, 29–30
Luria, A. R. 103
Lyons, J. 7, 68, 69–70, 71, 72, 74, 75, 78, 80–1, 82–3, 84, 92, 93, 94

Mace, J. 15, 42, 204, 216, 217, 218, 227
Mackie, R. 14, 202–3
McLachlan, K. 158, 168–9
'maktab' literacy 11–12, 129, 130–1, 132–57, 159, 160, 171, 172–8, 180, 221–2
'maktabs' (Islamic/Koranic schools) 11, 12, 129, 130, 132–57, 171, 173, 174, 175, 176, 178, 179, 180, 221
Marchetti, P. 206
memory 10, 47, 99, 104, 220
and oral tradition 48, 82, 99
and rote learning 142–4, 153
and written record 3, 10, 46, 50, 82, 110–21
'mir ab' (water foreman) 160, 165–6
mnemonic devices 48, 98, 102, 133, 152
morphemes 91
'Mullah Nasr-ed-Din' stories 142–4, 152

'non-literate' 35, 45, 54, 56, 57, 60, 79, 110, 157
see also 'literate'
numeracy 133, 183, 207

'objectivity', cognitive skill 7, 40, 53, 55–6, 64, 70, 72, 73, 74–5, 77, 78, 80, 81, 82, 83, 84, 88, 93, 94, 102, 148, 224

Olson, D. 4, 7, 27, 43, 70, 74, 75, 85, 87, 90, 93, 94, 103, 104, 117, 185, 224
and 'autonomous' model 3, 19, 20, 24, 28, 29, 35, 38, 39, 40, 41, 42, 43, 81, 219
and 'essayists' 76–7, 83–4, 93
oral culture 9, 20–4, 30, 35, 37, 39, 45, 47–9, 53, 81–2, 94, 97, 98–9, 117–19, 122, 125, 133, 135–6, 137–9, 141–2, 151
see also communication, oral modes
Osborn, J. 22
Oxenham, J. 13–14, 183, 184–6

Parkin, D. 163
Parry, J. 60, 77, 98–102, 135–6, 137, 144, 146, 147, 151
Persepolis Symposium *see* Unesco
phones/phonemes 36, 38, 51, 91, 98, 133
Piaget 2, 23, 37
Polanyi, M. 25
Popper, K. 102, 118
'World Three' 4, 76, 85, 86, 90, 99
psychology, and study of literacy 3, 9, 14, 34, 44, 61, 87, 102–4, 196, 218
Pulgrum, E. 35–6, 70–1
Puranas 100, 102, 146
Putnam, H. 85

Ramus systems 51
'rationality', cognitive skill 2, 4, 14, 19–43, 84, 117, 224
reading 9, 75–6, 90, 105, 108, 134, 175, 183, 190, 194, 219, 231
theory 120, 122–3, 133
see also writing
'restricted' literacy 5, 45, 61, 62–3, 64, 109–10, 130, 135, 142
'ritualised' literacy 6, 52, 61
Rizvi, S. A. 136
Romaine, S. 78, 79, 80
Rommetveit, R. 7, 84–7
Ronduen, P. 199, 201
Rosen, H. 4, 38
Ryle, G. 94

schooling, and literacy 2, 10, 11, 12, 19, 103–4, 186, 219–20
in nineteenth century Canada 105–10
in the UK 108, 153–6, 213–14
in the USA 121–5, 213–14
and the Wolof 3, 20–4, 29, 31–4, 36, 37, 38
see also 'dabestan'; 'maktabs'; teaching literacy
Scribner, S. *see* Cole, M.
Sepah-ye Danesh (Education Corps) 199–202, 205, 207

Smith, B. 39
Smith, M. 10
social control, and literacy 4, 8, 42, 105, 107, 108
sociolinguistics, and literacy 26, 28, 87, 88, 91, 101
speech 35, 66–8, 69
see also writing
Staton, J. 223–4
Stubbs, M. 4, 7, 24, 87, 88–9, 90, 91, 108, 218

'tajers' (village entrepreneurs) 12, 166–8, 171, 172, 173, 174, 175, 176, 177–8, 179
teaching literacy 2, 11, 15, 23, 107–9, 129–30, 192–4, 196–212, 215–16, 218–19, 221, 222, 223
see also schooling
Third World 73, 112, 146, 184, 185, 187, 189
'Tosi ol Mosa'el' (commentary) 137, 141, 151
Turton, D. 41, 57

UN survey 169–70
Unesco 13, 14, 103, 183
concept of 'functional' literacy 13, 183, 184, 187–8, 189, 191, 193, 194, 195, 196–7, 208

Persepolis Symposium 183–4, 186, 187–8, 190, 191, 194, 203, 208
see also literacy campaigns

Veda 98–102, 135, 136, 146
Viscusi, M. 188–95
Vygotsky, L. 103

Weber, H. 203
Williams, J. A. 136, 139, 140
Williams, R. 96
Wilson, B. 77
Wood, E. and N. 55, 56
Write First Time 223, 224, 227
writing 20, 36, 38, 47, 48, 56–7, 84, 89–90, 91, 93, 94, 97, 101, 102, 115–21, 139, 151–2, 172–6, 183, 231
'essay-text' form 1, 41, 130
and 'logic' 5, 44, 50, 53, 64
and 'objectivity' 81–3, 94
and oral memory 82–3, 98, 111–14, 120–1, 122, 142, 151
and reading 1, 2, 8, 21, 75–6, 87, 101, 105, 113, 115, 120–1, 152, 174, 180, 215, 219, 220, 224, 225
Semitic system 50, 52
and speech 7, 66–8, 69, 73, 74, 75, 87–8, 91–2, 153

Lightning Source UK Ltd.
Milton Keynes UK
UKOW041111130613

212190UK00001B/50/A